Don't Save Anything

THE WORKS OF JAMES SALTER

The Hunters

The Arm of Flesh

A Sport and a Pastime

Light Years

Solo Faces

Dusk and Other Stories

Still Such

Burning the Days

Cassada

Gods of Tin

Last Night

There and Then: The Travel Writing of James Salter

Life Is Meals: A Food Lover's Book of Days (with Kay Eldredge)

*Memorable Days: The Selected Letters of
James Salter and Robert Phelps*

All That Is

Collected Stories

The Art of Fiction (with an introduction by John Casey)

Don't Save Anything

Uncollected Essays, Articles, and Profiles

JAMES SALTER

With a Preface by Kay Eldredge Salter

COUNTERPOINT PRESS

Berkeley, California

Don't Save Anything

Copyright © 2017 by The Estate of James Salter
Preface copyright © 2017 by Kay Eldredge Salter

Library of Congress Cataloging-in-Publication Data
Names: Salter, James, author.
Title: Don't save anything : uncollected essays, articles, and profiles /
    James Salter.
Other titles: Do not save anything
Description: First Counterpoint hardcover edition. I Berkeley, CA :
    Counterpoint Press, 2017.
Identifiers: LCCN 2017017393 I ISBN 9781619029361
Classification: LCC PS3569.A4622 A6 2017 I DDC 818/.5409—dc23
LC record available at https://lccn.loc.gov/2017017393

Jacket designed by Zoe Norvell
Book designed by Mark McGarry

COUNTERPOINT
2560 Ninth Street, Suite 318
Berkeley, CA 94710
www.counterpointpress.com

Printed in the United States of America
Distributed by Publishers Group West

10 9 8 7 6 5 4 3 2 1

Contents

THE LIFE · 187

FRANCE · 223

ASPEN · 247

WRITING AND WHAT'S AHEAD · 275

Preface

Boxes kept surfacing. I'd forgotten there was so much. It was after Jim's death at ninety, in June 2015, that I began to go through the many boxes of papers, most in obvious places. I gradually found others tucked away and then discovered still more boxes stored in places I could only get to with a ladder.

He used to advise, "Don't save anything." He was talking about phrases or names or incidents a writer might be reluctant to use, holding them instead for a possible later work. But in a practical sense, he had clearly saved everything, not only finished copies of all he'd published but also all his notes and drafts.

Much of Jim's work appeared in collected volumes while he was alive—excerpts from both his fiction and nonfiction—about life as a pilot in *Gods of Tin*, his travels in *There and Then*, the correspondence in *Memorable Days* with a man he came to know first through letters, and the short stories in the PEN/Faulkner winner *Dusk and Other Stories* and, later, *Last Night*. And of course, there's his memoir *Burning the Days*. In it he wrote about only ten of the many people or experiences or eras he might have chosen, taking as his guide the filmmaker Jean Renoir's quote: "The only things that are important in life are the things you remember." That had been the structure, too, of his novel *Light Years*.

Years before that had been his decision to commit his life to writing. He said it was the hardest he'd ever made—resigning from a promising career in the Air Force where he'd spent over a dozen years, first at West Point and then as a fighter pilot in the Korean War. Only thirty-one and a lieutenant colonel, he turned his back on it to focus his hopes and energy on writing. He did it encouraged by his first published novel, *The Hunters*, based on his experiences in Korea, and on the sale of the book to the movies for a film starring Kirk Douglas.

Jim was married, with two very young daughters. He had an Air Force pension. He joined the reserves out of nostalgia, to get out of the house, and for the pay. He tried selling swimming pools. He and a friend made documentary films, even one that won a prize at Venice, called *Team, Team, Team*.

In the meantime, he was writing, trying to convince himself that he could really do it. His second novel was a derivative homage to William Faulkner. Decades after it was published, he rewrote it, unwilling to let it stand in its original form, and renamed it *Cassada*.

In 1961, when the Berlin Wall was built overnight to divide the city, Jim was recalled and sent to Europe. Out of that, he wrote a third novel, *A Sport and a Pastime*. It was the first book that was what he'd imagined it might be and that finally allowed him to believe in himself as a writer.

At the beginning of the 1970s, Robert Ginna, the first editor-in-chief of *People* magazine, invited Jim to write for it. The subjects included serious writers, and Ginna sent Jim to Switzerland, France, and England to interview Vladimir Nabokov, Graham Greene, and Antonia Fraser. It would be Jim's first journalism.

As I reread the published pieces, I remembered the stories that Jim told over dinner of all that had happened. The interviews had been arranged before his arrival in Europe, but suddenly everything fell apart. Greene had seen a spoof of *People* called *PeepHole* and avoided their meeting until a note from Jim, slipped under the door of Greene's Paris apartment, brought him around. Their talk produced not only the article for *People* but a bonus: Greene arranged for Jim's novel *Light Years* to finally be published in Britain.

Then on to Montreux and the hotel where Nabokov and his wife Vera lived. But when Jim telephoned to confirm his appointment with her husband, Vera Nabokov told him he had to submit his questions in writing. Jim explained he'd done that and had received no answer. Her husband wasn't well, she said. Still, she'd ask him about doing the interview. Jim expected her to merely pretend to ask, then return to the phone to say Nabokov couldn't do it. Instead, she specified the next day and a time they could meet, warning Jim that he could take no notes or record any of the conversation. The two men hit it off, and Nabokov even proposed a second "julep," as he called their drinks. But Jim regretfully rushed to the station to catch his train back to Paris. He missed the train and instead sat down with a notebook to feverishly scribble down everything Nabokov had said, telling himself that if Capote could claim to have remembered every word of a night with Marlon Brando, surely he could recall an hour with Nabokov.

Every story Jim wrote had a backstory. When he researched the development of the artificial heart, he went to dinner at the home of its inventor, Robert Jarvik, who decided to cook naked and insisted that Jim also jettison his clothes. Jim wrote about Robert Redford when Redford was still relatively unknown, the two men traveling together in search of material for Jim's screenplay for *Downhill Racer*. Jim had imagined a character like Billy Kidd at the heart of the film, but Redford had a different idea and singled out a young skier who looked a lot like himself: Spider Sabich. The film still plays on late-night television, generating residuals that "can almost buy lunch," as Jim liked to say. Redford became a star with *Butch Cassidy and the Sundance Kid* and remained a friend. When Jim received the lifetime achievement award at *The Paris Review* annual gala in 2011, Redford gave the keynote speech.

Jim also wrote about the lure of the movies. Dazzled by the European filmmakers of the '60s, he was asked to write films himself and even directed one called *Three* that starred the young Charlotte Rampling and the equally young and then unknown Sam Waterston. The experience convinced Jim he never wanted to direct again, but he wrote other screenplays until, with hopes of leaving writing more lasting, he eventually gave up all involvement in film to concentrate on what mattered most to him—novels and stories—while still writing occasional journalism and essays.

His articles appeared in *Esquire, Food & Wine, The New Yorker, Men's Journal, The Paris Review,* others. He wrote about important figures of Alpine climbing, about French brothels before World War I, about other writers he admired, among them one of his favorites, Isaac Babel.

With every piece, either assigned or of his own choice, Jim gave it all he had, which was considerable. He did thorough reading and research, but there were also times when articles took the form of essays that meant delving deep into his own memories and feelings—about the confluence of men and women, about his life in Aspen, about his experiences in France.

Don't Save Anything is a volume of the best of Jim's nonfiction— articles, essays, and profiles published individually but never collected in one place until now. Those many boxes were overflowing with papers, but in the end, it's not really a matter of quantity. These pieces reveal some of the breadth and depth of Jim's endless interest in the world and the people in it, especially those who are dedicated and passionate and who try to do something. One of the great pleasures in writing nonfiction is the writer's adventure of exploration, of learning about things he doesn't know, then writing them down. That's what you'll find here.

KAY ELDREDGE SALTER

Why I Write

Some for Glory, Some for Praise

"To write! What a marvelous thing!" When he was old and forgotten, living in a rundown house in the dreary suburbs of Paris, Léautaud wrote these lines. He was unmarried, childless, alone. The world of the theater in which he had worked as a critic for years was now dark for him, but from the ruins of his life these words rose. To *write*!

One thinks of many writers who might have said this, Anne Sexton, even though she committed suicide, or Hemingway or Virginia Woolf, who both did also, or Faulkner, scorned in his rural town, or the wreckage that was Fitzgerald in the end. The thing that is marvelous is literature, which is like the sea, and the exaltation of being near it, whether you are a powerful swimmer or wading by the shore. The act of writing, though often tedious, can still provide extraordinary pleasure. For me that comes line by line at the tip of a pen, which is what I like to write with, and the page on which the lines are written, the pages, can be the most valuable thing I will ever own.

The cynics say that if you do not write for money you are a dabbler or a fool, but this is not true. To see one's work in print is the real desire, to have it read. The remuneration is of less importance; no one was paid for the samizdats. Money is but one form of approval.

It is such a long time that I have been writing that I don't remember the beginning. It was not a matter of doing what my father knew how to do. He had gone to Rutgers, West Point, and then MIT, and I don't think in my lifetime I ever saw him reading a novel. He read newspapers, the *Sun*, the *World-Telegram*, there were at least a dozen in New York in those days. His task was laid out for him: to rise in the world.

Nor was my mother an avid reader. She read to me as a child, of course, and in time I read the books that were published in popular series, *The Hardy Boys* and *Bomba, the Jungle Boy*. I recall little about them. I did not read *Ivanhoe*, *Treasure Island*, *Kim*, or *The Scottish Chiefs*, though two or three of them were given to me. I had six volumes of a collection called *My Bookhouse*, edited by Olive Beaupré Miller, whose name is not to be found among the various Millers— Mrs. Alice, Henry, Joaquin, Joe—in *The Reader's Encyclopedia*, but who was responsible for what knowledge I had of Cervantes, Dickens, Tolstoy, Homer, and the others whose work was excerpted. The contents also included folktales, fairy tales, parts of the Bible, and more. When I read of writers who when young were given the freedom of their fathers' or friends' libraries, I think of *Bookhouse*, which was that for me. It was not an education but the introduction to one.

There were also poems, and in grammar school we had to memorize and then stand up and recite well-known poems. Many of these I still know, including Kipling's "If," which my father paid me a dollar to learn. Language is acquired, like other things, through the act of imitating, and rhythm and elegance may come in part from poems.

I could draw quite well as a boy and even, though uninstructed, paint. What impulse made me do this, and where the ability came from—although my father could draw a little—I cannot say. My desire to write, apparent at the age of seven or eight, likely came from the same source. I made crude books, as many children do, with awkward printing and drawings, from small sheets of paper, folded and sewn together.

In prep school we were poets, at least many of my friends and I were, ardent and profound. There were elegies but no love poems—those came later. I had some early success. In a national poetry contest I won honorable mention, and sold two poems to *Poetry* magazine.

All this was a phase, in nearly every case to be soon outgrown. In 1939 the war had broken out, and by 1941 we were in it. I ended up at West Point. The old life vanished; the new one had little use for poetry. I did read, and as an upperclassman wrote a few short stories. I had seen some in the Academy magazine and felt I could do better, and after the first one, the editor asked for more. When I became an officer there was, at first, no time for writing, nor was there the privacy. Beyond that was a greater inhibition: it was alien to the life. I had been commissioned in the Army Air Force and in the early days was a transport pilot, later switching into fighters. With that I felt I had found my role.

Stationed in Florida in about 1950, I happened to see in a bookshop window in Pensacola a boldly displayed novel called *The Town and the City* by John Kerouac. The name. There had been a Jack Kerouac at prep school, and he had written some stories. On the back of the jacket was a photograph, a gentle, almost yearning face with eyes cast downward. I recognized it instantly. I remember a feeling of envy. Kerouac was only a few years older than I was. Somehow he had written this impressive-looking novel. I bought the book and eagerly read it. It owed a lot to Thomas Wolfe—*Look Homeward, Angel* and others—who was a major figure then, but still it was an achievement. I took it as a mark of what might be done.

I had gotten married, and in the embrace of a more orderly life, on occasional weekends or in the evenings, I began to write again. The Korean War broke out. When I was sent over I took a small typewriter with me, thinking that if I was killed, the pages I had been writing would be a memorial. They were immature pages, to say the least. A few years later, the novel they were part of was rejected by the publishers, but one of them suggested that if I were to write another novel they would be interested in seeing it. Another novel. That might be years.

I had a journal I had kept while flying combat missions. It contained some description, but there was little shape to it. The war had the central role. One afternoon, in Florida again—I was there on temporary duty—I came back from the flight line, sat down on my cot, and began to hurriedly write out a page or so of outline that had suddenly occurred to me. It would be a novel about idealism, the true and the untrue, spare and in authentic prose. What had been missing but was missing no longer was the plot.

Why was I writing? It was not for glory; I had seen what I took to be real glory. It was not for acclaim. I knew that if the book was published, it would have to be under a pseudonym; I did not want to jeopardize a career by becoming known as a writer. I had heard the derisive references to "God-Is-My-Copilot" Scott. The ethic of fighter squadrons was drink and daring; anything else was suspect. Still, I thought of myself as more than just a pilot and imagined a book that would be in every way admirable. It would be evident that someone among the ranks of pilots had written it, an exceptional figure, unknown, but I would have the satisfaction of knowing who it was.

I wrote when I could find time. Some of the book was written at a fighter base on Long Island, the rest of it in Europe, when I was stationed in Germany. A lieutenant in my squadron who lived in the apartment adjoining ours could hear the typewriter late at night through the bedroom wall. "What are you doing," he asked one day, "writing a book?" It was meant as a joke. Nothing could be more unlikely. I was the experienced operations officer. Next step was squadron commander.

The Hunters was published by Harper and Brothers in late 1956. A section of the book appeared first in *Collier's*. Word of it spread immediately. With the rest I sat speculating as to who the writer might be, someone who had served in Korea, with the Fourth Group, probably.

The reviews were good. I was thirty-two years old, the father of a child, with my wife expecting another. I had been flying fighters for seven years. I decided I had had enough. The childhood urge to write had never died, in fact, it had proven itself. I discussed it with my wife, who, with only a partial understanding of what was involved, did not attempt to change my mind. Upon leaving Europe, I resigned my commission with the aim of becoming a writer.

It was the most difficult act of my life. Latent in me, I suppose, there was always the belief that writing was greater than other things, or at least would prove to be greater in the end. Call it a delusion if you like, but within me was an insistence that whatever we did, the things that were said, the dawns, the cities, the lives, all of it had to be drawn together, made into pages, or it was in danger of not existing, of never having been. There comes a time when you realize that everything is a dream, and only those things preserved in writing have any possibility of being real.

Of the actual hard business of writing I knew very little. The first book had been a gift. I missed the active life terribly, and after a long struggle a second book was completed. It was a failure. Jean Stafford, one of the judges for a prize for which it had been routinely submitted, left the manuscript on an airplane. The book made no sense to her, she said. But there was no turning back.

A Sport and a Pastime was published six years later. It, too, did not sell. A few thousand copies, that was all. It stayed in print, however, and one by one, slowly, foreign publishers bought it. Finally, Modern Library.

The use of literature, Emerson wrote, is to afford us a platform whence we may command a view of our present life, a purchase by which we may move it. Perhaps this is true, but I would claim something broader. Literature is the river of civilization, its Tigris and Nile. Those who follow it, and I am inclined to say those only, pass by the glories.

Over the years I have been a writer for a succession of reasons. In the beginning, as I have said, I wrote to be admired, even if not known. Once I had decided to be a writer, I wrote hoping for acceptance, approval.

Gertrude Stein, when asked why she wrote, replied, "For praise." Lorca said he wrote to be loved. Faulkner said a writer wrote for glory. I may at times have written for those reasons, it's hard to know. Overall I write because I see the world in a certain way that no dialogue or series of them can begin to describe, that no book can fully render, though the greatest books thrill in their attempt.

A great book may be an accident, but a good one is a possibility, and it is thinking of that that one writes. In short, to achieve. The rest takes care of itself, and so much praise is given to insignificant things that there is hardly any sense in striving for it.

In the end, writing is like a prison, an island from which you will never be released but which is a kind of paradise: the solitude, the thoughts, the incredible joy of putting into words the essence of what you for the moment understand and with your whole heart want to believe.

Why I Write: Thoughts on the Craft of Fiction
1999

On Other Writers

The Writing Teacher

Iowa City, along its river, is a beautiful town. There are brick-lined streets in a neighborhood called Goosetown, once Czech, where geese were kept in the deep backyards. Ample old houses remain and huge trees. Downtown there are wide streets, restaurants, shops, and a wonderful bookstore, Prairie Lights, but the chief business is really the University of Iowa, within which, small but renowned, lies its jewel, the Writers' Workshop. Originally established in 1936, the workshop is the preeminent writing school in the country, although it is almost universally believed that writing cannot be taught, and in fact it is not really taught there; it is practiced. Kurt Vonnegut, one in the long list of famous writers who have been on the workshop's faculty, liked to say he couldn't teach people to write but, like an old golf pro, he could go around with them and perhaps take a few strokes off their game.

There have been numerous old pros at Iowa over the years, many of them former students, and if you were lucky enough to have studied there, you might have sat across from John Cheever or Philip Roth, John Irving, Raymond Carver, Joy Williams or others discussing or demolishing what you or a classmate had written.

Afterward you might drink with them at the Old Mill or the Fox-head, tirelessly continuing the talk. You may not have been learning to write, but you were certainly learning something.

Frank Conroy, tall, unflappable, and urbane, was head of the workshop for eighteen years, from 1987 until a few months ago, and his stamp is firmly on it. He came to Iowa from the directorship of the literary program at the National Endowment for the Arts and a few teaching jobs before that, and more remotely from the literary scene in New York, the bar at Elaine's, innumerable parties, jazz joints, where he began as a brash outsider but made friends and eventually a name for himself with the publication of *Stop-Time*, a startlingly fresh, enduring memoir of youth, in 1967.

Admission to the two-year program at the Writers' Workshop is made on the basis of an example of submitted writing. As director, to guarantee the quality of students, which translated ultimately into the reputation of the school, Conroy read every submission and made final decisions himself. It was the way the great cities of Europe were built, not by committee but by royal decree. The faculty was assembled the same way. There were permanent members, Frank being one of them, but others were there by invitation for a year or two. The workshop ran like a clock, due also to a chief administrator, Connie Brothers, who looked after all the details Frank could treat somewhat offhandedly and who acted as a kind of foster mother for the students. Between them was the power.

In a dark wooden booth at the Foxhead one night, the air blue with cigarette smoke and the clatter of pool balls, Frank confided to me that he had just gotten an advance for the novel he was then writing, $250,000. Suddenly I could see that he was no ordinary academic. We sat drinking with Joseph Brodsky another night, the jukebox playing and a bell at the bar being rung every time someone ordered a local beer called Dubuque Star. Brodsky had come to Iowa City to read. He was not the only Nobel laureate to do so. Derek Walcott came and Seamus Heaney, who read to a crowd that overflowed onto half the stage. While it did not rival Stockholm, the invitation to Iowa City was a distinction. Almost every week someone of interest arrived to read, and there were dinners with them beforehand.

The dinners at Frank's house were best, seven or eight people, often including a visitor, martinis made in a silver shaker that had belonged to Frank's father. The talk was usually about writing. Objectivity came up more than once and the existence of truth, or God's truth, as Frank called it. No one could know that, the complete truth. It was too vast and complex. "All we know is what we think we know," he said; there was really no such thing as truth or fact. He told me he had written that his mother and stepfather had gone to Cuba to buy a piano or something—actually it was for her to have an abortion. But what he wrote was what he thought was true. "For me, it was true," he said.

"Who is the Dostoyevsky in American writing today?" Jorie Graham wanted to know.

Various names were brought up. Mailer, Frank proposed—among other things, he was Frank's friend. There was argument; voices became louder and louder. The next day I called to apologize for becoming excited. Maggie Conroy answered.

"Oh, who can imagine anyone getting excited about Norman Mailer," she said soothingly.

She had aplomb. She had been an actress and had grown up partly in South America. Her face was filled with even temperament and intelligence. Marguerite, Frank sometimes called her, suggesting her authority. They had no secrets from each other, even things in the past. "When we first got started," he said, "we just sat down and told each other everything. It took weeks. Everything."

"And after that we had nothing to talk about," she added wryly.

I taught twice at the Writers' Workshop, the last time in 1989, but Frank and I became good friends and stayed in touch. Then a letter came, very brief. It looked like it was all over, he said. Colon cancer had been diagnosed. There were four stages and he had the worst, stage four.

That was two years ago. He underwent surgery and the rest of it. The workshop began to look for a new director, someone who could fill Frank's shoes and deal equally well with those below and above, the deans, presidents, donors. Eventually Frank was told that his condition seemed stabilized and, though he was not cured, he might go on for a number of years. That didn't happen. There came the point when he was told that nothing further could be done. He decided to let nature take its course.

We had lunch in March, Frank and Maggie, my wife and I, in the comfortable, light-filled house that had been bought with the money from the novel. He looked the same, though a little weak. Behind the glasses his eyes were alert. The lick of boyish hair hung over his forehead. He wondered, he said, how it was going to be, whether the pain would be too great, whether he would be able to be himself until the end. He had been hoping to go to Nantucket, where they always spent the summer, but it didn't look as if he would be able to. Maggie and Tim, their son, would be going without him.

That was more or less the end. He went upstairs for the weeks that followed and died on April 6. He was sixty-nine. Maggie had lain down beside him for the final hours. There are not many people you would do that with.

The New York Times Sunday Book Review
March 8, 2005

Odessa, Mon Amour

Isaac Babel was stocky with a broad, kindly face and a forehead creased with horizontal lines. He wore steel-rimmed glasses, like a bookworm or an accountant, and had a soft, high-pitched voice with a slight lisp. For a time, in the 1920s, following the publication of his *Red Cavalry* stories, he was the most famous writer in Russia, and anything of his that appeared in print attracted great attention. Knopf published the translation of *Red Cavalry* in 1929, and its combination of startling beauty and great violence, delivered with an unsettling resignation, disturbed readers, including Lionel Trilling, who wrote about the exceptional talent, even genius, that it represented. Babel was a writer of the Revolution, a child of it, in fact, caught up in its idealism and equality, but over time he became disillusioned and less ardent.

For Babel, writing was an agony. He wrote and rewrote endlessly, often completing only a quarter of a page in a day, and he sometimes rose at night to reread pages. He was constantly searching for the right word or expression, significant, simple, and beautiful, as he said. He believed, among other things, in punctuation, the period, principally. No steel could pierce the human heart, he wrote, as deeply as a period in exactly the right place. The strength came not when you could no longer add a sentence but when you could no longer take one away. He loved Expressionist colors, green stars, blue palms, blood red clay, sunsets thick as jam, and his images explode from the page, as in the celebrated opening lines of "My First Goose":

> Savitsky, Commander of the VI Division, rose when he saw me, and I wondered at the beauty of his giant's body. He rose, the purple of his riding breeches and the crimson of his little tilted cap and the decorations on his chest cleaving the hut as a standard cleaves the sky. A smell of scent and the sickly sweet freshness of soap emanated from him. His long legs were like girls sheathed to the neck in shining riding boots.

Savitsky, the theatrical, bold commander, flower *and iron*, Babel writes admiringly, is based on a real figure, Semyon Timoshenko, who rose to become a marshal of the Red Army and to appear on the cover of *Time*. Other actual figures, Budyonny and Voroshilov, under their own names, are there as well. In his 1920 diary, on which the *Red Cavalry* stories were based, Babel jotted:

> Divisional Commander Timoshenko at HQ. A colorful figure. A colossus in red half-leather trousers, red cap, well-built, former platoon commander, was at one time a machine gunner, an artillery ensign.

He had no imagination and couldn't invent, he had to know everything, down to the last detail, he said, and Ilya Ehrenburg, who was his friend, agreed that Babel hardly changed anything but illuminated it with a kind of wisdom. It was more than that, it was with a unique talent. *Beauty, scent,* and *the sickly sweet freshness of soap* were added, and the half-leather trousers were transformed into an erotic image that sends electricity in both directions. He aimed, Babel said, at an intelligent reader with taste, more exactly a very intelligent woman who had absolute taste, just as certain people have absolute pitch.

Despite his ordinary appearance, women were attracted to him. He had love affairs, a son with a beautiful actress, Tamara Kashirina, a daughter with his wife, who had left Russia in 1925 and was living in Paris, studying art, and a second daughter with a "second wife," Antonina Pirozhkova, fifteen years younger than Babel and with whom he lived the last four years of his life. There is a rich element of sensuality in Babel's writing, sometimes implicit, glimpsed, sometimes clear. Prostitutes figure in stories, most notably in "My First Fee," a masterpiece published only in 1963, long after his death. The story takes a familiar subject, the first introduction to sex, and makes it both comedic and gorgeous. The narrator impulsively lies his way into the affection of a worn, savvy streetwalker, who ends up teaching him the tricks of the trade and calling him "sister." "Chink," "The Bathroom Window," and "An Evening with the Empress" have prostitutes in them, and "Dante Street" has all the aroma of a brothel, or something close to it. In Paris once, Babel stopped in front of a well-known brothel in Montmartre and, looking through the open windows—it was daytime—remarked to his companion that he wondered if they kept books in such a place. It would be fascinating to see them, he said, they could be a wonderful chapter in a novel. His curiosity was endless and intense. He wanted women to show him the contents of their handbags for what they might reveal, and he liked people to tell him the story of their first love. Everything is in terms of people in his writing, and his real interests were love and death. Like Maupassant and Flaubert, whom he revered, he was a realist. The *Red Cavalry* stories are stark and disturbing, completely out of step with modern sensibilities, and yet they are shot through with a strange kindness. No writer is more realistic and at the same time, even in the same sentence, romantic.

Babel was born in 1894 in Odessa, a port city on the Black Sea, in a poor neighborhood called the Moldavanka, which he made famous in his stories. Odessa had a large Jewish population, and Babel is a Jewish writer, though not in the way of Isaac Singer or Sholem Aleichem. In the diary he writes of feeling happy among the beset Jews of eastern Poland, who, along with their history, would be almost completely exterminated twenty years later. *Enormous faces and black beards. Every house remains in my heart. Clusters of Jews. Their faces—this is the ghetto and we are an ancient people.* In a ruined synagogue he sits, almost praying—it has an irresistible effect on him, though he writes as a Russian and a loyal communist much of the time.

He grew up having witnessed, in 1905, the great pogroms, massacres of Jews, that were sanctioned by the czarist government, although he and his family escaped harm—all brilliantly and almost innocently described in "The Story of My Dovecote" and "First Love." Babel's father was a tractor salesman, and Babel studied French, English, and German as a child. His first stories were written in French, perhaps from the influence of Maupassant and Flaubert.

There were restrictions for Jews, quotas, cities they were prohibited from living in, but the overthrow of the czarist regime broke down doors, if not prejudices. Babel had made his way to St. Petersburg in 1916, the year before the Revolution, and his early stories were published there in Maxim Gorky's literary magazine, *Letopis*.

Babel became a favorite of Gorky, who recognized his talent and advised him to go out and get some experience of life. Gorky himself had plenty of it, a bitter childhood and years of hard work. His famous play *The Lower Depths* made his name in 1902, and he became *the* writer of the Revolution, Babel's champion, and always a devoted Marxist, until his death in the fateful year of 1936 under somewhat mysterious circumstances. His judgment had been simple: "Babel is the great hope of Russian literature."

In 1920, with credentials as a war correspondent and under the assumed, very Russian name of Kiril Lyutov, Babel spent three and a half months, from June into September, with the First Cavalry Army, commanded by a legendary mustached Cossack, Semyon Budyonny. In late May Budyonny had ridden into eastern Poland from the Ukraine in a campaign against the Poles, who had moved forces into the disputed border regions. It was also a first move in the Soviets' plan to spread communism. Russia was thought to be a less than ideal place for a true workers' revolution, being too archaic. The new order would take hold better in a more industrialized society: Germany. Russia was only a temporary base for it.

There were early successes, and then defeats in the fall of 1920 that led to retreat. Amid the chaos, battles, rapes, and massacres, Babel traveled, writing articles for a government newspaper and keeping, in a plain, lined notebook, an intense, hasty diary of which it could be said that, as with other great writers, he threw away a novel on every page. *Describe* he is continually reminding himself, *describe.* The fifty-four opening pages have been lost, and with them Babel's first impressions, but from the beginning there is the muted horror: they are in Zhitomir, the western Ukraine.

> The Poles entered the town, stayed for three days, there was a pogrom, they cut off beards, that's usual, assembled 45 Jews in the marketplace, led them to the slaughteryard, tortures, cut out tongues, wails heard all over the square. They set fire to 6 houses, I went to look at Koniuchowski's house on Cathedral Street, they machine-gunned those who tried to rescue people. The yardman, into whose arms a mother dropped a child from a burning window, was bayoneted, the priest put a ladder up against the back wall, they escaped that way.

It's summer, fields of wheat. Down the road at a hard trot, eight abreast, an endless column of Cossacks are coming with their top-knots, carbines, long swords, and ragged clothes, the dust rising behind. Divisions are attacking, orders being sent out, dead and wounded men, nurses on horseback. *By one of the cottages—a cow, recently calved, with its throat cut. Bluish teats on the ground, just skin. Indescribable pity! A murdered young mother.* Death is everywhere. The images are like Goya's in his passionate series of etchings *Desastres de la Guerra*, the mutilation and murder, and above all, a kind of hopeless understanding and even forgiveness.

There are thirty-four staggering stories in *Red Cavalry*, which

opens like a cannon shot, crossing the River Zbrucz into Poland. The
blackened river roars, twisting itself into foamy knots at the falls.

> The bridges were down, and we waded across the river. On the
> waves rested a majestic moon. The horses were in to the cruppers,
> and the noisy torrent gurgled among hundreds of horses' legs. Some-
> body sank, loudly defaming the Mother of God. The river was dotted
> with the black patches of wagons, and was full of confused sounds.

Certain figures reappear, Savitsky, the long-legged division commander, disgraced and living with a Cossack woman he has lured
away from a Jew in the commissariat ("The Story of a Horse, Parts I
and II"). Sasha, the girlfriend of the squadrons, with her *shapely, cast-
iron legs*; Afonka Bida, the platoon commander, who shoots a gravely
wounded comrade who is pleading for death rather than being left
behind and caught alive by the Poles ("The Death of a Dolgushov").

He was leaning up against a tree, his boots thrust out apart.
Without lowering his eyes from mine he warily rolled back his shirt.
His belly had been torn out. The entrails hung over his knees, and
the heartbeats were visible.

Afonka talks to him briefly, takes some papers offered to him,
puts them in his boot, and shoots the wounded man in the mouth.
Lyutov/Babel, the narrator, had been unable to do it. *"Get out of my
sight,"* Afonka says, *"or I'll kill you. You guys in specs have about as much
pity for chaps like us as a cat has for a mouse."*

Along the way on a bowlegged horse rides Brigade Commander
Maslak, suffused with drunken blood and the putrescence of his
greasy humors. His abdomen rested upon the silver-plated saddle-
bow like a big tomcat.

Along the way also are peasant girls whom a soldier describes
sympathetically ("Salt"):

> Look at them two girls cringe at present on account of what they
> went through from us this night. Look at our wives in the wheat

plains of the Kuban that are spending their women's strength without their husbands, and the husbands, alone too, all through dire necessity violating the girls as come into their lives.

In one of the final stories there is the death of a prince, actually a rabbi's son who had commanded a scratch regiment but was defeated. Swarms of retreating troops are clambering alongside to get aboard the Political Section train as it passes through them. Babel is tossing them potatoes and, when there are no more, Trotsky's leaflets. Only a single man stretches a filthy hand to catch one. It's Elijah, son of the Rabbi of Zhitomir, beneath a heavy soldier's pack. Defying regulations, they pull him aboard and lay him on the floor, *the long, shamed body of the dying man . . . and Cossacks in loose red trousers set straight the clothes that were dropping off him.* The female typists stare dully at his sexual organs. He had been a member of the Party, he manages to tell Babel, but at first he couldn't leave his mother.

> "And now, Elijah?" "When there's a revolution on, a mother's an episode," he whispered. He died before we reached Rovno. He—that last of the Princes—died among his poetry, phylacteries, and coarse foot wrappings. We buried him at some forgotten station. And I, who can scarce contain the tempests of my imagination within this age-old body of mine, I was there beside my brother when he breathed his last *("The Rabbi's Son")*.

The *Red Cavalry* stories were written in 1923–1924. Babel had withdrawn to the Caucasus with his wife and was living in a house above Batum. The stories brought immediate fame as well as the disapproval of Budyonny, who wrote denouncing the depiction of the Cossacks. Gorky defended Babel, who was now a public figure and to some extent privileged. This period, the 1920s, was the most productive in Babel's life. In the Odessa stories and others, written before *Red Cavalry* and after, the canvas is broadened: there is childhood, first love, family, remembrance, and Benya Krik, known as the King, a legendary gangster in an orange suit and wearing a bracelet set with diamonds, who comes to call on one of the rich men in Odessa, Zender Eichbaum, to ask for his daughter's hand. The old man has a slight stroke at this but recovers. *He was good for another twenty years.*

> "Listen, Eichbaum," said the King. "When you die I will bury you in the First Jewish Cemetery, right by the entrance. I will raise you, Eichbaum, a monument of pink marble. I will make you an elder of the Brody Synagogue . . . No thief will walk the street you live on. I will build you a villa where the streetcar line ends. Remember, Eichbaum, you were no rabbi in your young days. People have forged wills, but why talk about it? And the King shall be your son-in-law—no milksop, but the King."

Babel himself was the heir of Maupassant, for whom he named one of his greatest stories. In it is Raisa Bendersky, who tells the penniless narrator that Maupassant is the only passion of her life.

> Black-haired with pink eyes and a wide bosom, she is one of those charming Jewesses who have come to us from Kiev and Poltava, from the opulent steppe-towns full of chestnut trees and acacias. The money made by their clever husbands is transformed by these women into a pink layer of fat on the belly, the back of the neck, and the well-rounded shoulders. Their subtle sleepy smiles drive officers from the local garrisons crazy.

Together they translate Maupassant from a shelf of twenty-nine morocco-bound volumes, and a week or two later on a climactic night when the others have gone to the theater, Raisa appears in an evening dress, holding out her arms:

> "I'm drunk, darling." Her body swayed like a snake's dancing to music. She tossed her marcelled hair about, and suddenly, with a

tinkle of rings, slumped into a chair with ancient Russian carvings. Scars glowed on her powdered back.

They are alone, drinking glass after glass of muscatel. She holds out her glass. *"Mon vieux, to Maupassant."* He kisses her on the lips, which quiver and swell. *"You're funny," she mumbled.* The inevitable perhaps happens. The ending, however, is not that but something unexpected and amazing.

Drawing conclusions, Chekhov said, is up to the jury, that is, the readers. My only job is to be talented.

So it is with Babel. The stories submit themselves. Life is life, Babel says, and on dark velvet presents marvelous jewels. As it happened, the Holocaust followed a few years after him. What he saw and felt was a presentiment. He wrote the merciful and unforgivable at the same time. The furnace doors swing open, and a fierce, frightening heat comes forth, but the incandescence brightens life like the sun.

By the 1930s the optimism of the Revolution had hardened into grim reality as Stalin tightened his grip. Soviet orthodoxy ruled, together with the secret police, and the independence of writers disappeared. In 1936 in great, Inquisition-like trials, former high officials, Party rivals, and men who had been prominent in the Revolution confessed sins and were executed. The terror was in full force. Nikolai Yezhov became head of the notorious NKVD. His wife, Evgenia Gladun, had an earlier love affair with Babel and remained friendly. He was a guest at their house a number of times, driven in part by a curiosity about how things were going higher up in the ominous times. A great knell was Gorky's death in June of 1936. "Now they are not going to let me live," Babel predicted. The former minister of defense, Marshal Tukhachevsky, and other top commanders were arrested, tried in secret, and executed. Then Yezhov himself was replaced by a brutal Georgian, Lavrentiy Beria, and subsequently arrested. In his obligatory confession he implicated Babel. Early in the morning of May 15, 1939, Babel was arrested and charged with espionage. The stories he had been working on, his notebooks and diaries, were all confiscated. Like other prisoners he was allowed no visitors. Stalin worked late and sometimes made telephone calls from his offices in the Kremlin, one night to Ilya Ehrenburg. Was Babel a good writer? Stalin asked.

"A wonderful writer," Ehrenburg replied.

"*Zhalko* [pity]," Stalin said and hung up.

The verdict had already been decided. Babel remained in prison, without communication of any kind, for eight months. He made a forced confession that he tried unsuccessfully to retract. The police photograph of him shows a swollen face and dark, bruised eyes—his eyeglasses, without which he could barely see, had been taken from him. An indictment was handed to him on January 25, 1940, and the next day there was a twenty-minute agony called a trial with no lawyer or witnesses. The sentence was death, to be carried out imme-diately. His final words were a plea: "Let me finish my work . . ."

What he felt as he walked to the chamber or courtyard in which he would be executed, shaken and alone, we cannot know. It may have been memories, his wife, daughter, even the fate of the folders of manuscripts that had been taken from him. Then, standing or kneeling near a wall, like countless others, he was shot. His wife and daughter were told that he had been convicted but sentenced by the military tribunal to "ten years without the right to correspond." Despite rumors that he was alive in the camps and purportedly seen there by witnesses, his true fate remained unknown until 1954, after Stalin's death, when Babel was officially rehabilitated, the facts made public, and the verdict set aside. Despite searches in the KGB archives, his manuscripts have never been found. It was claimed that they had been burned.

There are writers one always goes back to, the pages never lose their power. For me, Babel is one such.

Narrative Magazine
Spring 2009

Like a Retired Confidential Agent, Graham Greene Hides Quietly in Paris

The greatest living English writer resides in a large and somewhat sparsely furnished apartment on the second floor of a bourgeois building in Paris on the Boulevard Malesherbes. Though he has owned it for years, his name is missing from the inked list of tenants in the concierge's window downstairs. On his telephone, in place of a number, is a blank disk. Like a retired informer or spy or the principal figure in a notorious criminal case, Graham Greene lives in anonymity and quiet.

He was seventy-one last October and is extremely guarded about his personal life. Still, most facts about so famous a man are well-known. He is the son of a schoolmaster and has two grown children, a son and a daughter. He has been separated from his wife for more than twenty-five years.

Through the large windows one can see the bare branches of trees and the celebrated blue of the Paris sky. Greene wears an old cardigan sweater and gray trousers. His eyes, behind horn-rimmed glasses, are a pale, watery blue. Thin hair, the faded color of an old coat, is gray on the sides. From his photographs one recognizes him instantly; he looks like a prisoner long confined.

Greene's speech is soft and reserved with a vague scholarly impediment. There is a certain sense of loneliness, especially when he is talking of domestic life: "very desirable, but marriage is a bit tricky," he says. "Yes, one is always looking for a happy couple. It's hard to find a man and woman one likes equally, but marvelous when you do."

This season the Royal Shakespeare Company in London put on his new play, *The Return of A. J. Raffles*. It's a comedy about the famous gentleman thief created by E. W. Hornung, brother-in-law of the man who wrote Sherlock Holmes. Holmes had Dr. Watson, and Raffles also had a devoted chronicler and accomplice with the more appealing name of Bunny. The Raffles stories were enormously popular, in which Hornung wrote a classic line that will probably live as long as his dashing criminal. Of Conan Doyle's master detective, he punned, "Though he might be more humble, there is no police like Holmes."

This is Greene's fifth play and was not well received by most of the critics. Among its predecessors are *The Living Room*, *The Potting Shed*, and *The Complaisant Lover*. He has had partial success in the theater. Like another great Catholic writer, François Mauriac, he came to it late. He was forty-nine when *The Living Room* was first produced in London. It was a sensation, though it failed in New York the following year, 1954. "A dreadful flop," he admits. "It was very miscast. I've never had much success in America with plays."

With everything else, his serious novels, his thrillers or "entertainments" as he once preferred to call them, his films, he has had enormous success. Almost alone among important writers, Greene has had a long and close connection with the movies. It's a kind of love-hate relationship, he confesses. Many of his books (*The Third Man*, *Our Man in Havana*, *The Comedians*, *Orient Express*) have been turned into films, not all of them satisfactorily as far as he is concerned, though he has scripted a number of them and collaborated on the making of others.

In addition, there were three years during which he reviewed films for British journals and the famous suit brought against him by Shirley Temple when she was the moppet darling of Hollywood. He wrote, in effect, that she had an erotic appeal to a nation of dirty old men. He had to hide out in Mexico because of it.

Nevertheless, he still finds films interesting. "I go to them much more than to the theater. I liked *Chinatown* and *The Last Detail*. I like Nicholson, Polanski . . . I like Milos Forman. I've never been enthusiastic for Hitchcock. His plots don't stand up. When you leave the theater you're always saying, but why didn't he ring the police? Some old films do stand up. *Casablanca*. And I saw on TV last year Murnau's *Dracula* and I thought it was terrific."

On the table a tray of ice cubes is slowly melting. There is a drink in Greene's hand. He's had this apartment for ten years; before that he always lived in hotels. He likes the neighborhood, it has rather a village atmosphere. There's a very good butcher, a good *boulangerie*. He is fond of food and wine. "If I eat, I must drink," he explains, and also it is a great help in getting people to talk.

Every real writer creates a world. Greene's is a relentless one of sinning and divided men that is made bearable only through God and His mercy. In book after book there is forgiveness for the repentant sinner at the final hour. In the course of writing them all Greene has become, following his conversion at the age of twenty-two, the most important Catholic novelist alive. He has a dazzling sense of story, fine dialogue, and an eye for detail. He doesn't joke. He is too involved in his obsessions. Irony, yes, there is often that, and even a kind of comedy, but beneath it is a schoolmaster's firm will. Above all, his characters live. Scobie, the doomed policeman in *The Heart of the Matter*. The whiskey priest and his pursuer in *The Power and the Glory*. Pinkie in *Brighton Rock*. Coral Musker. Dr. Czinner. They are people one never forgets.

The writing table at which Greene works is almost bare. There is a TV on a set of library steps, three or four chairs, some paintings on the wall, but the principal decoration is books. The shelves hold Boswell, Ibsen, and H. G. Wells, as well as Greene's great favorites, Henry James and Conrad. Of James, he has said that he "is as solitary in the history of the novel as Shakespeare in the history of poetry." And as for Joseph Conrad, the Polish sea captain who carved out an immortal niche in the literature of a country not his own, Greene stopped reading him in 1932 because he was simply too influential a force.

The mystery writers Edgar Wallace and John Buchan (*The Thirty-Nine Steps*) must also be counted as influences. Wallace was a phenomenally popular writer. There was a time when one of every five books sold in England was his. From him Greene learned a great deal: the restrained voice, the variety of characters, the technique of advancing a narrative, and, perhaps most of all, the mysterious ability to create a legend.

Greene still reads a lot, three or four books a week, and notes them in his diary, putting down a little tick or cross in judgment. Among the Americans, he likes Kurt Vonnegut. Gore Vidal: "I like his essays." Alison Lurie. Philip Roth, not much. Bellow, he finds rather difficult. As for his own work, even coming from a long-lived family it is not easy, he admits, to think of starting on a book these days. "The fears," he says simply, "not knowing whether one will live to see the end of it."

He has been a published writer since 1929 with his first novel, *The Man Within*. There have been novels, travel books, thrillers, films, plays, short stories, and autobiography as well as essays and reviews. His output has been protean and the breadth of his travel and experience, vast. Many of his settings are foreign. *The Honorary Consul*, for instance, resulted from a three months' trip to South America. Though his command of Spanish covers only the present tense, he was visiting in Argentina and saw the town of Corrientes one day while going up the river to Asunción. Corrientes became the scene of the book. He has been in Africa, Mexico, Russia, and China ("I found it depressing"), served as an intelligence officer in Sierra Leone during the war, smoked opium in Indochina where he went as a correspondent regularly beginning in 1951, and flew in French bombers between Saigon and Hanoi. He has been an editor in a publishing house, a film reviewer, a critic, a life as varied and glamorous as that of André Malraux, another great literary and political figure. Like Malraux, he asks to be read as a political writer and has set his fiction firmly in that world. The lesson in the books of Graham Greene is the great lesson of the times: one must take sides.

He has been extremely generous towards other writers. He was Nabokov's champion in England when Nabokov was little known. Those he admires, he praises freely, Jean Rhys, for instance. "Yes, I like her very much. She's a writer's writer." Or Evelyn Waugh, the best stylist of their generation, he says. "In the Mediterranean you can see a pebble fifteen feet down. His style was like that."

A voyager in every sense of the word, laureate of the downtrodden and betrayed, Greene is a writer concerned with serious human problems who has lashed out fiercely against escapist fiction. "Life is violent and art has to reflect that violence," he says. At the same time, only a warm human touch together with a deep knowledge of how the world works could have won for him such immense popularity. In his books one feels the breath of a great belief that is enough to justify life, that will not protect one but that ties one to an order and meaning never to be extinguished.

He sits now in the twilight, both of work and of dreams. "With the approach of death I care less and less about religious truth. One hasn't long to wait for revelation or darkness . . ." The great moral and political question during his lifetime has been that of socialism. He has shared the hope of many sincere men that the cruel Communist dictatorships will pass and a more or less democratic form take their place, the end that Marx promised but that has remained ever distant.

He admired Allende. He was a man trying, as Czechoslovakia's Dubcek had tried, to bring forth a humane socialism. "Allende was a man with a sense of humor, a man who liked women, who liked practical jokes. He had the support of the cardinal. He had the support of a great body of the priests. He was not so histrionic as Castro. There was complete freedom of the press."

But Allende is gone; the Americans helped to overthrow him. Dubcek is gone. Portugal is teetering on the edge of the abyss. There are dark clouds over what remains of Western Europe. "I have my doubts of socialism now," he says. "It has to be either Communism or the welfare state, it seems."

And staggering England, what will become of her? He almost sighs. "I have a feeling that somehow, like the war, we will find a way through." He is like one of his own solitary heroes, concealing untold depths of unhappiness and strength.

He was always an outsider. Even the Catholicism which shapes his great works is gritty and heretical. It is the hard way he has written of, difficult solutions, difficult joys. He has no part of the casual view of life, hedonistic, mindless, glittering. He writes of the necessity to be "informed by a religious conscience," and it is overwhelming. He is a man who has managed to live his life with honor in an era which does not recognize honor, a man who has found something to remain true to. He quietly recites a bit of Arthur Clough:

> *We are most hopeless who had once most hope,*
> *And most beliefless that had most believed.*

"Isn't that the way it is now?" he asks.

People
January 19, 1976

An Old Magician Named Nabokov
Lives and Writes in Splendid Exile

The Montreux Palace Hotel was built in an age when it was thought that things would last. It is on the very shores of Switzerland's Lake Geneva, its balconies and iron railings look across the water, its yellow-ocher awnings are a touch of color in the winter light. It is like a great sanitarium or museum. There are Bechstein pianos in the public rooms, a private silver collection, a Salon de Bridge. This is the hotel where the novelist Vladimir Vladimirovich Nabokov and his wife, Véra, live. They have been here for fourteen years. One imagines his large and brooding reflection in the polished glass of bookcases near the reception desk where there are bound volumes of the *Illustrated London News* from the years 1849 to 1887, copies of *Great Expectations, The Chess Games of Greco,* and a book called *Things Past,* by the Duchess of Sermoneta.

Though old, the hotel is marvelously kept up and, in certain portions, even modernized. Its business now is mainly conventions and, in the summer, tours, but there is still a thin migration of old clients, ancient couples and remnants of families who ask for certain rooms when they come and sometimes certain maids. For Nabokov, a man who rode as a child on the great European express trains, who had private tutors, estates, and inherited millions which disappeared in the Russian revolution, this is a return to his sources. It is a place to retire to, with Visconti's Mahler and the long-dead figures of La Belle Époque, Edward VII, D'Annunzio, the munitions kings where all stroll by the lake and play miniature golf, home at last.

Nabokov, the Wizard of Montreux, the Russian émigré whom critics have called "our only living genius" and "the greatest living American novelist," submits unwillingly to interviews. He prefers to conduct such exchanges on paper, writing and rewriting the answers "and some of the questions," as he wryly says. From time to time, though, there is a visitor. "My husband does not ad lib," Mrs. Nabokov warns on the telephone. She is his companion, guardian, and acolyte. "He is very busy," she adds.

His newest book, *Tyrants Destroyed*, has just been published, a collection of thirteen stories. All but one were written in Russian between 1924 and 1939 and have been translated by Nabokov and his son, Dmitri. It is the penultimate work from a famous writer who seems busy bricking up any remaining chinks in the wall of his reputation. These recent books are not cornerstones, but they are, as always, beautifully written and call for frequent trips to the dictionary.

Nabokov deals in painterly colors, in marvelous details and tones. ". . . the last time I went swimming," he writes in one story, "was not at Hungerburg but in the river Luga. Muzhiks came running out of the water, frog-legged, hands crossed over their private parts: *pudor agrestis*. Their teeth chattered as they pulled on their shirts over their wet bodies. Nice to go bathing in the river toward evening, especially under a warm rain that makes silent circles, each spreading and encroaching upon the next . . ." He is a visual, sensual writer calling forever upon the past.

Whereas American entertainers such as Truman Capote or Gore Vidal, taking advantage of their fluency and known charm, appear freely on television and give us a more or less close look at the splendors of literary life, Nabokov is a more elusive figure. It is not that he is less attractive, and his English is impeccable. But he is aloof by nature, a compulsive revisionist, and he feels for some reason insecure with nothing between himself and an audience except unrehearsed speech. When he gave his lectures on modern fiction at Cornell, he read them from cards typed by his wife. "My husband," Véra Nabokov finally agrees, "will meet you at four o'clock in the green room next to the bar."

The great chandeliers hang silent. The tables in the vast dining room overlooking the lake are spread with white cloth and silver as if for dinners before the war. At a little after four, into the green room with the slow walk of aged people, the Nabokovs come. He wears a navy blue cardigan, a blue-checked shirt, gray slacks, and a tie. His shoes have crepe soles. He is balding, with a fringe of gray hair. His hazel-green eyes are watering, oysterous, as he says. He is seventy-five, born on the same day as Shakespeare, April 23. He is at the end of a great career, a career half-carved out of a language not his own. Only Conrad comes to mind as someone comparable (although Beckett, going the other way, has chosen to write in French), but Conrad, a native Pole, was a duffer in English compared to Nabokov's prodigious command of an adopted tongue.

Véra has blue eyes and a birdlike profile. Her hair is completely white. They are soon to celebrate a wedding anniversary, "our golden," Nabokov says. They met in Berlin and married there in 1925, but they might as easily have met in Leningrad. "We went to the same dancing class, didn't we?" he asks. It has not been an unhappy marriage then? "That is the understatement of the century," Nabokov smiles.

He is currently at work on the French translation of his novel *Ada*, which was published in 1969. It is the memoir of a philosopher, Van Veen, who fell in love when he was fourteen with his cousin, Ada, then twelve, who turns out to be his sister, and on and off their lives are entwined into old age, until he is ninety-seven and she ninety-five. "My fattest and most complex book," he says. It is also his preferred masterpiece, although the public still chooses *Lolita*.

This translation has already taken five years. Vera says that her husband is going over it line by line. "You see some terrible booboos," he moans. Nabokov knows French and German perfectly and, with his revisions, is content about the translations in these languages. His son, Dmitri, was unfortunately too busy to check the Italian edition; the horrors of the Turkish and Japanese Nabokov does not like to imagine.

He regards himself as an American novelist, and from the comfort of Switzerland professes great love and nostalgia for the United States, where he spent eighteen years, from 1940 to 1958. He prizes his U.S. passport, but here he remains, in the artistic vaults where rest such other international treasures as Chaplin and, when he was alive, Noel Coward, not to mention lesser pieces of bric-a-brac. He sips a gin and tonic. "It's only an accident that we're here," he explains. His wife had been here in 1914 with her family, and when the two of them passed through in 1961, she said, why not stay for a while? They have been here ever since. "I introduced kidding into Montreux," he says.

Novelists, like dictators, have long reigns. It is remarkable to think of Nabokov's first book, a collection of love poems, appearing in his native Russia in 1914. Soon after, he and his family were forced to flee as a result of the Bolshevik uprising and the civil war. He took a degree at Cambridge and then settled in the émigré colony in Berlin. He wrote nine novels in Russian, beginning with *Mary*, in 1926, and including *Glory*, *The Defense*, and *Laughter in the Dark*. He had a certain reputation and a fully developed gift when he left for America in 1940 to lecture at Stanford. The war burst behind him.

Though his first novel written in English, *The Real Life of Sebastian Knight*, in 1941, went almost unnoticed, and his next, *Bend Sinister*, made minor ripples, the stunning *Speak, Memory*, an autobiography of his lost youth, attracted respectful attention. It was during the last part of ten years at Cornell that he cruised the American West during the summers in a 1952 Buick, looking for butterflies, his wife driving and Nabokov beside her making notes as they journeyed through Wyoming, Utah, Arizona, the motels, the drugstores, the small towns. The result was *Lolita*, which at first was rejected everywhere, like many classics, and had to be published by the Olympia Press in Paris (Nabokov later quarreled with and abandoned his publisher, Maurice Girodias). A tremendous success and later a film directed by Stanley Kubrick, the book made the writer famous. Nabokov coquettishly demurs. "I am not a famous writer," he says, "Lolita was a famous little girl. You know what it is to be a famous writer in Montreux? An American woman comes up on the street and cries out, 'Mr. Malamud! I'd know you anywhere.'"

He is a man of celebrated prejudices. He abhors student activists, hippies, confessions, heart-to-heart talks. He never gives autographs. On his list of detested writers are some of the most brilliant who have ever lived: Cervantes, Dostoyevsky, Faulkner, and Henry James. His opinions are probably the most conservative, among important writers, of any since Evelyn Waugh's. "You will die in dreadful pain and complete isolation," his fellow exile, the Nobel Prize winner Ivan Bunin, told him. Far from pain these days and beyond isolation, Nabokov is frequently mentioned for that same award. "After all, you're the secret pride of Russia," he has written of someone unmistakably like himself. He is far from being cold or uncaring. Outraged at the arrest last year of the writer Maramzin, he sent this as yet unpublished cable to the Soviet writers' union: "Am appalled to learn that yet another writer martyred just for being a writer. Maramzin's immediate release indispensable to prevent an atrocious new crime." The answer was silence.

Last year Nabokov published *Look at the Harlequins!*, his thirty-seventh book. It is the chronicle of a Russian émigré writer named Vadim Vadimych whose life, though he had four devastating wives, has many aspects that fascinate by their clear similarity to the life of Vladimir Vladimirovich. The typical Nabokovian fare is here in abundance, clever games of words, sly jokes, lofty knowledge, all as written by a "scornful and austere author, whose homework in Paris had never received its due." It is probably one of the final steps toward a goal that so many lesser writers have striven to achieve: Nabokov has joined the current of history not by rushing to take part in political actions or appearing in the news but by quietly working for decades, a lifetime, until his voice seems as loud as the detested Stalin's, almost as loud as the lies. Deprived of his own land, of his language, he has conquered something greater. As his aunt in *Harlequins!* told young Vadim, "Play! Invent the world! Invent reality!" Nabokov has done that. He has won.

"I get up at six o'clock," he says. He dabs at his eyes. "I work until nine. Then we have breakfast together. Then I take a bath. Perhaps an hour's work afterward. A walk, and then a delicious siesta for about two and a half hours. And then three hours of work in the afternoon. In the summer we hunt butterflies." They have a cook who comes to their apartment, or Vera does the cooking. "We do not attach too much importance to food or wine." His favorite dish is bacon and eggs. They see no movies. They own no TV.

They have very few friends in Montreux, he admits. They prefer it that way. They never entertain. He doesn't need friends who read books; rather, he likes bright people, "people who understand jokes." Vera doesn't laugh, he says resignedly. "She is married to one of the great clowns of all time, but she never laughs."

The light is fading, there is no one else in the room or the room beyond. The hotel has many mirrors, some of them on doors, so it is like a house of illusion, part vision, part reflection, and rich with dreams.

People
March 17, 1975

From Lady Antonia's Golden Brow Springs Another Figure of History

"A *well-written* life," Thomas Carlyle said, "is almost as rare as a well-spent one." He might just as easily have turned it around and, whichever way, it would perfectly fit Lady Antonia Fraser, one of the most dazzling and aristocratic ornaments of London society, whose biography, *Mary Queen of Scots*, was a roaring bestseller a few years ago. Its success astonished those who knew Antonia as the darling of glittering dinner parties and a woman much talked about for a number of reasons, none of them being remarkable literary talent. (The gossip these days is about Lady Antonia and Robert Stephens, estranged husband of actress Maggie Smith.)

To prove it had been no fluke, she sat down in the small pink and white study off her Kensington bedroom and wrote a biography of Oliver Cromwell, the obscure country gentleman who went to Parliament when he was twenty-eight, turned into a leader and soldier of genius, and upended English history. It too became a bestseller.

This week yet another life by Antonia Fraser, a beautifully illustrated *King James VI of Scotland, I of England*, is being published in the U.S. She combines careful research with great readability and, as a result, is both popular and academically respectable.

No one should be surprised to discover that Antonia, forty-two, is still another twig of a remarkable literary tree. She is the daughter of the Earl of Longford, a sometime Labour cabinet minister and respected author (*Peace by Ordeal*). Her mother, Elizabeth Longford, is the masterly biographer of Queen Victoria and Wellington. Rachel Billington, her sister, is the author of several novels (the latest, *Beautiful*). A brother, Thomas Pakenham—the earl's family name—occupies the family seat in Ireland and writes such works of history as *The Year of Liberty*.

Lady Longford taught Antonia to read at the age of three, with extraordinary results. Today she devours printed matter at the incredible rate of 3,000 words a minute—Jack Kennedy was once famous for a mere 1,200. She can polish off a heavy work of scholarship in an afternoon. "We've often talked about it," Antonia says, "and wondered if my mother made some mistake, I read so fast. It's made me more enemies." People on the train who would never dream of talking to an elegant stranger watch her briskly turning pages and lean forward to say, "Excuse me, you can't be reading that book."

"I think U.S. fiction is better than ours," she says, seated in her large, light-filled house. There are books and flowers everywhere. The lampshades are askew. She likes Saul Bellow and Alison Lurie. She speaks with the faintest lisp, delicious as a whisper. "But English biography is better, I think. The climate for it is somehow right, perhaps like the Irish climate is said to be good for complexions." During the war she was sent to a boys' school, the famous Dragon School in Oxford, where she bathed in cold water, played rugby, and received a no-nonsense education. It was an experience which left her without the least sense of female inadequacy; part of her famous charm is this genuine ease, a kind of fond assurance that lies dozing in the blood.

She describes herself as hopelessly spoiled. She has six children, three boys and three girls, and a husband, Hugh Fraser, a Conservative MP with an important political career. Spoiled she may be, passing along a hallway of her house and gesturing vaguely toward a door, "There is a rumor that's the kitchen," but she also works extremely hard. Three years of research went into *Mary Queen of Scots*, even more into *Cromwell: The Lord Protector*. Like most good writers, Antonia Fraser works steadily—literary achievement is the triumph of the ant. In her case it means rising at eight, seeing her children and husband off, and then she is at it from nine until twelve thirty every day. In the afternoon there's a large family tea with her children, precisely at four. She works both in London and at the Scottish country house near Inverness where the family spends weekends and holidays. She is a Virgo. "Order appeals to me," she says. "Either to have it or impose it."

Her favorite biography is Mrs. Elizabeth Gaskell's *Life of Charlotte Brontë*, with Painter's *Proust* perhaps second. Her style is modeled on Gibbon's and is very Latin-based. "Those ablative absolutes," she moans. She was twenty and smoking cigars at Oxford when she read the Brontë and was stunned by it; she remembers thinking, gosh, this is what a biography should be. She reread it while writing *Mary Queen of Scots*.

As if all this were not enough, she is chairman of the Society of Authors and campaigning fiercely for public lending rights which would pay writers for the number of times their books are taken out of libraries. Such a system in one form or another already exists in other places—Scandinavia, Australia, West Germany. There is opposition.

"Alas," she laments, "the librarians are dead against it." The librarians of England have reason to fear. Against them, at the head of her fellow writers, witty, engaging, and armed with the personal friendship of many politicians, is that most powerful of foes: a beautiful and clever woman, determined to have her way.

It is Friday. In the favorite restaurant where she has lunched at the best table, they are holding out her cape. "I must run," she apologizes. "If I don't catch the train my husband will shoot me. Which he is equipped to do." She is off for Scotland with six new books packed in her bags.

"You'll read all those?"

"Oh, no," she says, smiling. "But in case the train breaks down . . ."

People
February 24, 1975

Ben Sonnenberg Jr.

In the firmament when I was a schoolboy were names like Achilles and Caesar, and Horatio, standing alone at the bridge. In the more immediate world there were Lindbergh, Jack Dempsey, and Scott of the Antarctic, writing with frozen fingers the heartbreaking fare-well letter. When Dempsey's eyes were swollen shut at the end of the championship fight with Tunney, a fight he had lost, he asked his handler to lead him across the ring so he could shake Tunney's hand. Class.

In the grown-up world, I was surrounded by heroes: all-Americans, halfbacks who'd played with Bear Bryant, Medal of Honor and DSC winners, top aces like Bud Mahurin, Boots Blesse, Kasler, and Low. There were men who'd been on the Ploesti or Doolittle raid or landed on Guadalcanal. Heroes in their youth, acting out of natural impulse, so to speak, even if it meant greater courage and skill than others possessed. Oddly enough, none of them seemed particularly heroic at the time. They wore it, almost all of them, lightly. But the more they recede into legend, the greater they become.

There's another style of heroism I find myself admiring: not the particular act or achievement, but the long, hopeless struggle almost beyond imagining, the battle that has no end.

I first met Ben Sonnenberg Jr. before he had any idea of what would be asked of him. It was about 1973. He was dandyish, well-off, in his thirties, several times married, a man with a certain loftiness, prodigiously read, a sometime playwright, raised in a handsome house in New York's Gramercy Park, disapproved of by a very successful father.

I don't remember when it was diagnosed, but there were the early signs: tripping slightly on a crack in the sidewalk, after a while the use of a cane, then two canes, the difficulty in getting out of a taxi, the process of somehow making it to the door of the restaurant and then falling across a table inside. In the end, a wheelchair, but how far from the real end this was.

He had MS, areas of the brain and spinal cord degenerating, the nerve fibers losing their covering and unable to transmit impulses.

Slowly, year by year, all that he possessed of physical ability was taken away. He became bedridden. He could no longer raise a hand in greeting, or feed himself, or even turn the page of a book. Absolutely everything had to be done for him.

Meanwhile, he never complained. He did not speak of the indignities, the nightmare of hygiene, the injustice of it all, the despair— these seemed not to exist. Instead, he founded and edited a literary magazine, *Grand Street*. He celebrated his birthday with an annual party, saw people, wrote, entertained. Perhaps he pitied himself, but he let no one else pity him. I think of Stephen Hawking, but I don't know him. I think of Helen Keller, but hers was a life of optimism, a life that was enlarging. Ben Sonnenberg's is of a long forced retreat.

I see him occasionally now, not like Richard Howard, who comes to read to him, not like Susan Minot and closer friends, but I am often near him. I think of him frequently. It's hard to explain, but I am jealous of him. I am jealous of his bravery and spirit. A hero is, among other things, someone favored by the gods. Greater, perhaps, is one crushed by them who, despite it, triumphs.

Men's Journal
May 2001

Life for Author Han Suyin Has Been a Sometimes Hard But Always Many Splendored Thing

In the China in which she was born, mile after mile of peasants sat in the branches of trees above the great floods. They were motionless, waiting for death as the train on its high embankment sped past. They did not wave or shout for help. No one would help them. Nothing would change.

In the China of her marriage to a fanatic young Nationalist officer, a husband could kill his wife—it was not unusual to beat her on their wedding night to teach her meekness and submission. China was a backward country, corrupt, poor, half-controlled by foreigners. Its problems were too immense to be solved.

Those Chinas have vanished.

And Rosalie Chou, the ugly-duckling daughter of a Chinese railway official and his Belgian wife, disappeared also to become, after incredible experiences, Han Suyin, doctor, writer, and a woman of her time.

Animated, beautiful, well-dressed, she gestures frequently as she talks. It is difficult to believe that she was once so plain she was told by her mother that she would have to earn her own living, she was too ugly ever to marry. How do these dazzling metamorphoses

43

occur? She was always intelligent, always pretty and defiant, but the awkward child who could never learn to dance somehow became a handsome young woman with a brilliant smile and white teeth—North China teeth—not a cavity in them to this day. They're very uneven, she insists; she is not beautiful, her features are uninteresting. "My eyebrows are too short, like Chou Enlai's." She moves her graying hair to reveal them.

Han Suyin, fifty-nine, is most famous perhaps for her bestselling novel *A Many-Splendored Thing*, published in 1952 and transformed into both a movie and a popular song. But she has also written a series of autobiographies, very moving in both their humanity and their vast detail. *The Crippled Tree* was the first, and *A Mortal Flower* and *Birdless Summer* followed.

She has just brought out *Wind in the Tower*, the second and concluding volume of her biography of Mao Tse-tung, whose death came almost on the eve of publication. An admittedly sympathetic work, it was eight years in the writing, and at what a moment it has appeared! Obscurity covers China: once again, fierce struggles, new paths. Mao seems certain to be the sacred figure whose legacy will be sought after for years to come. It is extraordinary how little of him is really known—the only intimate accounts are still those of Edgar Snow, the American reporter of the Far East who died in 1972.

Han Suyin did not know Mao personally. She had never read a word he'd written when one night on a Peking street she bought a pamphlet called *On the Correct Handling of Contradictions among the People*. It was 1957. She was practicing medicine in Malaya and Singapore and had gone back to China to see for herself if the new ruler was to be another Stalin, ruthless and bloody. "I would die in my soul if I did not return to see for myself."

It was one of the turning points of her life. She was fascinated by the man, his vision, his ideas. The story of Mao began to possess her, "a story that really shook me—the love of Mao for his people."

She saw Mao only once, in a room with forty other writers, and he did not speak. She met Chou Enlai many times, and she knew firsthand the era. She has become a kind of apologist for China now—with friends in Peking in high places, although she has enemies too, she admits. The extreme left does not like her, probably because of her European life and privileges. She has never returned to China to live. But the left is in eclipse. As always, she has been fortunate.

There were eight children in her family. One-half of them survived. "The average," she comments, "in those days." She had a brother who died of convulsions when the French doctor refused to come. "I'm not going to bother myself for a dirty Eurasian," he said. There were only three mixed couples living on the Peking-Hankow railway line, and the Eurasian children were despised. "We were looked upon as prostitutes and freaks."

Her mother named her Mathilde Rosalie Claire Elizabeth Genevieve Chou, and her father gave her the Chinese name of Chou Yueh-ping, which means guest of the moon. (In China the family name always comes first—there are only 186 surnames for all Chinese.) Their mother made the little girls remove their earrings every night. If warlords or bandits came they would rip them out of their earlobes. Rosalie—she preferred that name—went to a convent school and was raised as a Catholic. She read only pious works, "and once, Jules Verne." In 1935 she won a scholarship to go to Belgium—there were four or five students chosen a year—and she began her medical studies. She had dreamed of becoming a doctor since the age of twelve when every Sunday on the way to church the Chous had to fight their way through hordes of beggars. "I wanted to cure them."

The high-bourgeois family of her mother refused to accept her at first, but she eventually conquered them. One of her uncles, a diamond merchant in Amsterdam, wrote in a letter, "This girl is intelligent," and before long she was an ornament at family dinners. She was sitting one day in a park in Brussels, far from the China which had been invaded in her absence by a powerful new Japan. Above her were the tall, summery trees of the Bois Fort. "How peaceful it all is," her boyfriend sighed. She suddenly smashed her teacup. "I'm going to China!" she announced.

"The true me is inner-motivated," she explains. "My craziest decisions—things that appear crazy—I've thought about for months."

The voyage home was by boat from Marseilles. Onboard, in first class, was a young Chinese man who had been attending Sandhurst. He was returning to serve China, he told her. "So am I," she said. His name was Tang Pao-huang, and he came from a landowning family, part of the ruling elite. He was sincere, handsome, intensely patriotic. He proposed when they reached Hong Kong, and in a rapture of idealism they were wed. His true nature was soon revealed. He was, in fact, a demon, a cold fanatic filled with absolute loyalty and devotion to the leader, Chiang Kai-shek. In time he was to become one of the generalissimo's aides and eventually to find death in battle against the Communists in 1947. For the seven years they were together, he beat her.

Chiang Kai-shek had a ferocious temper. Everyone was terrified of him, Han recalls. This was the China in which six young writers, members of a leftist organization, were made to dig their own graves by Chiang's men and then were bound, thrown into the holes, and buried alive. Suyin and her husband lived in the wartime capital, Chungking. "A woman of talent is not a virtuous woman," he told her. He was ashamed of her, mortified that she had not immediately become pregnant, but despite everything she could not leave him. He would have killed her. She worked as a midwife, and Tang, to explain her frequent absences, invented a daughter for her. One day in Cheng-tu she bought one—children were for sale everywhere then—a year-old baby, beautiful but covered with sores and so pathetically hungry she cried when she saw a bowl of rice. Even today, thirty-five years later, Han Suyin's voice falters and her eyes fill with tears as she remembers. She paid a thousand Chinese dollars for her daughter. "Everybody said, 'Oh, you've paid too much. You could have got her for 200.'"

She wrote her first novel, *Destination Chungking*, during this period. It was widely praised and her talent was immediately evident. But only in London, where her husband had been sent as military attaché, was she finally able to break free. She refused to return to China with him in 1945. Did she not fear for her life then? "Ah, but this was in England," she says with a lovely smile. She went back to school to complete her medical education, graduating with honors in 1948, by then a widow. She was thirty-one.

Because it was the doorstep to China, by now Communist, she settled in Hong Kong and began her practice. She fell in love with a married British correspondent, and the story of their affair, written at night on the kitchen table, became *A Many-Splendored Thing*. Her lover was killed in Korea. Han Suyin married Leonard Comber, another Englishman, on the rebound—and because she thought her daughter, then twelve, needed a father. She was living in Malaya, running two clinics and working from early morning until night, charging one dollar a visit while other doctors charged $15. After work, she wrote. "It amused me," she explains. The reason is plainly deeper. "I do what I want. That's the leitmotiv of my life."

There is a long tradition in literature of doctors who have been writers, some good and some great. Rabelais and Chekhov, for example, Céline and Conan Doyle, A. J. Cronin and Somerset Maugham. "I don't think of myself as a writer," she protests, and the name she chose, Suyin, means simple sound. Nevertheless, she wrote four more novels between 1956 and 1963, none of them quite as successful as her bestseller, and then she turned to the autobiographies. Her marriage to Comber ended in amicable divorce. "He was a nice man," she says. "He spoke five languages, but our relationship bored me to tears."

She lives now in an apartment in Lausanne with her third husband, Vincent Ruthnaswamy, an ex-colonel in the Indian army, broad, deeply burnished, and a man of considerable tact. They met in Nepal where he was building roads. Medicine is behind her; she has not practiced since 1964. She and her husband travel, spending about four months a year in Lausanne. They have a house in India and a small apartment in Flims in the Swiss mountains. The apartments are rented. "I don't believe in accumulating property after sixty," she explains. She is rushing things a bit. Most women would be happy to look like her at forty.

Szechwan is her province; her father's family is from there. An isolated region deep in the mountains, it has often during its history been independent, with close ties to Tibet. The Yangtze flows from there and many great legends of China come from there as well. The people are different. "We are the Italians of China," she says. "We eat more red pepper than anyone else. Also, we are not afraid to die." She turns to her husband. "Don't you think it's better than other places in China?" "Yes," he says shrewdly. "It's very Indian."

Her day begins at seven. She wakes and has coffee. For an hour she does housework and then settles down to her correspondence, using the dining room table. "My husband has his typewriter on the desk," she explains, "and since he is a man, he should have the place of honor." Vincent doesn't smile as she says this but on his face is a certain mixture of forbearance and disbelief. "Every twenty minutes or so I get up," she says, "and do something else. I think it's good for the figure."

Vincent cooks the lunch, and from two o'clock on she works. There are no Saturdays or Sundays. It is always work; no matter where they are living. They see few movies or plays, go out rarely, seldom entertain. She has too much to do: the next volume of her autobiography and a novel about India. Who knows what the future will bring? As another famous doctor, this one fictional, wrote: "To live life to the end is not a childish task." That was Zhivago.

People
November 8, 1976

D'Annunzio, the Immortal Who Died

He was born in a backward province, in a town of no consequence. His father was a politician and lecher, his mother one of those saintly women that Italy is famous for. He was one of five children. None of the others ever amounted to much. He had his first glimpse of glory at sixteen, the glory of Pushkin and Balzac that never tarnishes, and he was never to lose sight of it, even in the final years of his life when toothless and senile he died on a day he had predicted.

When I visited Gabriele D'Annunzio's villa which overlooks Lake Garda in northern Italy, it was November 1976. The big hotels along the lake were closed for the winter, the guides—the villa is now a national monument—stood around the cloakroom in their overcoats with newspapers stuffed in their pockets. D'Annunzio bought this villa just after the First World War when it was not much more than a small farmhouse. He named it the *Vittoriale* which meant roughly, "signifying victory," and set about enlarging and rebuilding it to his taste. It is filled with books, sculpture, grand pianos, bas-reliefs, and all the memorabilia of his life, even the airplane in which he flew over Vienna.

On the days I was there, few other visitors appeared. The grounds

were empty except for an occasional workman. In one of the out-
lying buildings a large exhibition of photographs of D'Annunzio's
life was in its final, unattended days. I had taken a tour of the main
house the day before and now wanted to go through slowly with a
notebook. The guide had wandered off and I was alone in a room
when a man engaged in replacing a light bulb suddenly noticed me
and, straightening up, demanded what was I doing? Photography or
making notes was absolutely forbidden, he said. An argument began
and finally the guide agreed we would have to obtain permission.
We walked down to the administrative offices near the gate. The
president of the *Vittoriale* was not in but an assistant, a woman in her
fifties, came out to see us. I explained that I was a writer interested
in D'Annunzio. I had taken the tour and was merely going through
again and making notes. I showed her some pages.

Ah. If I had only written for permission, she told me, everything
would have been all right. As it was, she was sorry, she could not
permit it.

"But what objection," I said, "can there be to making notes?"

"Don't you see, if we let you do it then all the writers will want
to come and do it," she said.

"Of course," I said. "How obvious."

No one wrote like D'Annunzio; no one, not even Byron, led so
scandalous and unforgivable a life, and no one has seen his legend
vanish more quickly. He was not just the national poet of Italy, he
was a Great Poet, that phenomenon which appears only once in a
century like a comet, and he saw himself rise and rise further still
until he seemed to be as bright as anything in the heavens. At the
time of his fame, in the period just before and after the First World
War, he was the most romantic and perhaps the greatest figure of
the century. But the verdict seems to have come in early. He will not
stand with Dante. He will not stand with Wagner. He will not stand
with Napoleon.

Gabriele D'Annunzio was born in Pescara, a town in the Abruzzi,
in 1863. It was the same year in which Cavafy was born, Chekhov

was three. Joseph Conrad six, and Tolstoy was thirty-four. He was the youngest child and a superior student. In those days education was classical. He read Latin and Greek, he knew French perfectly and some English. He had, from the first, an extraordinary ear, an eye that was smitten by beauty, and a desire that was to earn him a place in literature. His first book of poetry was published while he was still in school. It was youthful, passionate, and well-written. He sent a copy with a flattering inscription to the reigning poet of the time, Carducci, and was noticed by the critics. One called him an extraordinary talent. Another, in a phrase that could be applied to him throughout his life, said he deserved a medal and a sound thrashing. With a taste for the extravagant which was to be both his strength and weakness, he sent a false report of his death to a newspaper. Obituaries appeared throughout the country. He was launched.

In Rome he was the very picture of a young poet, romantic and unspoiled, but within a few years the skimpy black suit had vanished and he was summoning waiters in cafés with imperious raps of the cane and borrowing money from them as well. He met the great Carducci who had been his model. He married, in a great scandal and over the fierce objections of her family, the very eligible daughter of the Duke of Gallese. He had no money and expensive tastes. Soon after his marriage he began the series of love affairs that were to continue uninterrupted for more than thirty years and were to include some of the most highly placed women of his time. Meanwhile, he was writing, volume after volume of poetry, journalism, and in 1888 the first novel, *Il Piacere* (*The Child of Pleasure*).

His writing was opulent, dazzling, sensuous. He made no distinction, he used to say, between the soul and the flesh. It was a fatal lack. He had abandoned his wife and three children. His mistresses, the important ones, began with a beautiful, middle-class Roman he had first caught sight of standing outside a bookstore. There followed a Sicilian princess, then Eleonora Duse and a marchesa whose father was nothing less than prime minister. All of these and the ones after were infamous. He stood trial for adultery. He fought duels. He was detested by fellow writers, by decent people, the church, many crit-ics, and not a few husbands. He was amoral, grasping, shrewd, and the greatest writer in Italy.

As is the case with all Don Juans, his power came from within. He was anything but handsome. He was short, baldheaded, with bulging eyes and a prominent nose. His hips were broader than his shoulders. His teeth were described as yellow, white, and black. There was something faintly vulgar about him, something ordi-nary. And yet, women wrecked their lives for him and, abandoned, remembered him forever. It was quite simple: he was a god, and they believed he was. Their letters, their vows, their acts of self-immolation are all the same. The intoxicant he used was his fame.

By 1898 he had settled in a villa outside of Florence where he was to remain for twelve years, the most productive of his life. It was the *periodo solare*, his years of the sun. Duse had a house close by and their collaboration was one of both spirit and flesh. She was, next to Sarah Bernhardt, the most celebrated actress in the world. "A noble creature, chosen by me, who ruined herself for me," he later wrote. It was D'Annunzio's practice to take his novels directly from his personal life. Like George Sand, he wrote his notes almost literally on the body of his partner. In the case of Duse, he did not even wait until they had separated, but in 1900 published *Il Fuoco* (*The Fire*), which revealed brutally frank details of their relationship. "I love you but I shall make use of you," the hero says. It was a huge success and immediately translated into six languages.

During the same period, however, he wrote plays for her, almost one a year, and the poetry which is considered to be his imperish-able achievement. When in 1910, hopelessly in debt from years of lavish spending, he went to France, he took with him a world rep-utation. He spent five years of self-imposed exile there. They were years of excess, even for a man who was used to everything. Then in 1914 the war broke upon France like a thunderstorm.

Now began one of the most exalted phases of his life. Though he was a voluptuary, there was another side to D'Annunzio. He came, it must be remembered, from a region that was both primitive and violent. Virility was his creed. He believed Italy was a great nation, that it had been and was to be again. For a young nation the path to greatness was war. Though the horrors of the conflict were already apparent, D'Annunzio did all he could to bring Italy into it. His fiery speeches in Genoa and Rome were a major factor. On May 23, 1915, Italy joined the Allies.

In anguish at the bitterness of no longer being young and exhausted by years of pleasure, he nevertheless succeeded in joining the army. He was fifty-three. The military authorities recognized he would be of greater value if allowed to fill an unconventional role, and as a result he saw action on land, at sea, and in the air. Although he was in a privileged position, there is no question of his valor. He won the highest decorations. He lost an eye in an aircraft accident. The apogee of his military career was a spectacular raid over Vienna in which he led his squadron and dropped leaflets instead of bombs.

In the end he was disappointed. The fever of the war was over. Like many other men he found it difficult to face peace. Italy had spent too much, there was little to show for it. A year after the war he had one final adventure, he led a force of volunteers, the *arditi*, into Fiume, a seaport east of Trieste, to seize it for Italy. For over a year he remained there, making speeches from a balcony and refusing to be dislodged. The government finally took courage and moved against him. He capitulated. He was not punished.

When Mussolini, with whom he had been on intimate terms, seized power in 1922, D'Annunzio had already withdrawn to the villa where he remained for the rest of his life. Although he may have had a certain contempt for the Fascists, he had inspired them, helped prepare the ground for them, and was sympathetic with their aims. He continued to write; a national edition of his works comprised some forty-nine volumes.

He was still the greatest of heroes to two generations of Italians. In 1924 he was made a prince, a hereditary title, the Prince of Montenevoso. He fervently supported the Italian invasion of Ethiopia. His teeth were gone, he was a trembling old man, addicted to cocaine. The last photographs show someone looking close to ninety, the nose swollen in a collapsed face, the chin that of a tortoise. The *Vittoriale*, he had enlarged with state funds into a museum and monument. It was, as well, a mausoleum, a shrine, a tomb like that of the kings. He died suddenly on March 1, 1938, and lay in state in the uniform of a general of the air force. On his finger was his mother's gold ring. On the photograph of her kept near his bed was written, *non pianger piu* . . . from a line of Dante's, "Weep no more, your beloved son is coming home."

Ariel. A name he called himself and often signed, sometimes as Gabriel Ariel. In every poet, to some degree, there is this lyric angel and the sheer beauty of language is his domain.

Bacca a Luisa. The last of the women. She was a young pianist that he met in Venice during the war and who was with him thereafter. D'Annunzio was passionately devoted to music. He believed the Italian language possessed musical elements that were Wagnerian in their power. He felt himself, in fact, to be the heir to Wagner whose death in Venice with the hero carrying the coffin is the closing scene of one of the novels.

Canto Novo (New Song). The second book of poems, published when he was nineteen. In it was exuberance, sensuality, and an assured voice which cried, ". . . Sing of the immense joy of living, of being strong, of being young, of biting the fruits of the earth, with strong, white, ravenous teeth . . ." Suddenly he was famous.

Capponcina. The villa on a hillside at Settignano, overlooking Florence. The city at that time had great cultural prestige. He remodeled the villa, which was rented, to conform to his taste. The rooms were various shades of gold, there was heavy furniture, statuary, pillows, brocade, and bric-a-brac of every description. He had horses, servants, dogs, and two apartments in town. He lived the life of a *gran signore*, traveling frequently, often with Duse, and writing prodigiously, plays, novels, his greatest poems. From the furnace of his mind, as he said. Towards the end, when Duse had been replaced, the scale of living went from extravagant to ruinous and favorite horses were sleeping on Persian rugs. In 1911, when he had gone to France, the contents of the villa were put up at auction to satisfy the creditors. Everything was sold, furnishings, horses, pictures, even the dogs.

Duse, Eleonora. She was born in a hotel and died in one. The child of traveling players, her name was on posters when she was six. At sixteen she played Juliet in Verona and scattered roses on the body of Romeo; her ascension had begun. She was plain, with a high forehead, faded-looking, austere. She used no makeup. She made herself up morally, she used to say. She was Bernhardt's great rival, playing in competition in the same city on many occasions and once in the same theater. They died within a year of each other, Bernhardt in 1923, Duse in 1924.

When she was twenty she was seduced by a newspaper publisher and had a child, who died. She carried the coffin to the cemetery herself, it was in Marina di Pisa, a small seaside town where she would later go with D'Annunzio. When she was twenty-three she married a minor actor. They had a daughter. The husband, she ultimately left in Buenos Aires. She formed her own company and became the mistress of the poet Arrigo Boito. Divorce was nonexistent in Italy then, they could not marry. She was playing Ibsen, Shakespeare, Sardou and Dumas and reading the morning papers in an old shawl and tortoise-shell glasses. There were tours to England, America, all of Europe.

She had been urged to read D'Annunzio by a friend and found herself both attracted and repelled. Boito was eighteen years her

senior, wise, idealistic, paternal. Now came the incandescent young
poet trailing scandalous relationships and an immense reputation.
Amori et dolori sacra—26 Settembre 1895—Hotel Royal Danieli—Venezia
is written in his notebooks with an asterisk. Sacred love and pain. It
was the night they became lovers. Even before this she had recognized in him the inspired poet the theater had been waiting for and
he at last had found his heroine.

In the nine years that they were together, he wrote many plays
for her and she determinedly kept them in her repertoire even
though they were unsuccessful, even sending him money and false
reports from half-empty houses in America. His best play, *La Figlia di
Iorio*, he gave to another actress, just as he had given an earlier one
to Bernhardt. Still they traveled and went on tour. They planned a
national theater they would have at Albano, immortal plays beneath
the stars. Meanwhile, beneath her nose he was writing the novel
that exposed her before the world. She could have stopped its publication but chose not to. What was her suffering, she said, compared
to the question of giving Italian literature another masterpiece? At
the same time she felt soiled and ashamed. The character in the
novel, who was called Foscarina, had invaded her life.

The following year she put out 400,000 lire, then an enormous
sum, to open his newest play. "To the divine Eleonora Duse," it was
dedicated. By 1903 his unfaithfulness was flagrant. It was the end.
In desperation she wrote to her successor begging for a share of
D'Annunzio's life. She then disappeared, in a sense, into tours and
distant cities. After several years she retired and bought a small house
in the country. Rilke tried to raise money for a theater for her but
was unsuccessful. She had a slight limp. During the war she acted a
little and worked in hospitals. Her path crossed D'Annunzio's once,
in Udine; he passed in a cheering crowd. Their last meeting was in
Milan. She was in her sixties and wanted to produce one of his plays.
As he left her he is reported to have said, "How you have loved me!"

She was on tour in America when she died, in Pittsburgh, on
April 21, 1924. Her body was returned to Italy and is buried in the

cemetery of Asolo, in the theater where we will all act someday, as she liked to say. All of D'Annunzio's letters to her were burned. To the end, though, she still blessed him, the great giver of life who had made her what she was. Before him, she said, she had not existed.

Exile. 1910 to 1915. He went first to Paris where he lived at the Hotel Meurice and quickly met everyone of importance. This was the Paris of Isadora Duncan, Proust, Diaghilev, and Stravinsky. He divided his time between the capital and a small summer resort near Bordeaux and resumed the life he had been living in Italy, mirrors, divans, damasks, women in emeralds and pearls. He seduced and was seduced. He caught syphilis. He raced greyhounds. Also, he triumphed. He was a figure, a cult. Plays poured forth, vast works of pretension and self-indulgence. Among these the grandest was *The Martyrdom of St. Sebastian.*

Fantasia. The yacht on which he went to Greece, with four companions including his French translator, Herelle, in 1895. D'Annunzio spent the days lying naked in the hot sun and having the sailors cool him with buckets of water. The conversation was mostly of cities and women and on a vulgar level. They read little or nothing and asked the guides to take them to brothels. In Athens they visited museums—the treasures of Mycenae had recently been discovered by Schliemann. From this trip and from notebooks that contained laundry lists and women's addresses came the first book of the *Laudi,* the series that includes D'Annunzio's finest work. When he returned with Duse some years later, he gave a speech saying that he owed to Greece the maturity of his mind.

Father. Francesco Paolo D'Annunzio, mayor of Pescara, landowner and bankrupt. He was born Rapagnetta but took the name of an

uncle who had adopted him, providing his son with a priceless legacy although Gabriele D'Annunzio was called Rapagnetta by detrac-
tors all his life. The father had small eyes, full lips, dyed hair when
he was older, and an unquenchable sexual appetite. He arranged to
send his son to the finest school, however, and paid for the printing
of his first book of poems. He died in 1893. D'Annunzio did not
return home in time for the funeral.

Flying. He flew for the first time in 1909 with the American pilot
Glenn Curtiss. He experienced rapture, comparable only to the purest sensations of art and love, he said.

Some of his best descriptions are those of pilots who were his comrades and whom he could still recall vividly even when an old man.

Genoa. It was here he came in 1915, returning from exile in France
with his eyes blindfolded as he neared the border should the emotion of seeing his homeland again prove too powerful. Here he
delivered the first of the orations that helped to bring Italy into the
war. Italy had an alliance with the Central Powers but had entered
into negotiations with the Allies to see who would offer the most
for her participation. It is likely D'Annunzio knew of this; his speech
had been submitted for government approval. The occasion was the
anniversary of Garibaldi's sailing fifty years earlier, there were some
of his white-bearded veterans in the crowd. D'Annunzio was not
just a writer standing up to speak. He had taken curtain calls, delivered eulogies, gone on lecture tours. He was an actor playing the
role of his life. The reaction of the crowd was frenzied. He felt the
drunkenness that comes from a feverish mob. He went on to Rome
where 40,000 people were waiting for him at the station. "No!" he
cried in a speech, "We will not be a museum, a hotel, a vacation
resort, a horizon painted Prussian blue where foreigners come for
their honeymoons . . ." He was constantly interrupted by applause.

His rooms at the hotel were drowned in flowers. He was summoned to meet the king who held out his hand, D'Annunzio said, to the good fighter who expressed the feelings of his people. A few days later Italy was at war.

Hardouin, Maria. Daughter of the Duke of Gallese, she was for fifty-five years the wife of D'Annunzio and his widow for sixteen. As a young girl she was slender, blonde, and unassuming. D'Annunzio had been invited to the family palace by her mother. The daughter was then eighteen with a taste for poetry and art. Soon they were exchanging notes and meeting secretly. They tried to elope but were caught. The affair was made even more infamous by D'Annunzio's poem, "Sin of May," that told of a blonde virgin and the gift she gave the poet, not to mention newspaper articles and his many confidences to friends. Three months pregnant and over the fierce objections of her father she was married without dowry in an almost empty church. After the honeymoon they settled for a while in Pescara. There were a few years of happiness, but she had made a terrible mistake, she would have done better to buy his books than to marry him, she later said. She discovered the first infidelities from a letter which fell out of his pocket. She bore him three sons; by the time the last one arrived D'Annunzio merely telegraphed instructions as to its naming.

Il Fuoco (The Fire). The most swinish book ever written, as one critic said. The scene is Venice, an autumnal city where a famous actress past her prime is desperate and wandering. The Hero is tormented by never having possessed her just after one of her triumphs on the stage when she was still hot from the breath of the crowd. Duse was five years older than he, but in the novel D'Annunzio makes it twenty. It was a work of pure invention, he insisted. People did not understand the real essence of the book which was "an act of gratitude."

La figlia di Iorio (The Daughter of Iorio). His most successful play and the only one which remains popular. He wrote it in thirty-three feverish days at Nettuno in the summer of 1903. The summer was his favorite time for work. He would begin at four in the afternoon, have a light meal at eight, and work until dawn. He preferred to be near the sea.

Laudi (Praises). The four books which contain the best of D'Annunzio's poetry. They were part of a projected series of seven, each to bear the name of one of the Pleiades. The full title is *In Praise of Sky, Sea, Earth, and Heroes.* Of the four, *Alcyone*, published in 1904, is generally conceded to be the finest. It describes the sensations of a Tuscan summer, the sounds, smells, glare, the burning noons. Many of the poems are of astonishing beauty, and when asked in old age which of his works he would like to see preserved, he said, *"Alcyone."*

Leone, Elvira. The dark-haired woman he had seen in front of a bookstore, she was the first important mistress. He saw her a second time at a concert. It was the spring of 1887, she was just recovering from a long illness. Within a week he had possessed her and renamed her Barbara. They had seven days of love in a small hotel in Albano. Their desire was, in his words, irreparable and unhealable. She was separated from her husband and lived with her parents. She would come to D'Annunzio in the room where he worked and give herself to him. He made detailed notes of her body which she found and read. These, as well as her letters, he used in a novel, *Il trionfo della morte* (*The Triumph of Death*), in which she is the heroine. "There is but one intoxication on earth," the hero says, "the certainty, the absolute unshakable certainty of possessing another human being."

Libyan War. In 1911, stimulated by the conquests of her powerful neighbors, Italy entered the final phase of the colonial era like the last stock buyer before the crash. Italian regiments sailed for North Africa to fight for the desert, and D'Annunzio's poems in praise of the adventure, written from exile and published prominently in the pages of the *Corriere della Sera*, made him a national poet at last.

Le Martyre de Saint Sebastien (The Martyrdom of Saint Sebastian). A zeppelin of the theater, written in French, in five "mansions," as the acts were called, with music by Debussy and a cast of two hundred. It was created for the dancer Ida Rubinstein. The costumes and decor were by Bakst. A glittering audience attended the premiere on May 22, 1911, and it was three in the morning when the last curtain fell. Proust found it boring despite the climax when the dancer was bound half naked to a tree and, avid for martyrdom, died beneath a rain of arrows. There were only ten performances although it reappeared after the war in Milan and more recently in Paris.

Mistresses. A hysterical Sicilian princess with whom D'Annunzio had two children followed Barbara Leone. Her name was Maria Gravina. She had run away from her husband and it was he who had them tried for adultery; they were convicted but never went to prison. She was moody, suicidal, and jealous to the point of madness, she used to wait for D'Annunzio with a loaded revolver in her hand. After six years he finally parted from her by packing a small suitcase and saying he was going to Rome for twenty-four hours. He never returned. Next came Duse and after her, the tall, blonde Alessandra di Rudini who came to the Capponcina on a path the servants had strewn with rose petals, D'Annunzio at her side in a suit of white silk. She was a widow at twenty-six and a noted horseman. Nike, he called her. It was she who introduced D'Annunzio to the Lake Garda region where she had a house.

Nathalie de Goloubeff was Russian, a singer, she had been sculpted by Rodin. She had two children and a rich husband; D'Annunzio always preferred other men's wives, proven women, as it were. She dreamed of performing in his *Phaedra*. She began learning the part, had costumes made, took singing lessons. Telegrams with secret words flew between them. Mixed with fervent expression were powerful erotic acts. "A great naked bee with beautiful tresses," he called her. When, after several years, he became indifferent, she retired to a farm outside Paris where she cared for his greyhounds and pitied her lost life. He sometimes visited her there. Until 1932 she held on to the farm though the dogs were gone and she had lost everything in the Russian revolution.

He would weep if he saw her again, she wrote. She sold his letters, stipulating that they not be published during his lifetime. She died a beggar in a small hotel in Meudon in 1941. Among her few possessions was a handsome dog collar with the name of their great greyhound, Agitator, that had won at St. Cloud.

Montesquiou, Robert de. The tall, arrogant, homosexual poet who was the model for Proust's Baron de Charlus. He introduced D'Annunzio to the society of Paris in 1910 and was his greatest champion. It was Montesquiou who took him to the dressing room of Ida Rubinstein after a performance of the ballet *Cleopatra.* D'Annunzio fell to his knees and, looking up at the boyish body, the long legs, the narrow head, whispered, *"Saint Sebastien."*

Mussolini. Their paths crossed after the war when Mussolini was editor of *Popolo d'Italia* and still a Socialist. He supported D'Annunzio's march into Fiume and even encouraged him to go further, to overthrow the government in Rome. Dear Comrade, it was, and My

Dear Friend. D'Annunzio did not have the talent or instinct for such a coup, however. Mussolini later cooperated with the government to bring the Fiume occupation to an end. From this time on he was central to D'Annunzio's life, paying him, flattering him, and in a sense confining him. He made a number of visits to the *Vittoriale*, the last in March 1938 when he walked behind the coffin.

Ortona. D'Annunzio's mother's birthplace near Pescara and the seat of his candidacy for parliament in 1899. He ran successfully as a conservative. He was not and never had intended to be only a poet; the world had to understand that he was capable of everything. His political career consisted of two speeches, a duel, and a dramatic change of party when he walked across the Chamber of Deputies from the right to the left, from death to life, he said. In the following election he ran from a district of Florence and was soundly defeated.

Vienna. It was described as one of the greatest exploits of the war. The mission had been cancelled several times. At last the weather was right. On August 12, 1918, the planes took off at dawn, one by one, and reached the Austrian capital by midmorning. "Over Vienna a pale mist lay," D'Annunzio reported. "Our manifestos drifted down like leaves falling in autumn."

> People of Vienna. We are flying over Vienna and could drop tons of bombs, on the contrary, we leave a salutation and a flag with its colors of liberty . . .

There was scrambling in the streets for the leaflets. Seven hundred miles, the newspapers hailed, with two crossings of the Alps and the stormy Adriatic. D'Annunzio delivered a speech: "We passed in our flight . . . the Isonzo, like a ribbon fallen from heaven, and forgotten Sabotino . . . Caporetto, like the Despair, which climbed up to tear our wings, all our slaughterhouses, our cemeteries, our Calvaries, our holy places. No, comrades, don't weep . . . Remember, remember, remember . . ." Elated by his success he planned a series of flights over all the capitals of Europe, flying directly over Mont Blanc, the highest point on the continent, as a symbol, but the war ended.

World War I. He saw action on land, with the 77th Regiment. He led a raid by torpedo boats against the harbor of Buccari. He commanded a flying squadron, made speeches to troops, won medals, fell to his knees to kiss the earth of battlefields. In Venice, while convalescing and half-blind, he wrote on slips of paper handed to him by his daughter the book that is regarded as his finest prose, *Notturno* (*Nocturne*). The war exhilarated him. At the head of his bed was a banner, on the dressing table, talismans and perfume. He flew in patent-leather boots with high heels and sometimes held the bombs between his knees. In the air over Italy he was battered by his age, the passions of his heroines crashing back to him, the memories, the trampled lives. He had no fear, he said, because he expected every mission to be his last and he could desire no greater glory than to die for Italy with "her beautiful limbs, from which harvests, artists and heroes were born." Death, he described as the male genius to whom youth was consecrated. Blood, wounds, and sacrifice, they were woven into themes to create an invincible nation, a great Italy rejoicing in just battle. "You with us," the blue and white banner of his squadron said, "We with you."

He had seduced a nation. He had as much as anyone brought his country into war. And afterwards the seizure of Fiume. He had spent himself. He had always considered himself a god and behaved as one, but physically and psychologically he was exhausted. The cloak of heroism which he had fashioned for himself had become heavy. With such a cloak, how much further could he march?

He went as far as Lake Garda. His uniforms are there, his letters from Rostand and Anatole France, his signed copies of Wagner's librettos. His death mask is there, as well, the nose larger, the eyes closed and at peace or at least in repose like a performer resting, like a gambler who need no longer play.

The Paris Review
Fall/Winter 1978

West Point and Beyond

Cool Heads

As a pilot I came close to being killed twice, once in a spectacular training crash and the second time in combat, in Korea, though
oddly enough not by the enemy. It was the airplane itself that almost
killed me. This was an F86, a Sabre, the first swept-wing fighter and
at the time the best we had.

I was coming back from a mission and turning steep onto final at
about five hundred feet. The landing gear and flaps had just come
down when suddenly, without warning, the controls froze. The stick
would not budge; it felt as if it was set in concrete. I was headed
straight for the ground. There was no time to call or say anything. I
might have ejected with a chance my chute would open in time, but
I was afraid I was too low. In those last seconds I shoved the throttle
forward and trimmed back on the stick, the only possible chance,
however slight, of moving the horizontal stabilizer and getting the
nose up enough to clear the ground. At the same time I pulled up
the gear. This last, almost insignificant detail saved me. Something
had gone haywire in the hydraulic system and extending the landing gear somehow froze the stick.

I climbed shakily and at a safe altitude tested it. There was the identical result.

"K14 Tower, I'm having some control problems. I'm declaring an emergency and would like permission to make a straight-in."

I don't know what my voice sounded like. In my memory, which is the only record, it was as calm as one could hope for. Why this, instead of, "Oh, my God! You know what happened? I nearly killed myself out here!" For one thing, other planes were trying to land; no one was interested in my emotional state. I was an element leader. This was a veteran wing.

You were trained to be cool. It was a mark, in fact a requirement. Frightened, inaccurate transmissions could clutter the air, spread confusion. Extreme coolness was greatly admired. It showed nerve, ability, control. After the event, sometimes hours after, the fear that had been subdued might make its appearance. A pilot I knew bailed out once at three hundred feet with his plane literally tumbling end over end. His chute barely blossomed before he hit. To his leader who'd circled back and was passing over he held out an upraised thumb—I'm OK. It was not until he was in the club that evening that his knees began to shake uncontrollably.

I made a straight-in approach to K14 that day, rounded out a little above the runway, and at the last moment extended the gear. The stick froze and the plane settled in to a smooth landing.

My knees didn't shake afterwards. It had all been too quick for that. Fear is more likely, more distinct when you see the enemy turning towards you from far off, many of them. They see you and are coming to kill you. Anyone can feel fear. There were jolts of it when the MIGs were firing and getting in behind you, and sometimes between missions, I felt a simmering fear for no apparent reason, but it would soon give way to normal concerns. The point is to go on. We had pilots—a few—who were unable to do that, but I never asked them why. They were, in a way, outcasts. They lived with their own nightmares, sleeplessness, concealed shame.

Afterwards, back in the states, I carried a feeling of superiority.

I'd been a flight leader in combat, I had a victory, I'd been in the thick of it. Slowly all that faded. In the years of ordinary life that followed I worried, felt anxiety, sometimes lost heart, but the facing of fear in the raw sense never came up. The lessons I had learned didn't translate. I was living in a different hierarchy with different values. Deep inside however there still exists that ethic, long drummed in and well-remembered: don't lose your nerve and, more important, don't appear to be losing it. As the beach boys in Hawaii used to say, "Cool head main ting."

Joe
1999

An Army Mule Named Sid Berry
Takes Command at the Point

Douglas MacArthur sat in this room. Through the windows, the Hudson is visible, the great gray river that American revolutionary forces at West Point once guarded. It is a large room, somber, paneled in oak. At one end a fireplace, in pale, gothic stone. On all four walls, high up, a solid band of portraits, each exactly the same size, of the men who have been superintendents of West Point.

This is the heart room a cadet never sees. The only way to see it, they say, is if you're the first captain or getting kicked out of school. There's one other way: you become Supe.

The new Supe is Sidney Berry, who at age forty-eight is one of the youngest major generals in the army. Behind him lies a brilliant record as a field commander. His hair is gray, going to white and cut exceedingly short. His face radiates intelligence, a cold face, proud, unyielding. On his finger is a heavy gold wedding band; on his wrist a chronometer that gleams like a surgical instrument. His arms are revealed by short khaki sleeves. They are sinewy. The word "Ranger" is on the point of one shoulder. Maxwell Taylor was forty-four when he became superintendent—four years younger than

Berry. Robert E. Lee was forty-five; Westmoreland, forty-six. Douglas MacArthur was thirty-nine.

Numbers do not prove everything, but this year over 11,000
young men applied for admission to West Point—a record. Something like 6,100 were nominated by their congressmen, and 1,435
were finally admitted, one of the largest classes ever.

"The country, the army, and West Point have emerged from
Vietnam," Berry says. "We are looking ahead." But since he recently
took over as superintendent, Berry must look as much to the present as to the future. He is, in a sense, still in training—just like the
new cadets in their first summer, whose faint sounds can be heard
from the far-off parade grounds. These roaring hot days of July and
August have long been known as Beast Barracks, "beast" being
cadet slang for an incoming fourth classman. They are the crucible
months. The ancient tradition was for them to be filled with unending humiliation and debasement, as if a man had to be reduced to
nothing before he could be recreated. Over the years this has gradually changed. The hazing, like many things from a time now past,
was once far more fierce.

And it was impractical. The task here is to produce the best possible soldier leader. It is approached somewhat like breeding cattle.
The good points are preserved, the bad are gotten rid of. The day of
highhanded authority is over. The emphasis now will be on building upon the natural dignity of the young men. There is no longer
a place at West Point for learning what cannot be of later use in the
army. This does not mean things academic, for the curriculum has
been broadened and enriched considerably and a cadet has more
freedom to choose among courses than ever before. It is the technique and attitudes of leadership, things that have always been the
academy's special interest, that now demand fresh definition and
attention.

They call West Point "The Factory," both in admiration and scorn;
it is dedicating itself to making certain that everything learned there

is transferable to the career which follows. "Career" is a word Berry hates. He is a man of ideals. His conscience is written all over him, like that of a fine Southern lawyer. "'Service' is the key word," he says quietly, "something other than personal gain." But Berry, as he well knows, must address himself to a new army that has emerged from Vietnam. A chastened army. A volunteer army. An army with a radically new racial composition, nearly 20 percent black.

When Berry was a first classman in 1948, there was hardly a black face in the Corps. Between 1900 and 1969, only seventy black men graduated. Today 268 out of some 4,300 cadets, about 6 percent, are black—including 82 in the incoming class. Berry would like to see the proportion of blacks and other minority groups become at least as great as in the population at large. "We are encouraging all minority groups in every way to enter."

Berry was not an outstanding athlete. Academically he was in the middle of the crowd. But he was well liked and popular. "Setting his standards by his father and Wendell Willkie . . ." the yearbook reads. He rose to be a cadet captain.

He was sent to the occupation forces in Japan. It seemed a kind of exile. Everyone was requesting duty in Germany. Nobody had foreseen the Korean War. For Berry it was a great piece of fortune, the first of many. One needs luck to go with ability. Luck may even be part of ability, in fact. When in the later days Napoleon no longer knew all the officers in his army who were being promoted to general, he would put a mark by names he did not recognize and ask in the margin, "Is he lucky?" Berry was wounded in Korea and twice promoted on the battlefield, from first lieutenant to major. Fifteen years later he was wounded again in Vietnam—shrapnel, sixteen holes. The man next to him was killed. He has won a Distinguished Service Medal, the Silver Star—four times—and the Air Medal an improbable forty-two times. The days are gone when a single bit of ribbon on a man's chest was a sign of heroic achievement. But wounds are still not cheap. And perhaps, God willing, he is lucky.

The superintendency has often served as a stepping-stone to the very top. Berry has all the credentials. He was military assistant to Secretary of Defense Robert McNamara in the Pentagon. He earned a master's degree at Columbia. He taught history. The proper mixture of education, exposure at high levels, the sound of guns. Like a racehorse making its move, he began to come to the front. He was the first in his class at the academy to earn a general's star.

He begins, in his careful, undramatic way, to tell a story about a Vietnamese officer he knew who was given command of a division known as "the coup division" near Saigon. The moral turns out to be, in his words, that "generals must become more politically aware but not more politically involved." He admires George Marshall, a man of strong principles and soldierly attitudes—"one of the outstanding men of this century," he says simply. And Omar Bradley, Lee and Grant, strike him as leaders of great integrity.

"The symbol of the army," he explains, "is the mule. The mule is stubborn. It works hard. It's basically a very honest animal."

Now, at this moment, the vivid caricatures of *Dr. Strangelove*—or the threat of holocaust—are worlds away.

The heat of afternoon lies over the green fields of West Point. There are grass cutters at work. The smell of the fairway. A question floats forth, apparently simple, though behind it is a certain amount of suspicion and guile. Could we have won in Vietnam?

The answer comes promptly: "No."

And the reason?

"The political understanding and the staying power of the Communists," Berry says, "were greater than those of our forces."

This must certainly have been one of the more knowledgeable admissions made by any field or flag officer involved in Vietnam. There were generals who wanted in both Korea and Vietnam to go the whole way, to take on China. It would have to be done sooner or later, they argued. Berry was and is not one of these. It would have been crazy, in his view.

He is a man one trusts. Like many soldiers, he comes from the south, from Hattiesburg, Mississippi. His wife is from Decatur, Georgia. They have two daughters and a son.

It was his children who brought him Dostoevsky and Hermann Hesse—and a book he has read more than once, *War and Peace*. He seems to have read without passion, however. One senses he reads to broaden himself, dutifully, as if trying to learn a foreign language.

"I identify with Prince Andrei," he says, referring to the nobleman in *War and Peace* whose bravery in battle was immortalized by Tolstoi.

The mule works hard. It is patient.

Vietnam is past. The presidents who committed us to it are gone, their advisers, their ministers of war; Kissinger is the only important exception. The army suffered badly there. Frustration and defeat. The loss of a sound moral position. The dissatisfaction, even the contempt of much of the country, especially the young, focused on it.

Resignation figures of West Point graduates rose sharply, going up to about 37 percent in the class of 1966. There was a four-year service commitment after graduation, so officers from this class could only begin to leave the army in 1971. Indications now are that the percentage of resigning officers is beginning to go down.

Berry has most recently come from commanding a division, the 101st Airborne at Fort Campbell, Kentucky. The army was buffeted during Vietnam, he admits, but the 101st is far healthier now than it was a year ago, and it will be even healthier a year from now, he promises.

This image of a fighting general himself—behind him the years of dusty encampments, bloody battles, daring escapes, and obedient routine—this dedicated life as it is revealed in his character and face is perhaps the real lesson he will somehow impart to cadets. Among them is probably one who will someday sit in this very office when Sidney Berry is a photograph high on the wall, above the Whistler sketches, the Catlin landscapes. It is a life that is a proof of things which no longer seem to exist.

The cadets come from the great cities now, and from sprawling suburbs. The rural and agrarian character of the Corps is changing. These new young men know little of nature and the kind of everyday hardship that used to be part of American life. West Point can no longer attract the great football players either, or even the very top students, perhaps. Can it compensate, in part, by the fiber of those who do come? And where can they now be found? For a long moment, Berry stands at the window embrasure, cold gray eyes looking out over West Point. Once a fortress that guarded a river, it became a school to guard a nation. There are trophies everywhere, cannon taken in Mexico, the cannon that fired the last shot at Appomattox. Tradition and glory. Enormous eagles carved onto the buildings. An oxide-green General Patton standing near the library.

The afternoon is fading. The light on the river is stilled. Berry is reflecting. He thinks, perhaps, of the America which lies beyond the cities, which seems to be shrinking but which, when one enters it, is as endless as the sea.

"There are still a lot of Hattiesburgs around the country," he says.

People
September 2, 1974

Ike the Unlikely

He possessed, like his boss, an invincible smile. The era had two of them. Roosevelt's was the hail of a champion. Ike's, they say, was worth twenty divisions.

Generals never smile. That was only one of the rules he broke. MacArthur didn't smile. Bradley either, it wasn't his nature—besides, his teeth were false. Ike smiled all the way, and his smile was instant and true. Even de Gaulle, a man not easily taken in, was impressed by him and sensed both generosity and warmth.

He never really commanded like Napoleon or Grant. "He let his generals in the field fight the war for him," MacArthur commented disdainfully, while "he drank tea with kings and queens." In an even more acidic mood he described him as the "best clerk I ever had."

We see the grand MacArthur striding through the surf onto the shore of the Philippines, fulfilling his pledge, trouser legs soaked, weathered hat on his head, the legendary figure who fought back from stunning defeat across a battlefield that was an ocean so vast that men's perceptions could barely cross it and who even after victory did not return home but chose to remain in Tokyo as proconsul and govern the shattered Japanese. He did it magnificently and with remarkable discernment, knowing it would be the capstone of a great career. While poor Eisenhower, whose dream of the future was merely a quiet cottage, had to oversee the demobilization, accepted the presidency of Columbia, for which he was ill-suited, recovered his poise to some extent in command of NATO, and finally lifting his head to the shouts was swept to the presidency by an adoring public. Thus the farm boy and the last of the aristocrats.

He was born in obscurity in northern Texas, one of seven children, all boys, in a family that always had to struggle and soon moved back to Kansas. From his mother Eisenhower inherited his chin, high forehead, and steady gaze. She was a hardworking, honest, no-nonsense woman, a pacifist who eventually became a Jehovah's Witness. "He that conquereth his own soul is greater than he who taketh a city," she told her son.

It was 1890, bread cost three cents a loaf. The plains were still crude and raw, the railroad the sole connection with the rest of the world. He was born into a home where the Bible was read daily, into a town that still lived by the frontier ethic, and into a world where man's temporal role could be summed up in one word: *work*. As a boy he grew vegetables behind the house and sold them. He worked in the Belle Springs Creamery, where his father was also employed, after school. Together with his brother he tried to earn enough money so that one of them could go to college, the other to follow afterward. Years later he was asked by someone if he was really a conservative. "Any of you fellows ever grow up working on a farm?" he asked.

At the urging of a friend, he took the exam for Annapolis and for West Point too while he was at it. It turned out he was too old for the naval academy, but the first man for West Point failed the physical and Eisenhower got the appointment. He arrived in June 1911. He had come mainly for a free education. Here he is, making his first, brief appearance as a running back for Army: sandy hair, five feet eleven inches, stocky, called Ike by his classmates. As a measure of his indistinguishability, there were four other "Ikes" in the class.

There were also nicknames like Nigger, Jew, Dago, and Chink. It was the class of 1915, the class they later said "the stars fell on." In what could pass for a gentleman's world, a backwater world as was the army it fed into, they rode horses, studied geology, engineering, natural philosophy, and hygiene, and pitched tents for the summer at the far end of the Plain. It was a closed world that held a certain comradeship and mystery.

He did not seem destined for greatness. Academically he was only average. He was not one of the cadet pantheon; neither was Bradley. He was well enough liked, confident, breezy. He preferred poker to dancing, and his classmates noted that he was fond of shooting the bull.

Caught up in the rising swell of the First World War, he was given training assignments and rose to become lieutenant colonel on his twenty-eighth birthday, but the war ended and he had suffered the classic grief of young officers—he had not seen action. The army quickly shrank. Everyone was demoted. He reverted to the rank of captain and together with Mamie vanished down the dusty roads that led to routine and remote posts—Leavenworth, Camp Meade, Fort Benning—while Jimmy Walker, Lindbergh, and Babe Ruth strode the stage. Lingering behind him, like a faint epitaph, was the opinion of one of his instructors at West Point who, like the others, had found him unremarkable: "We saw in Eisenhower a not uncommon type, a man who would thoroughly enjoy his army life . . ." But not much besides.

The most important group in the United States Army of the '20s and '30s was Pershing's men, the officers who had found his favor either before or during the war. George Marshall, who had been in his headquarters in France, was one. Douglas MacArthur, though he had performed brilliantly as a troop commander, a dashing and gallant figure right out of *Journey's End* rising to become the youngest brigadier general in the army, was not. He was too vivid, too pushy, too iconoclastic. He and Marshall never liked each other. They had much in common—both were aloof, puritanical, driven. Marshall, however, had hardly a single watt of military glory. It was the "loftiness and beauty of his character" that stood out, as Dean Acheson noted. MacArthur was not without character, but the thing that shone so unmistakably from him was ambition.

Another of Pershing's favorites was George Patton, who had gone to France as the old man's aide and wangled his way into the front lines, commanding the first tanks near the end of the war. Eisenhower met him in 1919 at Camp Meade. Patton was a temporary colonel, tall, glamorous, every inch a soldier. He was rich and so was his wife—he would always be known as the wealthiest man in the army. He owned a yacht, played polo, and taught ladies' riding classes. He was five years older than Eisenhower, with a high, squeaky voice and a foul mouth with which he loved to shock social gatherings, but he also had shrewdness and an intense love of his profession. It was at Patton's house one night that Eisenhower met and made an impression on a general named Conner, who a few months later invited him to come to Panama as his executive officer. He was the first of the two important sponsors Eisenhower was to have during his career.

Fox Conner was a Mississippian with the common touch who'd been Pershing's operations officer in France and had a reputation in the army as a brain. He was always quoted as saying that if we ever had another war he hoped to God we wouldn't have allies. In Panama he took Eisenhower under his wing, encouraging him to read and discussing with him strategy, commanders, and the fate of nations.

"Someplace along the line there Ike got serious—there isn't any question about that," one of his classmates remembered. It's uncertain exactly when or how this happened. It may have been due in part to the settling effect of marriage or to the death of his young son from scarlet fever a year before Panama. The change may have been something that was coming all along. What we do know is that when Conner arranged for him to get into Command and General Staff, the most important of the army schools, Eisenhower went, determined to do well. Those admitted were already an elect, and graduation high in the class was said to mark a man for future advancement. At the end of the year Eisenhower was number one.

George Marshall always kept a file of officers who impressed him and it's probable that Eisenhower's name first came to his attention at this time.

Known for years mainly as a coach of post football teams, Eisenhower was now viewed differently. The Army didn't exactly stand on its head for him, but in a few years he found himself in Washington working for the assistant secretary of war and then for the chief of staff, a man of dizzying ego, phenomenal memory, and comprehensive knowledge who liked to refer to himself in the third person—in short, MacArthur. They had adjoining offices with only a slatted door between them. When, on his retirement, MacArthur accepted the post of military adviser to the Philippines, he took Eisenhower with him for what MacArthur said would be a year or so.

They arrived in Manila in September 1935. Already balding, wearing a white suit and straw hat as did MacArthur, Ike is in many ways fully formed—the man who, unknown to himself, will command the war. He stands dutiful and frowning in the tropical sun as his renowned chief poses. He was twenty years into his profession now and still a major. Years later a woman asked him if he knew the celebrated MacArthur. Yes, he knew him, Eisenhower said, he'd studied dramatics under him for seven years.

In the Philippines they worked to create a defense force. There was little money or equipment, and as the hundreds of ordinary days drifted behind there began to appear, drawing closer and closer, the storm they all knew was coming. Everybody felt it. One evening on an antiquated radio Eisenhower heard Neville Chamberlain declaring war. The first flicker of lightning. In far-off Europe catastrophe had arrived.

Eisenhower went to MacArthur and requested to return to the States, feeling he would be needed more there. He left at the end of 1939 and began a series of assignments as what he had always been, a staff officer, first at regimental, then division and corps level. He bumped into Marshall at some maneuvers soon after getting back. Duty in the Far East, everyone knew, was duty with houseboys, servants, amahs. Even privates got spoiled. With the barest of smiles Marshall inquired, "Well, Eisenhower, have you learned to tie your shoes again?" It was only the second time they had met.

In the fall of 1941 in huge maneuvers held in Louisiana, Eisenhower stood out as chief of staff of the victorious Third Army. He got his promotion to brigadier general just as the dust of the maneuvers was settling. It was late September. Two months later, all negotiations at an impasse, a powerful Japanese strike force left port and slipped into the fog of the Northern Pacific under sealed orders that when opened read "Pearl Harbor."

It is easy to see in retrospect the confusion and fears, the long ordeal the end of which no one could foresee, the great wave that swept over the nation and half the world, the greatest event of the century: the Second World War.

Summoned abruptly from San Antonio to Washington a few days after the bombing of Pearl Harbor to fill a need in plans for someone who knew the Far East, Eisenhower went directly from the train station to Marshall's office. He was to face an immediate test. For twenty minutes Marshall outlined the grave situation in the Pacific with its nearly insoluble equations. Then he looked at Eisenhower and said only, "What should be our general line of action?"

Eisenhower had just arrived, he was unfamiliar with the latest plans, he had no staff. He hesitated for a moment and then said, "Give me a few hours."

Sitting in an empty office he thought at some length and then with one finger began to type out his recommendations. He went back to Marshall. The Philippines, with their weak forces, would probably fall, Eisenhower said. Nevertheless, everything possible should be done to help them hold out. This was important. All the peoples of Asia would be watching the coming battle there—they would accept defeat but not abandonment. Meanwhile, Australia was the key—it had to be built up as a base of operations and the long line of communications to it kept open at any cost. "In this last we dare not fail."

When he had finished, Marshall said just four words: "I agree with you."

Now began desperate days, during which they tried to find men, aircraft, equipment, and, above all, ships to carry them to distant garrisons. The news was worse and worse, naval disasters, staggering Japanese triumphs. The days were eighteen hours long and Eisenhower came home exhausted to his brother Milton's house in Falls Church for a sandwich at midnight. In three relentless months, however, he had Marshall's confidence and was wearing a second star.

Allied strategy was, Europe first—the defeat of Germany before anything else. The Americans favored a direct, cross-Channel invasion of the continent to which the British agreed in principle but with deeply ingrained reservations. For a nation that had known Gallipoli and would soon know Dieppe, the idea of a seaborne assault against a strongly defended mainland was not something to be viewed with enthusiasm. Ike had been responsible for drawing up plans for the invasion force to be built up in Britain and he offered Marshall a profile of the sort of officer who should be sent to command it, someone who was flexible, whom Marshall trusted completely, and who might further serve as Marshall's deputy when the former was named to lead the invasion (which was expected). A month later, an officer "then almost unknown," as Churchill called him, arrived in England and was welcomed at Chequers for the first time by the prime minister, who was wearing a siren suit and carpet slippers. That officer was Eisenhower.

They were to become very close, and it was always Ike's good fortune to have a supporter on one side as staunch as on the other. For his own part, he had come with the determination to get along with the British. You could call a British officer a bastard, the word was, but you could not call him a British bastard. He became a champion of Allied cooperation. It was not merely a question of the British agreeing to call lorries trucks and the Americans in exchange to call gasoline petrol, it was the task of hammering out an acceptable common strategy and bending difficult and proud commanders to fight side by side. The war was not waged in a spirit of pure harmony. Generals have ambitions. Nations have their goals.

Eisenhower was a major general when he came to England, almost a lowly rank. He was nearly fifty-two years old, he had never commanded troops, never seen a battle. In a matter of a few months, the invasion put aside for the time being, he found himself, quickly promoted, in a damp tunnel in Gibraltar waiting uneasily while fourteen convoys from both sides of the Atlantic, all bearing forces under his command, converged for simultaneous landings at Casablanca, Oran, and Algiers.

The invasion of North Africa had been hastily decided upon and planned, with Eisenhower as the logical commander since it was to appear as an American initiative. Actual military command, however, was in the hands of three experienced deputies, all British, for land, sea, and air.

There were problems with the colonial Vichy French, battles with the French fleet, and the usual early disgraces that go with poor officers and green troops. Americans dropped their weapons, abandoned equipment, and fled at Kasserine Pass. Eisenhower had neither the tactical nor strategic experience required, the chief of the British Imperial Staff, Alan Brooke, decided. He was putty in British hands, said Patton, who was also making his first appearance in the war; "I would rather be commanded by an Arab," Patton wrote in his diary. "I think less than nothing of Arabs." A depressed

Eisenhower kept repeating, "Anybody who wants the job of Allied commander in chief can have it." Nevertheless, he took full responsibility for the confusion and first defeats, and by spring, the supply situation better, the bad weather past, his reorganized forces had battled through Tunisia to meet Montgomery coming the other way. In the sudden, final collapse in May 1943, almost 250,000 Germans and Italians, many of them driving their own trucks in search of POW compounds, were taken prisoner. These were veterans, and with them went the Mediterranean.

Sicily was next, a less than brilliant campaign. The plan of invasion was uninspired—the Germans never could comprehend why the Strait of Messina had not been immediately seized to cut them off. The fighting was in the heat of summer, fierce and bloody. Patton, now an army commander, revealed some of his dash here and also his impulsiveness. Bradley, more temperate, would rise above him. Neither of them liked Montgomery: "pompous, abrasive, demanding, and almost insufferably vain," Bradley described him.

The campaign in Italy was more of the same—bad strategy, landings in the wrong places, lost opportunities. As Mediterranean Theater commander, Eisenhower was far from the center of things. Italy was a mere sideshow compared to the immense scale of the Russian front, where literally hundreds of divisions were engaged, and in the course of a battle the opposing armies might lose a division a day. Though assured there would be a second front in the spring, Stalin shrewdly demanded to know who its commander would be. That he would be American was understood, since the bulk of the forces were to be American. That it would probably be Marshall was also understood. But at the last moment Roosevelt decided otherwise. The principal figures had been in their roles too long to change. A deeply disappointed Marshall had the grace to send to Eisenhower as a memento the handwritten note that named him supreme commander.

Generals who do not fail, succeed. From the middle of the pack, past Clark, who was left mired in Italy, past Bradley, who had gotten a star first but was late getting to Europe, past the brash Patton, through all of it, gathering strength, experience, the feel of battles, learning to predominate in conference, perfecting the structure, prodding, cajoling, slowly becoming unchallenge-able, Ike made his way.

When he arrived back in London to take charge of the enormous planning, D-day was set for May 1, 1944, a mere three and a half months away.

The Germans knew it was coming. There were fifty-eight German divisions in France, all that could be taken from the east for what Hitler had told his generals would be the decisive battle of the war. If the Allies were defeated, they would never invade again, he pledged—the losses and the blow to morale would be devastating. The Germans could then transfer their entire strength to the grind-ing eastern front "to revolutionize the situation there." The waters off the French coast were dense with steel piles, stakes armed with mines, iron barriers. There were over four million land mines laid along the beaches, wire, concrete gun emplacements. At Dieppe, at Tarawa, these defenses had proved murderous.

To England, convoy after convoy had brought the heaviest of all things: armies, with their vehicles, tanks, mountains of munitions, guns. D-day had finally been set for the fifth of June. On that morn-ing tides, moon, everything would be right. But not, as it turned out, the weather. At the last moment the initial eight-division assault had to be postponed, and the following day, with only an uncertain pause in the winds and storm and the immense force leaning for-ward, as it were, Ike turned it over in his mind, pondered on des-tiny, and said at last, "Okay, let 'er rip."

He stood at an airfield in the darkness saluting each paratroop plane as it took off. In his pocket was a folded message on which he had scribbled a brief statement to be used in the event of disaster: the landings had failed and the troops, having done all that bravery and devotion could do, had been withdrawn. "If there is any blame or fault attached to the attempt, it is mine alone." These were the words, as historian John Keegan says, of a great soldier and a great man.

In France, dogs were barking in the windy darkness. Beneath the low clouds and the usual steady sound of aircraft crossing, the Germans were asleep, expecting a quiet night, when, at about two in the morning, into the country behind the beaches twenty-four thousand armed men came floating down. It was the airborne overture. The ships came at dawn, appearing out of the mist in numbers so great they could not be counted.

On the American beaches alone there were eight thousand casualties. Utah was not too bad, but Omaha was a bloodbath. The outcome was in doubt there for half the day. By that night, however, 150,000 Allied troops had gotten ashore. "Their road will be long and hard," Roosevelt broadcast to the nation that night, leading it in prayer. "Give us faith in Thee, faith in our sons, faith in each other . . ."

The campaign that began that day lasted for eleven months and became the greatest Allied victory of the war. Eisenhower held big cards and he played them correctly. His armies and his generals by that time were battle-hardened, but there was also considerable finesse. He deceived the Germans by keeping Patton, whom they feared, in England for a long time in command of a phantom army. When the battle of Normandy was over, Rommel was writing to his wife, "We're finished . . ."—even if the German High Command did not admit it, even though the life and death struggle went on. The Allies had more materiel, better intelligence, and, above all, command of the air, but the Germans were incomparable soldiers and for them there was no way out. Generals committed suicide and men by the tens of thousands died along the road.

That December saw the last great German offensive of the war.

Massed in absolute secrecy, under the cover of bad weather, three German armies fell on the four weak divisions that were stretched out to cover eighty-five miles of front in the Ardennes. It was an attack that Hitler personally had conceived and von Rundstedt commanded. Almost simultaneously the first V-2s began to fall on England.

It was just before Christmas. Ike had only that day received his fifth star and was celebrating by drinking champagne and playing bridge when the word came of what would become the Battle of the Bulge. At first neither he nor Bradley could believe what was happening, but soon the scope of the breakthrough became apparent. "Calamity," Alan Brooke admitted, "acted on Eisenhower like a restorative and brought out all the greatness in his character." There were black headlines in the newspapers and grave meetings, but Ike had come of age. He committed his strategic reserves to hold the critical area around Bastogne at all costs, which they did. At the end of a week the weather broke and fighter-bombers swarmed over the front. From this time on, Bradley noted, Montgomery or not, Ike ran the war.

On May 7, 1945, with Eisenhower refusing to see the German emissaries who had come to sign the surrender as he had refused to meet captured generals throughout the war, the road at last came to an end. The thrust into Europe, the crusade, as he called it, was over. There had been 586,628 American casualties during the campaign.

Perhaps he was not a great general. He was not a heroic one. He cannot be imagined crying to his troops, "Forty centuries look down upon you!" or "God for Harry! England and Saint George!" He was a new invention, the military manager, and the army was made over in his image. Those who think of him only as president, an old crock with a putter, fail to see the man as he really was. He was tough, resilient, wise. In a sense, the war used him up. For years he gave it every hour, every thought, every breath. It discovered him, and he is entombed in it, together with our greatest victory. The rest is epilogue.

He died on March 28, 1969, twenty-four years after the surrender. He was in Walter Reed Hospital, an invalid, ruined by heart attacks. His last words were, "I want to go. God take me."

Esquire
December 1983

Men and Women

Younger Women, Older Men

Raoul and Tommy stop by for a few minutes on the way back from the beach.
They come onto the porch with their girlfriends, one of whom looks eighteen.
Raoul is close to forty, worn, with gray hair. He hasn't shaved but somehow
seems stylish. It's probably worry—he owns two restaurants, the pressure is
always there. Tommy works in one of them. He's younger and Raoul is like
a father to him.

The girls are wearing sandals with heels and slight bikinis tight as string.
The sexual flux on the porch has violently changed, as with a powerful mag-
net, but they act unconcerned. In-ess, one says her name is, the one who looks
eighteen. She had a slight accent, South America, Rome? In any case, to the
other women she could be Kali, the goddess of destruction, wearing a gar-
land of skulls. Women fear girls in a way that men do not react to boys. Ines
stands there indifferently, nearly naked, her skin smooth and blemish-less.
The dog, inquisitively, is sniffing her feet. At last she seems to have found
something of interest. "Oh," she says, reaching down to pat him, "he's so
sweet."

Raoul slips a shirt on over his pale, skinny chest. He refuses a drink. He
says something to Ines, who nods. They're going to the American Hotel for
dinner. One can picture them there, not talking much but on display. The

two men are talking. They order a good wine—Raoul knows these things. This is all later, the last light lingering, the pleasant weariness from the sea, the food, the crowd. What happens afterward, one is forced to imagine. Raoul has never married though he has the ease of a married man. Tommy is separated from his wife.

When they have driven off there is a dampened spirit in the house. The women are somehow annoyed; a bruise, a tender spot, has been irritated. Their dignity has been injured in some way, or at least their feeling of confidence. Their husbands' thoughts have gone to where they should not be . . .

It is true that Héloïse was a mere sixteen when she began her immortal love affair with her smitten tutor, Abelard, who was thirty-nine, and that Ajax and Achilles, as has been pointed out, were both in love with their servant maids, but it is an unfortunate thing, this open attraction to young women, many of whom have barely gotten their teeth and claws and who, insufficiently warned, allow themselves to consort with older men whose interest in them cannot entirely be one of friendship. It is a perversion of the state that nature intended of amity and understanding between men and women, equipping them both as she did with the same heart, blood, and sinew as well as with similar limbs, desires, and powers of thought.

Having established this, let us go further.

There is something deeply moving, something innate and good in the image of a young couple, intelligent, even-tempered, filled with hope and rich expectations. They are the alpha pair, upon which all society is founded. Everything else is inferior to them, every choose-it-yourself paradise, the men who love men, women who love women, the radicals and sexual Bolsheviks raging in the streets.

It is an invincible pair but also highly volatile; youth is volatile. Their desires, which now seem so clearly focused on one another, are in fact teeming and infinite. Life is very long and the struggle fierce. So many things will conspire to pull them apart, so many crises for which there seem to be no rules.

The young shun the old, probably with reason since they are usually nothing more than themselves squeezed of vitality and lacking ideals. Still there are exceptions. There are older people who know things and have done things, and anyway they are not that old. At least they don't seem to be. There can be a natural and classic conjunction. A. J. Liebling in his beautiful chronicle of Paris, *Between Meals*, describes a great—though not important—French playwright and friend, Yves Mirande, who as a boy of seventeen fresh from the provinces was taken to bed by older women, in their twenties as it happened—as Madeleine Béjart did with the green Molière—made love to, and taught the rules. "When he was a ripe man," Liebling wrote of Mirande, "he returned the favor by making love to the young." In a sense this is like a career in education, studying for a doctorate and then afterward proceeding to instruct so that knowledge passes on more or less undiluted.

It is painful to recall life's pleasures once thought of as unshakable, such as ocean liners, the tango, and dry martinis, that have now been swept into the rubble, but the intoxicating relationship between experience and inexperience endures. There are few things more gratifying than being in the company of someone younger who admires you for your knowledge and is avid to have it shared. If you are lucky, it is a woman.

Des arrived with his new fiancée. She came in first, hair tousled, wearing a man's black overcoat and boots. When she took off the coat you saw how good-looking she was. She was from New Orleans and had a wonderful smile. Des and I kept talking nonstop, reminiscing, making jokes. "I see why you guys like each other," she said.

Later she had her bare feet up on the table, beautiful nude feet, long and white. We were on the second bottle of wine. She hadn't said very much and then—we must have somehow mentioned it earlier—out of nowhere, "What's so great about Louise Erdrich?" she wanted to know.

She was just starting to read books. All that was ahead of her, the new-

ness of it, the things you learned you could do, the real dimensions of life. Des was going to lay it all out.

How had he met her, I wondered—that's always the question.

The attraction to men of young women cannot be marked down solely under the heading of education, of course. Many other things are involved, including the imbalance. Happiness is often at its most intense when it is based on inequality, and one of the imperishable visions of it is of life among a burnished, graceful people not as advanced as we—among them are to be found servants with whom, as with slaves in the Koran, pleasure is permitted for those so disposed, the pleasure that simplifies everything: Tahiti, 1880; Bali, 1910; Mexico, 1930; Bangkok, 1950. . . .

Well, all that is struck down. It is part of the darkness of colonialism and perhaps racism. If you care to include it, there is sexism, too. Men's dream and ambition is to have women, as a cat's is to catch birds, but this is something that must be restrained. The slightest understanding of things shows that men will take what they are not prevented from taking, and all the force of society must be set against this impulse.

Not long ago I watched an instance of this—they are, after all, countless. It was at a wedding reception in Paris, in one of those apartments that are obtained only through inheritance: huge windows, silk on the walls, rooms and salons tumbling into one another, women in large hats, champagne. In the crowd the groom's niece, fifteen years old with a lovely broad face that seemed to hold nothing but purity, was boxed in against the wall by a wild Englishman of forty, heavy, with florid cheeks and curly black hair, who was talking to her passionately and without pause.

"We have to get him away from her," I heard a woman remark nervously, "he's mad as a hatter."

Mad, perhaps, but a member of the wedding party, and among the wives and divorcees he had found something more thrilling. The stitching had given way under one arm of his coat and he was telling her in inspired language of . . . who knows what? No one had ever paid her this kind of attention before, no adult. If he had just a day and a night, he was thinking feverishly, even only a night. If she drank just one more glass of dizzying champagne. . . .

My God, how awful! one thinks fearfully. But he will be dead in ten years most likely, from drink or a car accident, and everything he knew, the poems of Cavafy, the gossip of famous names, the best years for Pauillac, great music, restaurants in Lucca, all of it gone along with the books, pictures, and expensive suits, gone except for the things she remembers, and that is a lot. She will be only in her mid-twenties then with not a wrinkle or scar, not much taken from her and a great deal given, and perhaps she will come once, years later when she is older and has children, to visit the grave. Perhaps she will still have the note he left, the lines like those last few written by the heartsick narrator of *Lolita* telling her to be true to her husband, ". . . do not let other fellows touch you. Do not talk to strangers. I hope you will love your baby. I hope it will be a boy."

Alix came in in the evening, tall and smiling though she was tired. She had just finished work—she was housekeeping for the summer for someone who had rented a big place near Chilton. She did everything, took care of the cleaning, cooked—she hadn't known how to boil an egg but after a month she was doing dinners for twelve with fresh asparagus.

"What's so hard about cooking asparagus?"

"The sauce," she said airily.

She was a senior at Radcliffe. Her father was a lawyer. She had a brother who was at Duke. She'd come to the Vineyard to get away from Boston and also her boyfriend, Gordon. He was an investment banker and avid sailor. Also a model. "You can see what an identity crisis he has."

He called her all the time. "He called me tonight, in fact. He's still in love with me. He wants me to marry him. I'm not about to marry him, he's much too old. He's thirty-nine." She pushed back her hair and went on.

"He's great, but he always takes things a little too far you know? He goes just a little past where he should. He has one drink too many, he wants to go to just one more place, he looks at some other woman just a little too long . . .

"I remember he gave this big party, I mean all his friends. I wasn't nervous, men never make me nervous. I felt totally secure. It was my house, I was totally at ease. I was wearing this great dress cut down to here. Believe me, they noticed." Her breast touched one's arm as she talked. That was the thing, her body belonged to both of you, as if you were teammates, parts of it brushing you from time to time. *"Everybody was there and of course he had to invite his ex-girlfriend Sharon. You can imagine why. Anyway, it got late and there were four of us sitting there, Gordon and me and Sharon and her date, and it was like a contest who was going to go to bed first? Finally Sharon's date left and there were just the three of us. The two of them were whispering and finally Gordon said, 'Look, Alix, why don't you go up and go to bed? I'm going to talk to Sharon for a while; she has some problems she wants to talk about.'*

"So I went up and took off my clothes and put on a real sexy nightgown. After a while I went to the head of the stairs and called. I waited until he came to the bottom of the stairs and could see me, you know, and I said, 'Don't forget to put out the cat, will you?'

"He was great but you had to watch him all the time."

The thing that aristocrats have is the sum of their breeding, going back for centuries, so that what might be called random behavior is minimal in them. You can learn how, let us say, to put on a pair of gloves so that you can fool almost anybody, but how is one to learn acts that are wholly unrehearsed? It can't be done; you have to have the code, passed down through countless unions.

So it is with women. The millennia have created them and certain things are known to them instinctively, by reflex, as it were.

A woman, as the Russian proverb goes, is a complete civilization. Men may aspire to this but generally things come to them more slowly. Think of it as two long lines, one male and one female, placed side by side according to the degree of being civilized. The males will be opposite females much younger. In short, at the same age they are less far along. Their manners are unsettled and their speech artless. They may be kept for drinking at a future date but they require aging.

This is something women are always concerned with, the maturing, or let us say the perfection, of men. It should come as no surprise that in certain cases they may choose a wine that is ready to enjoy rather than one that must be laid down for five or ten years.

Men, on the other hand, are in the opposite position. As the Abbe de Brantome noted in his gallant tales, there is wood like ash and young elm that burns quite green and quickly, and there are others that will burn only with terrible difficulty. So it is, he observed, with girls and women: "Some, as soon as they are nicely green, mere saplings, ignite easily and burn so briskly that one would think they had imbibed love's heat and whorishness while still in their mothers' wombs," to such a point, he added, that they do not even wait until maturity to begin lovemaking. They are the tinder to which men supply the match. The French, expert in this as in other things, have a rule of thumb regarding the proper difference in age for couples: the woman's age should be one half that of the man's plus seven years. At first this yields nothing remarkable—a boy of twenty and a sweetheart seventeen—but it becomes a man of thirty and a woman twenty-two, a man of forty and a woman twenty-seven. The real intent may be to assure there can be children, but the formula has an appeal of its own.

I have never become cynical about them, Raymond Chandler wrote, "never ceased to respect them, never for a moment failed to realize that they face hazards in life which a man does not face, and therefore should be given a special tenderness and consideration." Though Chandler is a handful of generations back and died before the last of the statues in the temple were smashed, his words strike a chord. Women have a harder duty in this world. They have been given their beauty in recompense. Beauty in its brevity.

Isn't this the message of so many things, the ballet for instance, with its perfect grace? The dedication and labor of the dancers rewards them with an aura. Pliant and slender, they were made to be adored, but one cannot really—not ever—know them, for they are not what they seem—when the lights go down their reality disappears. As dancers and women they belong to that order which is the greatest of all, of things truly unpossessable.

Out on the field in the cold sunshine the soccer teams are playing, girls in shorts and numbered white shirts, shrill shouting and coltish legs. On the sidelines you have a chance to talk to your daughter's roommate for the first time. Her name is Avril. Long blond hair, fine brows. On her radiant jaw the light picks up a faint youthful down. She wears jeans and boots with high heels although she's already quite tall. She hasn't gone out for the team, she hasn't really gotten into anything, she admits. She hates the school, she suddenly says, looking out at the field, they have such senseless, stupid rules. It's something about a weekend and signing back in, but she doesn't really explain, she is already running awkwardly onto the field, the game is over and a loose huddle of sixteen-year-olds are shouting, "Ice-cold beer, makes you want to cheer! Ice-cold gin, makes you want to sin! Ice-cold duck . . . "

If it were not for the idiotic rules, and perhaps in spite of rules, Avril, not a day older, might be imagined in the etchings of Picasso's Vollard Suite, idyllic drawings with an irresistible purity of line. The bearded sculptor, his forehead barely creased, relaxes with his naked young model in bed or on a couch, fulfilled by her but not ardent, distracted in fact, in a kind of vague equilibrium with the joys of this earth— to paraphrase Kazantzakis—women, art, ideas. It is a depiction of immortality and the spareness of the furnishings essential for it.

Picasso's life itself might serve as an illustration. He is that sculptor, of course, and a large portion of his work is of one or another of the women in his life, all of whom were younger. Marie-Thérèse

Walter, who was his mistress and bore him a child, was seventeen when they met; he was forty-six. Françoise Gilot was twenty-one and Picasso was over sixty. The first, fatal interviews. Why not? He was rich, both in money and—more seductive—fame, probably the richest painter who ever lived. His pictures, masculine, frank, would be a logical target of feminism were it not for their greatness. Picasso, in fact, stands in the path of new ideas and relationships. The order he represents and is inseparable from is as archaic as the gender pronouns in the Bible. Why, for instance, didn't he paint women his own age? Why didn't Leonardo, why didn't Gauguin or Matisse? After all, there are women who cannot easily be imitated, who come down in the morning with a sly smile and ease, hair loose, face purified by sleep, needing coffee and talk. They have been in hotels, houses, countries, and risen from many forgotten nights; not all of them are interested in money or weary of men.

The floor bare, music blaring. Aerobics. The class is in three ranks, an ordinary class, salesgirls, housewives, the man who works in the auto parts store: common clay. Amid them, one long-nosed girl with a strong back, shapely legs: the sole swan. She's wearing white shorts, a green tank top over a white T-shirt. There's a slight tense sinew up where her legs join, the apex. Kick, kick, kick, higher, higher. Her movements are youthful, ecstatic, hands thrown out loosely as her leg sweeps free, fine hair leaping. From time to time she looks back and smiles at a dumpy woman behind her, her mother. During the last half of the class she rolls her T-shirt sleeves above the shoulder like an Oklahoma boy and looks down admiringly at her slender arms. What joy there is in her! The girlfriend by her side is of a separate species.

In the sit-ups she struggles, can't do them, and finally gives up and lies helpless, lanky calves flat on the floor. One wants to seize and embrace her, the life, the aimless perfection! Her name is scribbled on the roster beneath her mother's: Chris.

•

This glimpse of the divine standing dampened in the entry to an empty gym, skin glowing, pulse still a fraction high returning slowly to normal and making one think of the dreamlike descent from other heights. *Agnosco veteris vestigia flammae*, the poet says: I feel again a spark of that ancient flame. You cannot take your eyes from her. It will be such a long time before she becomes her mother, perhaps never.

In Thailand mistresses are an accepted part of the society, often a mark of riches. They are called small wives and their children bear no stigma, any more than those of French kings. But this is not Thailand and Chris and her retinue have walked out the door. It was fantasy, though others are not: high heels, black stockings, tight little skirt, a young woman and all the pleasure she brings. I have had two friends, both Yale men as it happens, who told me that they had never deceived their wives. I know a famous movie director, often married, who says the same thing. From time to time I think about this, especially since one of the Yale men also claimed he had never once in his life told a lie—of course, in his case an important motive had been removed. I am not praising faithlessness—that is too dangerous—only reflecting that these men seem less interesting, like those who don't drink. Certain faults, if you can call them that, make men intriguing, just as certain flaws make a more beautiful face. In any case, rules are only rules. We live in society but also in zoology. We will never escape that, and if we do, hope of salvation is gone.

There are complications, however, and the uncertainty of what to do about them. In the office, for instance. The end of the day, streets dark with people. The girl who works on the floor below. She comes in out of the cold with a smile, face flushed, and in the intimacy of the crowded bar says, "Hello, darling," and without a pause, "I love you. I'm so glad I met you." Her smooth skin, her legs, her apartment with its cat. The exhilaration, the thrilling nights without care. On the one side there exists a perfectly decent domestic life. On the other, the forbidden and inexpressibly sweet. The real temptation is not pleasure but the idea of capturing it, of abandoning everything and starting again.

There are advantages in being a man. In *Lysistrata*, with its sexual boycott more severe than any since, the women are credited with all the determination and most of the intelligence, but as the heroine herself says, when a soldier returns from the war, even though he has white hair he can quickly find a wife. With women it is different, she declares, women have but one summer.

I heard this same observation made by a European woman I know whose second husband had died. She was past the age of childbearing and though she had lost none of her charm, a woman of fifty, unlike a man, was used up, she commented, whereas a man that age could go out and begin again. It was perhaps unfair, but that was the way it was. I don't mean to heavy-handedly connect Aristophanes to a restaurant in Basel but merely to note the obvious at each end of a two-thousand-year span.

So he marries, not the wife of his youth, then, but someone who comes along later, the stunning ex-student or assistant or even the daughter of a friend. She is a potent object, this new wife, the dreams she excites in others, the envy, the unexpected things she can say, none of them familiar, none of the wearisome stories about house and children. The cities they will conquer together, the journeys, the sacred mornings! The glory of walking in with a young woman—power over her may wane, but the power of her, never. She is a pardon, a second chance. This time there is everything: happiness, reason, money enough. The years, not treating them equally, roll by. In the end the inevitable happens and he, unfortunately grown old, one day falters and drops in the traces. He dies. There are the photos on the piano, all in handsome frames, which the two ravishing children still in school identify: Daddy and Mommy before they got married, Daddy in his uniform—don't know where that was, the four of us at the lake, Daddy before he got sick . . .

There remains of the vanished father and the memories surrounding him something romantic, even exalted. Things that are gone acquire this patina, people, decades, cars. His white suit will always be white, his lined face kind and unaging. He will never become cranky, wear pants with baggy seats, or in any way diminish their love for him. And widowhood, for her, is not uncomfortable. There is the house, money, the children, and something she always had little of, time to spend by herself. It's a welcome thing and there are always friends.

She is still undeniably young, the house is a wonderful one, would she—this is a funny question—would she rather have married a younger man? the interviewer asks.

The shadow of something like reflection crosses her face and she shakes her head. "But I wouldn't mind one now," she says.

Esquire
March 1992

Karyl and Me

We first met—that's not the right word, I first became aware of her spectacular existence—at a seminar on film in Aspen in the late 1960s. She was sitting in an upper row, stunning face with high cheekbones, dark hair, rapt expression, and I was more aware of her than of anything of supposed importance that was being said. I didn't know who she was or anything about her, and it's been so long now that I don't remember how it happened that we first spoke or how I learned everything.

Her name was Karyl Roosevelt. She'd been married and divorced twice, the second time to a grandson of one of our greatest presidents, FDR, and she had four children. All this by the time she was barely thirty. She told intriguing stories about herself, some, at the beginning, not entirely true. She'd had intercourse with her second husband only eight times during their marriage, she said, and had gotten pregnant after three of them. She'd been born, she claimed, in Leadville, Colorado, and had an aunt who'd fallen in love, on a trip to Italy, with one of Mussolini's aides. It ended unhappily and the aunt tried to commit suicide by drowning herself. The creek, however, was only two feet deep.

What I didn't realize immediately was that her stories were the stirring of something hidden and unsuspected: literary talent. It turned out she was a born writer, but more of that later.

My real friends have always been men. I don't know how it could be otherwise. I went to boys' schools, was in the army, then married. My preference is for men—in a certain sense I never encountered a woman in the same life as mine.

The question is, what constitutes friendship? Some is nothing more than companionship, some is only a practical matter, some just lengthy acquaintance. Friendship is more than knowledge and intimacy. It belongs to the order of things that cannot be weighed, like sorrow, honor, and hope. It is a form of love. It lies in the heart. You can name certain of the essentials: trust, a shared view of the world, admiration, understanding, and something I value, a sense of humor. All of these are a part of it but none of them define it.

It all began with Karyl when she took the job of typing my manuscripts, I think for a dollar a page. She was a good typist and, at first, coolly efficient, but then she began to offer a comment or two. I learned that she liked to read. It was not just a quick dip into reading to make herself more interesting, she was avid. Still rarer was her taste; she knew what was good and why. I don't know at what point in her life this power to discriminate came into being. I somehow could not picture the ravishing high school girl she must have been, already focusing her life on men, as a serious reader. Somewhere along the way, however, what was latent emerged. I like to think it changed her life or at least prepared her for the second and third acts. Beauty is a great accomplishment, but knowledge—or should I broaden it and say culture—is at least as seductive.

We became friends in part I think because we did not become more. Is the other more? In the short term, yes, of course. In the long term, yes also, providing there is something additional. It was this additional we shared.

We have been friends for nearly thirty years. She has almost always been in someone's arms, not promiscuously but reliably. It's a quality I like. I recall an evening in our kitchen with the dishes. There we were amiably, Karyl, my wife, and I. A friend who had dropped by was curious. "What's Karyl doing here?" he took me aside to ask.

"She's living with us," I said for no real reason. I wanted to see his reaction.

"You must be out of your mind," he whispered.

She was always tremendously attractive, but youth at last made its exit. She moved to Chicago and for a time, for a novel almost, worked for Saul Bellow. Then she moved to New York. Our lives— this was in the 1980s—became even more closely entwined. She reviewed books. She was social secretary to a woman on Fifth Avenue. She worked for the ASPCA. Her stories were irresistible. The man who came in and said, "You got any snakes?" He wanted a real good one.

"A good one?"

"I wants to make a wallet," he said.

I called her there once and the phone rang for a long time. Finally it was picked up and someone went to get her. "They must have been killing cats," I said.

"Yes," she said. "They were killing the best dogs in the place."

It may not have been true but it was typical of her stoicism and contempt for what the world had become. She more or less believed, as Kazantzakis wrote, that *nobility, harmony, balance, the sweetness of life, happiness, are all virtues and graces which we must have the courage to bid goodbye*. They belonged to another age.

I had not been surprised when, before this, she had given me stories she'd written. Her letters—I judge a great deal from letters— had always been exceptional. You cannot teach someone to write any more than you can teach them to be interesting. Her writing was very good, it had her voice and tone. The sad thing was that she never believed in it or even in herself. She lacked the ego to persevere, ego strengthened by the knowledge that there is nothing else, it is write or disappear. I encouraged her with all my heart, as if we were swimmers far from shore and I had the endurance to make it but she did not. I understood why I had loved her and why she was immediately drawn to two close friends in New York I introduced her to. She fit right in. She belonged. Food, drink, gossip, scorn, travel—we breathed the same air. She turned to writing plays. A few were staged but not with great success. She was disappointed but you would never know it.

In the end we became—we have become—almost like stepbrother and sister. I was attracted to her in the beginning as a woman, but now her being a woman is significant mainly for the clear view she brings from the other side. The news, you might say. Her friends are women for the most part, and what she knows about them, sometimes marvelously wicked, is the attraction. A friend of hers, she said, decided to make a list of all the men she'd ever gone to bed with. One of the entries was *Tall Norwegian* and, beneath it, *His two friends*.

To me she once wrote, Without you, my own life would have been much smaller and darker.

I think of the lines of Robert Burns in one of his most famous poems, written two hundred years ago. "John Anderson My Jo, John" is the poem. *Jo* means "dear." We climbed the hill together, Burns wrote—I am simplifying the Scottish tongue—and many a happy day, John, we've had with one another.

> *Now we maun totter down, John,*
> *And hand in hand we'll go,*
> *And sleep together at the foot,*
> *John Anderson, my jo.*

After all the years, that is Karyl and me.

Modern Maturity
April–May–June 1997

When Evening Falls

A few nights ago at dinner, they were talking about an ardent young feminist. She was good-looking, with long hair, and went around in tight jeans and high calf-leather boots. After a lecture she gave one evening, she announced that she would accept questions only from the women in the audience—men, oppressors of women throughout the centuries, would not be permitted to speak. It didn't especially matter, since after two questions she abruptly decided that the lecture was over.

She was, at the time, involved in a love affair with a soft-spoken young composer. He happened to remark in company, when the subject somehow came up, that he had occasionally felt himself tempted by his female students. That brought the affair to a sudden end. She rose from the table, exclaiming with disgust that she never wanted to speak to him again, and so far as anyone knew, she never did.

I found myself wondering, among other things, what Jean Renoir might have made of this story; not what he would have thought of it but how it might have been handled in one of his films—as a human foible, probably, passionate and foolish. His great ability, in the thirty-five or so films he made during his lifetime, was to put things into very human terms. I never met Jean Renoir, who died in 1979 at the age of eighty-four, but I feel as if I knew him—he belongs to an order of people and things that I admire. In addition to his films, he wrote three books: a memoir of his father, an autobiography, and one novel, *The Notebooks of Captain Georges*, which happens also to be in the form of an autobiography.

It's about the love affair or, more correctly, the love of a lifetime between a young upper-class soldier and a straightforward, dark— *brun*, as the French say—somewhat fatalistic prostitute. He first notices her at a party with drunken comrades, one of whom has sex with her while she's seated on his lap, an act she accepts with indifference, even a trace of amusement—it's not known yet that she's a prostitute. Afterward, she calmly straightens her skirt and helps herself to more dessert. The soldier who has made love to her gets sick and leaves, and the narrator begins to talk to her. She has small white teeth in a generous mouth, and suddenly he feels an urge to kiss her, mostly out of curiosity, "the way one is tempted to give a sheet of newspaper to a goat, to see if it will eat it."

She wasn't expecting that, is her comment afterward. Didn't she like it? he asks.

"'Oh, I don't mind, but you aren't the type.'

"'Is there a type for kissing?'

"'Like anything else.'"

Her name is Agnes. One soon, like the narrator, falls in love with her. This takes place in a garrison town in France in the year preceding the First World War. Agnes is nineteen and works in the local brothel—there is a single one, as was often the case in small towns in France in those days. She is strong-minded, honest, and to a degree impossible to falsify, entirely herself. At first, she rejects Georges (it's only later that he becomes an officer), even when he comes to the brothel, although seeing the state he is in and knowing how unhealthy it is to allow it to be unrelieved, she politely takes care of that before he is made to go. Later, in a sudden about-face, she gives herself to him entirely without any illusion of it ever being more than what it is, but what it is, is a happiness greater than any she has ever known, and the same is so for him. It is "Madame Butterfly" in reverse—she is the one who is promised to someone else, a husband, as it happens, who has installed her in a brothel before going off to find the money to fulfill his dream of opening a hardware store someday.

The war steps in and takes Georges away, and though for a time they are reunited, in the end he loses her, as does her husband, and for the rest of his life never knows love like that again; such heights are reached once only.

Despite the banality of the book's plot, it is the human details that shine through. When she became naked, Georges recalls, letting the thin dressing gown fall away, there was a modesty in it and nothing of pride or the idea that her body was an incomparable gift. "She simply thought, 'He likes me to be naked and I am happy that it pleases him.'"

The book may be entirely fiction but seems to be based at least in part upon Renoir's experiences—like Georges, he was a cavalryman and was also wounded in the early days of the war. After recovering, he, like Georges, finished the war as an officer. He married Andrée Heuschling, one of his father's models, and she became the star of his first films; perhaps he transformed her into Agnes, perhaps Agnes was drawn from someone else. It doesn't really matter; one believes the book. Renoir is a man whose fiction is more credible than others' facts. The scenes of garrison life; the brothel, with its cozy atmosphere and odor of talcum, sweat, and cheap perfume; the waiter who ignores the girls because he is married to a "real woman" at home; the pompous little owner, with his moralizing and common sense—it is all done with brevity and style.

Like knowledge of the classical world, which comes to us through ruins and books, there are glimpses of this part of ordinary French life of fifty or a hundred years ago in architecture, painting, and writers' pages. Many such pages can be found in the two thick volumes of a grand album of French brothel days, *Maisons Closes*, written under the pseudonym Romi. In the 1930s, the author had been sent by a newspaper to investigate brothels nationwide. He visited a vast number and became their historian. In his book, one finds a provincial town on a river in the student days of 1926–27, described by Jean Loubes—14,000 inhabitants and one *maison publique* with four girls, a quartet, good-natured, not unintelligent, obliging and indiscreet. Through them, one could learn some absorbing things about the town's best citizens as well as the physical imperfections and desires of their wives. The beer was a bit expensive but good, and from rooms on the second floor as evening fell there was a view of the entire town, its roofs and enterprises, streets and quays. In these rooms, all cares and sadness fell away.

Les bordels, of which Aragon sang. Le Havre—Rue des Gallons, another writer remembers, the smell of women, urine, sour milk, the sea. Nothing, he says, can give an idea of the peace, the feeling of family life in a provincial brothel. One talked, laughed, gossiped, drank, discussed elections, played belote, which was to that world what bridge was to society, and on Sunday everyone went to Mass. When I become old, tired of the noise of Paris, of literary quarrels, news, salons, snobs, poets, and travel, I will bury myself in a provincial brothel . . . equivalent of the chamber of commerce. It carried, I know, along with the listings, advertisements for knee-high boots of supple leather, shoulder-length gloves, schoolgirl uniforms incomplete in certain places and suitable for reenactments of coming home from school. The Guide had no price on it. It was not for sale, though it was easy enough to get a copy.

It's uncertain when it was published for the last time, 1939 or perhaps 1945. Any need for it ended in 1946, with the law that closed all brothels, not abruptly but with an admirable compassion that permitted a grace period of one month for towns of 5,000 or

less, three months for those of up to 20,000, and six months for
those larger. It allowed men and women to prepare themselves for
the end of what the government now realized to have been a social
plague.

I remember when I was twenty, exiled to faded airfields and
towns on the Texas border where the most important figures were
the bank president and the Coca-Cola bottler, whose daughters,
if any, strolled in a world separate from ours. The weekends were
endless, with long, burning afternoons. We went across to Mexico,
to the restaurants and the cheap bars. There were usually women
in back or in a nearby house and always someone to take you to
them. I remember, in Mexico City, a girl from Havana with unforgettable white teeth. It was a little like Jean Renoir's novel or what
it might have been if written by someone without the humanity
and style.

"Je comprends la vie"—"I understand life"—Madame Anaïs con-
solingly said to Séverine, the young married woman nervously
presenting herself for occasional service in *Belle de Jour*. That is the
phrase that remains. There are some things that demand to take
place one way or another; it may be better to face them frankly. It
is not love, after all, that is the raison d'être of brothels; it is desire
and dreams.

Generally speaking, saints are less interesting than sinners, which
is what many of them were to begin with. Life has its turnabouts,
but there must be something to act against, a too-easy something, a
sensual life. Moderation is admirable, but when evening falls there
is the call of the boulevards, the lights, shapely legs. There is Henry
Miller on his arrival in Paris, "bewildered" and "poverty-stricken":
"A weird sort of contentment in those days. No appointments, no
invitations for dinner, no program, no dough. The golden period,
when I had not a single friend." He compared himself to a ghost
at a banquet, but before long he was able to sit down to the table
himself.

I never found a copy of the rose-colored Guide. In an odd way, the longer I looked for it, the less I needed to find it; I already knew it quite well. In the end, I decided to let the one destined for me stay hidden on an upper bookshelf or in the attic where it had been for so long. Some things are better imagined than seen, especially in the light of day.

GQ
February 1992

Talk of the Town on Bill Clinton

The indiscretions of famous men are of great interest, though usually they remain footnotes. As has been made clear, however, it was not only the president's indiscretion but his deplorable attempt to conceal and deny it that was fatal. From this a crime was concocted. I think of the time-tested formula of the father of a friend of mine: in the event of wrongdoing, a manly confession and a pious resolve. It might have been hoped that President Clinton would, when faced with the accusation, immediately come out with the whole truth. If he had been a member of the Grand Old Party—like Nixon, or Reagan, for that matter—he would surely have had the requisite moral fiber.

There are lies that presumably cause one to be descended into hell and lesser, even trivial, ones that cannot be judged as harshly and are often, in fact, a necessity. The president's quibblings and, in some cases, untruths were meant to keep his private and entirely legal behavior from being revealed. They were to save his reputation and to prevent considerable injury to Mrs. Clinton and their daughter.

Still, there remains the awful fact of what happened in the White House. The acts were certainly unexampled. They amounted to evidence of an illness, and Starr and his loyal associates did what they could for the good of the country and the furtherance of justice. Never mind that the country, and its leadership, was already good. As for justice, we know quite well from the Simpson case that it will always eventually triumph.

I recall a foreshadowing in a play of Wallace Shawn's some years ago, *Aunt Dan and Lemon*. In it the young protagonist imagines herself meeting Henry Kissinger. She would be fully prepared, she says, to be Kissinger's personal slave, something she feels he would like. He could have his pleasure of her with nothing in the way of preliminaries; she knows how busy he is—an exchange of glances would do. "He served humanity. I would serve him," she fantasizes. It is unsettling to have such thoughts committed to paper, not to speak of spoken aloud on the stage.

Jack Kennedy's moral strength, which was part of his immense appeal, was later found to be flawed. Before these revelations, he had set in motion huge undertakings—the flight to the moon, for instance. Had it been known how hollow he actually was, perhaps Oswald would not have been impelled to shoot him—it could have been expected that he would collapse of his own accord.

I was never a great admirer of Clinton. I felt that he had somehow failed to measure up: that it was all right to duck out of fighting in a war, but if you sneaked away from fighting you should not seek to be Commander-in-Chief. Perhaps these things are no longer that closely related. In any case, today, as he is being unmercifully flayed by men undoubtedly finer but a bit less generous, I am changing my opinion. I am impressed by his grit and unfaltering dedication to the duties for which he was twice elected. If he is also shameless, he is not alone in this. There is no real beauty without some slight imperfection.

The New Yorker
October 5, 1998

On the Edge

The Definitive Downhill: Toni Sailer

Kitzbühel is a handsome old town known for its fine skiing and unspoiled look. The latter is an inheritance of the centuries, but the fame of the skiing is owed in part to the great racers who came from there, most of them members of the celebrated Austrian team of the 1950s, which included Sailer, Molterer, and Pravda. Toni Sailer was the most unforgettable. In the 1956 Olympics, at Cortina d'Ampezzo, he swept the three Alpine events, the only man besides Jean-Claude Killy to do it. On the way, like Killy, he won the most famous of all downhill races, Kitzbühel's own race, the Hahnenkamm, a run of about two miles plunging through the dark firs of the Austrian Tyrol.

The Hahnenkamm is one of the oldest races, and indisputably the toughest. Characterized by extreme steepness at the start, abrupt changes of terrain, and difficult turns, it is a course that is respected and feared. It demands everything, courage, endurance, skill, and like all downhill races, a little more of yourself than you are able to give. If you win the Hahnenkamm, you have done something. Even to race in it is an achievement.

Last year, I was in Kitzbühel. I was covering the race, one of five hundred people occupied in doing it. I was trying to find someone who would take me down the course. (When the course is open, any thoroughly competent skier can do it.) I was looking for a coach or a friendly racer who could explain the details to me, the fine points only an insider would know.

"Why don't you go down with Sailer?" someone said. "Sailer?" He was running the children's ski school. Just go up and talk to him, they said. He had raced in the Hahnenkamm five times. He'd won it twice.

"Sailer?" I said, stalling. "Why not?" I went to the ski school, which was at the bottom of the slope, not far from the finish line. There was a little booth and I asked for Sailer. He wasn't around, so I left a note for him, tucking it into the top of a ski rack so that his name could be seen. Later in the day I came back. This time he was there. Sailer was forty-seven but looked much younger, with the handsome, cold face of a man who has seen the heights. The note, I noticed, was still on the ski rack, unread. I explained what I wanted, to go down the course with him and have him point out its real features. Sailer was taciturn. He seemed to show very little interest. Finally he said, "All right. Meet me here at eight tomorrow morning. On second thought, make it quarter to eight."

At seven the next morning I woke, having slept only fitfully. Outside the window children were walking to school along snowy paths in the dark. By the time I reached the meeting place it was daylight, a cold, January morning without shadow or promise of warmth. Not a soul was in sight. At exactly 7:45 a lone figure appeared carrying a pair of skis. It was Sailer. He greeted me economically and we started toward the cable car station. A few people, among them racers up for early practice, were already waiting.

Sailer, in his red parka and black pants, stood there and talked to some of them briefly, the young Austrian boys—he had been one of the team coaches for a while. Then he sat on a bench and began fastening his boots. Finally he took out two thin straps which he fastened with some care above his knees. I watched this with a vague feeling of uneasiness. We rode up in silence. Out the frosted window I could see the bare, glazed course, partly hidden by somber trees.

At the top he put on his skis without a word and headed for the small hill that went up to the starting area. We sidestepped up. The snow on top was trampled by the boots of racers who in previous days had been waiting there for their practice runs. Now it was vacant. As we began to cross it I finally stopped him to ask if we could talk for a minute about what we were going to do.

"We can talk better at the bottom," he said. He headed for the starting hut but I made one more attempt to engage him. How many times, I asked, had he skied this course? He thought for a moment. "1952," he said, "1953 . . ." "Not just the races. All the times. Counting practice." "Those don't matter," he said. The starting hut has no floor; it's set right on the snow. There is a railing down the middle to create a kind of waiting area on one side. Sailer glides around it and lines up in the gate. There he pauses and looks down the bleak, empty course. They have been working on it all week. Difficult to know what his thoughts are, his memories. He first won the race the year of his Olympic sweep when he won the downhill, normally a matter of hundredths, by 3.5 seconds, the slalom by 4 seconds, and the giant slalom by 6.2 seconds. It was the greatest individual performance ever. Nobody, one authority says, has ever come close to those time differences, especially in giant slalom, not even Stenmark. Killy won by razor-thin margins.

From the starting gate the course goes down sharply to a hard left turn that leads into an even steeper, narrower pitch, a breathtaker called the Mausefalle. After this is another, the Steilhang. Sailer stands with the tips of his skis hung out over nothing. My thoughts are close to panic. I feel as if we are about to step off a precipice.

Sailer turns his head and then offers something for the first time. "How are your edges?" he asks. "Sharp? Because it's all ice here. If they're not sharp, I don't think you're going to make it." And he is off. I watch in disbelief as he makes one or two confident turns and goes out of sight to the left at the bottom. My own skis are rented. I push them out over the edge. I had pictured us skiing slowly down the side of the course, shadowing it leisurely. It isn't going to be like that.

I push off. From the first moment it's like a car without brakes. On the frozen surface my edges won't hold. I try to turn, but the skis only clatter. Picking up speed, I can't make the last turn, fall at the bottom, and get up quickly. Sailer is standing there at the top of the Mausfalle.

"The ice isn't bad," he comments as I reach him, "it's grippy." When he was racing they used to pre-jump here and go most of the way down in the air. Now they press, holding their skis on the ground and taking the air as it comes. At the bottom it flattens suddenly—it's called a compression—driving the legs up into the body. There's no time for recovery. Three quick turns lead into the Steilhang, more difficult still. These turns are very important, Sailer comments, you have to make them correctly to keep up maximum speed. I nod reluctantly.

On the Steilhang is something unexpected: Austrian ski troops at work grooming the course. They are under the supervision of Willy Schaeffler, a former United States ski team coach now in his sixties. I know Schaeffler and am relieved to see him.

"What are you doing here?" he asks. We've stopped there beside him. "Toni's showing me the Hahnenkamm," I say casually. "Him? He doesn't know anything about the Hahnenkamm," Schaeffler says, to my alarm. "He's forgotten it all." He laughs at his own joke. Sailer says nothing. After a moment, merely, "Let's go." He lets his skis run down the rest of the Steilhang, some twenty or thirty yards, onto a relatively flat road through the woods. It feels like we are going sixty miles an hour. We are probably doing twenty. The tension is beginning to ease, however. The top part is the hardest—perhaps we're going to make it.

We come to another pitch, not so steep. It's called the Alteschneise—the Old Cut—and is where Sailer fell in 1958. He points to the approximate spot. He hit a fast place or bump, he doesn't know which—the course was narrower and rougher then and the skis just went out from under him.

Through the middle section it is relatively pleasant, the sort of terrain that lets you ski fast but doesn't oblige you to. And it's less icy. Wonderful skiing.

Ahead is the last big pitch at the Hausberg. It's the final test of the race and has a brutal compression at the bottom, where many racers have fallen and more than a few have ended their careers. Just before reaching it we see someone else on the course, a stocky figure in a blue ski suit who is gazing down the mountain almost pensively. It's the Austrian coach, Kahr, known as Downhill Charly— the Austrians have a proprietary feeling toward the event which they regard as their exclusive domain. Kahr and Sailer exchange a few quiet words like a couple of fishermen. The sun has just come up and is casting a shadow down at the bottom where, Kahr points out, the racers will be at their maximum speed, eighty-five or ninety miles an hour. One thing the two of them agree on: the snow is perfect. We go down the final steep pitch together. It's challenging but fairly wide. There is room to turn, and the compression is nothing because we cross it at an angle and at reasonable speed. The long straightaway to the finish is like applause.

True to his word, in a little restaurant at the foot of the slope Sailer talks about racing, what it was to be a great racer, what it takes to win. There are things you can learn from the coaches and things you can't learn. "Energy," he says. "Will."

We talk for half an hour. He seems very different here, almost amiable. He was the son of a roofer. He became a great champion, knew all the glamour, and now he is back in his hometown. They are cheering for others now. When he looks back on it, the races, the fame, the records that in all probability will never be equaled, when he looks back on all of that, what does he think of, I ask? He reflects for a moment.

"Well, I think it was a good thing to do it. Sport makes character," he says. I walk back to the hotel. It's barely nine o'clock. The early skiers are walking past me up toward the cable car. The day is beginning to take on winter brilliance, the snow sparkling, faces animated and bright.

"Did you do it? Did you go down with Sailer? How was it?" It will be true one day even if it isn't now. "The greatest run of my life," I say and go upstairs and back to bed.

The New York Times
November 7, 1982

At the Foot of Olympus:
Jarvik, Kolff, and DeVries

When Robert Jarvik, the designer of the artificial heart, came to
Salt Lake City in 1971 to go to work at the Institute for Biomedical
Engineering which is part of the University of Utah there, he and
his young wife were able to drive west with all of their possessions
loaded in the back of their car. The Institute itself was then four
years old, Jarvik was twenty-five, and Willem Kolff, for whom Jarvik over the next decade was going—unbeknownst to him at the
time—to design and build a whole series of artificial hearts, was
sixty. Neither man had met the other, they had only talked on the
phone. When Jarvik arrived, Kolff called him into his office, which
was in an old, converted World War II barracks, and told him simply
that his job would be to make an artificial heart.

"That's all he said," Jarvik recalls. He doesn't remember precisely
how he went about it. His only preconception was that it "ought to
be heart-shaped," so the first heart he made was shaped like that.

Jarvik did not invent the artificial heart. There were many models before his. The search had been going on for about forty years
and in the imagination of men much longer. The problem is quite
simple: the heart, as many authorities have observed, is merely a

pump. But what a pump. "This moves of itself," as Da Vinci wrote, "and does not stop unless forever. Marvellous instrument invented by the supreme Master." Governed by a faint electrical impulse, by glandular action, and by a dictum called Starling's Law (the volume of blood pumped by the heart depends on the volume returned by the veins which dilate in times of emotion or stress to increase the flow to the heart and hence its output), this most crucial organ is entirely muscle, weighs less than a pound, and beats tirelessly over 3 billion times between birth and death, unnoticed, uncared for, while we eat, dream, love, and pray. In an age of tremendous scientific discovery the heart has remained a kind of holy grail.

Although he had never built an artificial heart or even considered the problem, Jarvik was nevertheless a good choice for the job. The son of a Connecticut doctor, he had shown an aptitude for making things since early childhood and in high school he designed a surgical stapler, an instrument like a pair of graceful scissors meant to be held in one hand and to save time by clipping closed severed blood vessels during an operation. He continued to think about this device for years. The first time she went out with him in college, Elaine Jarvik recalls, he was talking about it. The history of the stapler is in a way the history of his life, connecting the various segments of it in a remarkable manner.

Unable to get into medical school in the states, Jarvik and his wife—they were married the day before they left—went to Italy where he entered the University of Bologna. He spent two years there. It was a difficult period. Neither he nor his wife spoke much Italian and they led what they describe as a hermetic existence.

"I didn't go to class very much," he says. "It was kind of an intolerable situation. It was very, very crowded." For the anatomy course the students would begin to gather in a courtyard an hour before class.

When the gates were opened everyone would rush into the building and down a long corridor lined with display cases containing thousands of skulls. "I refused to run. After a while I just stopped going and stayed home and studied."

He worked on the stapler there, however, and also when he returned to the States. He had come back still hoping to get into medical school here. Although Bologna was the oldest university in Italy with a medical school dating back to 1306, there was virtually no lab work—they couldn't obtain cadavers—and his father had arranged to have him do dissections at NYU. Jarvik showed the stapler to various people there, including a professor interested in biomechanics who promptly offered him a fellowship.

"I took it hoping that it would lead me to medical school at NYU," Jarvik says. "I got on the waiting list that year but I didn't get in."

He got a master's degree in biomechanics, and the next summer an executive of a surgical instrument company that was interested in the stapler, having failed in an attempt to help Jarvik get into Duke, called someone he knew in Utah, a Dutch doctor named Kolff who was head of a biomedical institute there. The idea was to have Kolff hire Jarvik. As a resident of Utah, he would have a better chance to be admitted to medical school there. The executive even offered to pay Jarvik's salary but Kolff, who was struggling to get his institute established, did not seem interested. Finally Jarvik called himself to plead for the job. He was advised to return to Bologna and get his degree. That was not what he wanted, Jarvik said, he wanted to work for Kolff.

"Do you have a car?" Kolff asked unexpectedly.

Jarvik said he had a Volvo.

"Oh, I see my administrator through the window," Kolff interrupted, adding, "How much money do you want?"

Jarvik pictured a man just walking past Kolff's window who would in a few seconds be gone, together with Jarvik's chances. "A hundred dollars a week," he said hastily.

Kolff told him to hold the line for a minute. In fact the administrator was sitting in an adjoining office with a glass window between him and Kolff. When he came back on the line, he said, "OK. When do you want to start?"

It was the Volvo, Jarvik is convinced. If he hadn't had a European car he wouldn't have gotten the job.

Willem Kolff is a unique figure in medicine. Tall, white-haired, paternal, and shrewd, he is best known as the inventor of the artificial kidney. This was in the Netherlands in 1943, during the German occupation. Kolff, who had graduated from medical school at Leyden five years earlier, was working in a small municipal hospital in Kampen, a town on the Zeider Zee, legendary, as he says, for its fools. A young patient of his slowly died of kidney failure, going blind first, and Kolff, deeply disturbed by the event, set out to try and devise something to help such cases. A man of wonderful energy and imagination, in Kolff these qualities are matched by an equally great compassion. His father was the director of a tuberculosis sanatorium with immense concern for the welfare of his patients, which Kolff feels he inherited. In his youth he didn't want to be a doctor because he didn't think he could bear watching people die. The example of his father's dedication, however, finally swayed him from his original conviction to become a zookeeper.

Kolff's first kidney machines, designed to remove waste products from the blood, were rotating drums wrapped with tubes of cellophane. The patient's blood circulated through the tubes and impurities were drawn through the permeable cellophane into a surrounding solution. Of the first fifteen patients the artificial kidney was tried on, only one survived, and that one might have done so anyway, Kolff admits. In 1945 there was finally an indisputable success, a sixty-seven-year-old woman who was saved. It happened to be a woman who had been a Nazi sympathizer and much hated, but she was a patient and Kolff treated her.

In wartime Holland things had to be made out of whatever was available. A local enamel factory built the tanks and the permeable membrane was sausage skin. This unorthodox approach is typical of Kolff. In Cleveland where he went a few years later to join the staff of the Cleveland Clinic, he used washing machines and fruit juice cans in the construction of more advanced models. Today there are more than 50,000 patients in the U.S. and 200,000 worldwide whose lives are dependent on the artificial kidney, and the list of Kolff's prizes and awards for this and other accomplishments fills nearly three pages, but he is still, because of his pragmatic methods, taken perhaps less seriously than he might be. Not an active surgeon, he is treated lightly by the star performers with their powerful egos. A tinkerer and an individualist, he has few champions in the bureaus of government where grant money is found. "I make gadgets," he says, looking out over his horn-rimmed glasses. "I'm not considered scientific."

In 1957, Kolff and an assistant named Tetsuzo Akutsu put the first artificial heart in the Western world into a dog which lived for an hour and a half. In the beginning the concept was so bizarre and outside the scientific mainstream that papers describing experiments were not even accepted by medical societies. But research continued and over the years Kolff found coworkers whom he managed to inspire and keep. The atmosphere in Cleveland was too conservative, however, and in 1967 he decided it was time to leave. He asked a friend where he could find a good, regional medical program and the answer was Utah. Encouraged by the medical school, the university, and the governor, he moved there, leaving behind everything he had built up during seventeen years, including a farm he loved.

In Cleveland, according to Dr. Clifford Kwan-Gett, who came with him to Utah, they had money but no space. Every time someone walked to the elevator, he had to move his chair. In Utah they had space but no money. "It took about three years to get going," Kolff agrees. He now has 120 people of different disciplines, doctors, engineers, social workers, and electronic specialists and a budget of over $5,000,000. Almost all of this money comes from government grants and contracts. About 20 percent of it goes to the artificial heart. Kolff's own salary is less than that of a mediocre shortstop: $63,000 a year. He has never made a penny from the artificial kidney—he never even bothered to take out a patent on it.

The artificial heart has come almost full circle. From obscure and dubious beginnings it advanced to a stage where, stimulated by testimony of the famous Houston surgeon, Dr. Michael DeBakey, Congress made it a national objective. For a feverish decade in the late '60s and early '70s, the National Institutes of Health coordinated the efforts of research centers and blue-chip technology corporations to build a device that would be as marvelous as the Apollo ship of the space program, except this would be for a voyage inward, to the center of man.

It had been estimated that up to 50,000 people a year might be recipients of artificial hearts, but delays, failures, and waning optimism in the nation at large finally caused the NIH to lower its aim and deemphasize the program. Kolff is not one to be discouraged by mere shifts in policy, however. He has gone doggedly on. More than any other man's, the heart is his. He finds a way around delays and cautious decisions. He has recently developed, despite government indifference, a portable artificial kidney which represents a considerable advance over bulkier models. It can be worn by the patient.

"The government now spends through Social Security more than one billion dollars a year on end-stage renal disease, but if I want ten thousand dollars to build a better artificial kidney, I can't get it."

Kolff begins his days with an 8 a.m. meeting of his staff. Around a long table sit a group of men and women, some in white coats, some in plaid shirts and jeans. In a mild voice with a slight accent, Kolff begins without fanfare.

"How are the calves?" he asks.

One of the sheep, it turns out, is having ventricular fibrillation. This is discussed for a minute or two, then the subject changes to the vacuum-molding method of making hearts. A short lecture on an electric motor they are interested in is delivered by an engineer.

There is mention of microcircuits, custom chips with 1,700 gates, and a new microprocessor.

"Do we have seven thousand dollars for this new computer?" Kolff asks.

"Well, we can probably find it somewhere," Jarvik replies. "It depends where we look for it."

If they fire the lecturer whose name is Jeff, it is suggested, they could probably get it from his salary.

"Barely," Jeff says, unperturbed.

There is talk about a two-by-five-inch emulator card which can do everything the chip does until the chip is available. Kolff is sitting on the edge of the table in a business suit and hiking boots.

"You call it an emulator card," he asks, making a note.

"Yes."

"I learn a new word every day."

Kolff is the sort of man who inspires affection. With his high forehead and face filled with confidence and humor, one feels he knows things, and not merely about the work to which he has devoted his life.

The first heart that Jarvik designed was never tried in an animal. The second was not very good, either. Developed from an idea of Kolff's, it was flat and in fact was called the pancake heart. Jarvik had begun work on another model when Kolff summoned him.

"When is your new heart going to be ready?" he asked. "We've been beaten. Dr. Nosé has beaten us."

Nosé was a former associate in Cleveland who stayed there when Kolff left. Experimenting with the idea of a flocked surface inside the heart that was meant to encourage an organic layer to form on it, he had had a calf that survived seventeen days, a record at the time. Kolff was determined to surpass it. Jarvik was by then in medical school—he had gotten in with Kolff's help—but he was still employed at the lab. All through Christmas that year he remembers working on the new heart.

The first calf they tried it in lived six days. It died from a massive blood clot—the inside of the heart hadn't been cleaned well enough in this case, but the formation of clots was a constant problem in the beginning. Jarvik and Kolff were using a smooth inner surface, as smooth and nonirritating to the blood as possible.

After four or five tries, just before the ASAIO (American Society for Artificial Internal Organs) meeting that year, they had a calf that went nineteen days.

"It was so exciting," Elaine Jarvik says, "those two weeks. It was so intense. Your parents called every night."

"Every day was a new milestone," Jarvik agrees.

All the early hearts were made of silicon rubber. Polyurethane was thought to be a better material, more durable, very abrasion resistant, smoother and less damaging to the blood, but the hearts made of it didn't stand up, the diaphragms broke after a few days or weeks on the tester. Then Jarvik had an idea. It was to use several layers of polyurethane with Dacron mesh between them for support. Pharmaceutical mesh cost too much so he bought some in a fabric store for $4.95 a yard.

The first calf they tried it in went three months. That was in 1974. The record had been thirty-six days.

The new heart was called the J-3.

"That was the first thing I did that was inventive," Jarvik says. "We used that heart, in that form, for quite a long time. We got up to about four, four and a half months."

Each animal was a journey into the unknown, a major operation, a complete medical history. Infection was coming in where the air lines that drove the heart entered the body, and there were still blood clots forming at the seam where the diaphragm joined the wall of the chamber. Kwan-Gett, who designed early hearts, had wanted to cover the inner surface with liquid polyurethane. There would be a shallow concave mold at the bottom of the heart and the polyurethane formed by it would be the diaphragm. Jarvik took this idea which had never worked for Kwan-Gett and made a heart. It was seamless, the J-5.

With it, in 1977, they got the first six-month survival, a calf named Abebe. There have been a lot of long-lived calves since— Sirius, Claudius, Romulus, Fumi Joe, among others, and Tennyson who lived 268 days, nearly nine months. There the record stands. All of the long survivors have been with J-5 hearts except Fumi Joe who had a J-7, the model designed for human implantation. One limitation has become the animal outgrowing the heart, becoming too large for it and dying of cardiac insufficiency. Sheep, though they are difficult to work with, might solve the problem. When Jarvik came to Salt Lake City no animal with an artificial heart had lived more than three days.

The next step will be in the hands of a tall (six-foot-five), whippet-lean surgeon named William DeVries. The chief of Cardiothoracic Surgery at Utah, he has had a long acquaintance with the artificial heart. "I just sort of grew up with it," he says. He was one of Kolff's first new employees and like Kwan-Gett built early hearts for him. When permission for clinical testing is received from the FDA, it will be DeVries who performs the actual operation.

DeVries is a Mormon and grew up in Salt Lake City. One of nine children, his father was a naval surgeon killed in the South Pacific during World War II. His mother is a nurse. DeVries himself has five children, coaches basketball, and is the legendary Westerner, lanky, drawling, straightforward. It was Kolff who stirred in him an interest in surgery. He was already in medical school when they met and later, with Kolff's assistance, he obtained a prestigious residency at Duke, "I probably wouldn't have got it by myself." When his residency was completed it was only natural that he return to Utah which, at Kolff's suggestion, he did. He had fully expected that an artificial heart would have been tried by then. "At the time I left the field," he says, "I felt sure one would be put in in a few years."

DeVries has operated on literally hundreds of animals including both Tennyson and Fumi Joe. His job has been to perfect the surgical techniques. "I know that I can put that artificial heart in better than anyone in the world right now," he says confidently. He does about 200 heart operations a year. Of these, perhaps 5 percent are high risk—patients whose chances in cardiac surgery are not good, generally someone with poor left ventricular function. If at the conclusion of surgery the patient cannot be brought off the heart-lung machine despite all efforts, if the heart cannot be made to beat again, in short if someone is to be given up for dead, then the artificial heart will be implanted, with prior consent, of course.

"Last year I had maybe three patients who would fit the criteria," DeVries says. He adds, "and they all died."

The final act will be his alone. He will select the potential recipient according to a carefully prepared profile, he will decide at the crucial moment if the heart will be used, he will put it in. Two consulting cardiologists will approve his decision, but apart from that, his authority will be complete.

The result, if successful, will be someone permanently tethered to an array of bulky mechanical equipment, a control box, a large compressor, backup compressor, standby tanks of compressed air for an emergency, and the rest. To many people this seems disturbing. Kolff has always said from the beginning, however, that the comfort and happiness of the patient come first. He has even said that he would give the patient a pair of scissors and not keep him from using them if that was what he wanted.

The publicity has already begun. "We do not seek it," Kolff says, "but it is unavoidable."

"There's been a tremendous amount . . . too much," DeVries agrees.

Appearances on national television, stories, interviews. Last summer Jarvik was asked to design a heart to be used in a movie with Donald Sutherland, *Threshold*, about a surgeon who perfects an indestructible heart. When the movie was being made Jarvik met Sutherland and Denton Cooley, probably the best-known cardiac surgeon in the world, who kept a patient alive for several days with an artificial heart while waiting for a transplant donor in 1968. Cooley had instructed Sutherland in surgical matters and even made a brief appearance in the film. They were having drinks in a hotel in Toronto and Jarvik, convinced that Cooley had never heard of him, asked how he had become involved in all this. Cooley's cold blue stare fixed on him.

"It's about me," he said.

The heart that Jarvik designed for *Threshold* is nuclear powered and the moment when the natural heart of the young woman who receives it is removed forever is a chilling one. This aspect of the artificial heart, that it represents an irreversible step, is one of the objections put forth against clinical testing. The NIH has shifted its support to an intermediate device which is, in effect, half a heart. It is a pump that can be temporarily attached to an ailing left ventricle to ease its work and allow it to recover—the natural heart would stay in situ. This is the LVAD, left ventricular assist device, now in limited use.

The LVAD makes sense but the results of it have not been very good. Used principally in Boston and Houston, about one patient in twenty has survived. Kolff's people feel it has its place just as transplants do, but there are hearts that the LVAD cannot help.

One of the problems has been that the LVAD is used on patients who have been on the heart-lung machine too long and on whom everything else has been tried. There is massive bleeding because the coagulating power of the blood is gone. Even the doctors who support it say that results would be better if the LVAD could be put in sooner.

This could also apply to the first use of the J-7. The patient may have been on the heart-lung machine for five or six hours before every alternative is exhausted and the artificial heart can be used. This is too long.

Jarvik is outspoken about disagreeing with the way it will be done. He would use it on a voluntary basis, straight off, someone with cardiomyopathy—progressive disease of the heart muscle. "If the patient is on bypass six or seven hours," he says, "I don't think he'll live." DeVries agrees it is a problem.

Still, everything has been practiced, everything anticipated. For a year and a half now DeVries has gone to St. Mark's, the abandoned hospital in which the artificial heart program is housed, to do an implant every week. He has done them in cadavers as well as animals. Early in May the J-7 was tested in a woman who had been declared dead because her brainwaves were flat. The operation was done by Kolff's son, Jack, who is a cardiac surgeon in Philadelphia. The heart was in for several hours, supported life, and worked well.

The scrub nurses have familiarized themselves with the operation, doorways have been checked to make sure the special equipment will fit through. When the FDA gives its permission, all systems will be go.

Not all medical opinion is favorable.

"What's happening in Utah is an aberration," says an important surgeon. "It's way out in left field . . . In fact, it's a very bad idea. Jarvik and DeVries are self-destructing. Old Kolff, he's retired and his contact with medicine has been peripheral . . . We're not at that stage where we're ready for it."

"There's room for the artificial heart but I think it should require more work," another says. "It took us five years to negotiate permission to implant the LVAD . . . Utah has a lot to learn."

There are considerations that are not purely scientific.

"We've sold four hearts to Argentina, to Favaloro," DeVries says. "His group may be the first to take one and put it in a patient. What if they say, you can't do it here, and Argentina does it?"

Dr. René Favaloro is the surgeon who developed the coronary bypass operation when he was in Cleveland. More than 100,000 are now performed annually in the U.S. The clock is ticking.

A grotesque optimism, a blind push towards progress, science for the sake of science, and a perfect faith in the undiscovered—these are disquieting but they are not what motivate the team in Utah. Kolff, Jarvik, and DeVries, all doctors and sons of doctors, represent in a strange way a kind of nineteenth-century idealism striving to perfect what they see as an eminently useful device. They are not pursuing monstrous visions to whatever end. Nor do they seek, as some critics say, to create a race of invalids. Their goal is simpler and more direct: to heal the sick. Forever? Hardly. The body will find ways to die despite an imperishable heart.

Typescript
May 26, 1981

Man Is His Own Star: Royal Robbins

In Yosemite there is a great hotel, the Ahwahnee, with beautiful windows and chateau-like grounds. In sitting rooms the size of churches there are tables from England, rugs from the Caucasus, and lamps made from antique Japanese jars. There is also, friends tell me, a ten-year wait for Christmas reservations.

There used to be a nightly display for guests: at nine in the evening the rangers would light a huge pyre of bark slabs and wood and push it over a cliff. This ceremony was known as the Firefall. At the far end of the valley, on the vertical 2,000-foot face of Half Dome, climbers attempting its first ascent could see this river of fire from whatever narrow ledge they were bivouacked on for the night, and they chose the time to flash signals to their friends on the ground.

The climbers were led by a young, hatchet-faced Californian, aggressive, supremely talented, who had been famous since his teens. They were five days on the face of Half Dome, tormented by its immense scale and by the summit overhangs which would have to be crossed somehow. On the fifth morning they stuffed their excess gear into a hauling bag and threw it into space. They watched it fall endlessly, never once touching the wall, and finally hit the ground. Then they pushed on and, by means of a narrow ledge barely a foot wide, hanging from it by their hands at the end, they at last reached the top. It was the first Grade VI climb in America, a climb of the highest level of endeavor. The year was 1957. The twenty-two-year-old leader was Royal Robbins.

I drove to Yosemite National Park with Robbins not long ago. We pulled off the road at an overlook near the entrance to the valley and sat there in silence gazing out at it. The great glacial cliffs, the forests, the deep valley floor were still far off and appeared smaller than I had expected. Still, it was very moving, this first image he was letting me have without a word of description or reminiscence, standing back from it as it were and allowing me to see it with my own eyes. He, of course, had seen it countless times. He had spent, by his own estimate, more than a year in Yosemite, half of it on one climb or another and more than sixty nights bivouacked on the big walls.

Robbins—even a chief rival calls him *"Numero uno"*—is forty-three now. He's medium sized, strong, with blue eyes and straight brown hair. There is something neat, even academic about him. With his glasses and beard, his fine ears and high forehead, he might be an anthropologist with important work behind him. In fact, he is a high school dropout; his education came later. He speaks in a low, somewhat reluctant voice. His responses are often just a single word.

Yosemite rock, which he began to point out as we drove along, is all smooth, steep, and glacially polished. There are few handholds, and a climber must make use of characteristic vertical cracks. These often run for long distances, varying in width from several inches to two or three feet and then narrowing to a line no broader than that of a pencil. A very technical and highly evolved method of climbing is necessary, and even then climbs are not easy.

"Great climbing," Robbins explained, "is steep rock without excessive difficulty. Yosemite steep climbs are often difficult. Yosemite tends to be discouraging and to require condition and endurance.

Also, it's not particularly exhilarating. They are problems you wrestle with rather than overcome with finesse."

To one who does not climb, of course, steepness seems to be the most difficult thing to accept, the most demoralizing. I had mentioned this on another occasion and Robbins had said that very often something that looks hard actually isn't.

"Steepness, for instance, isn't one of the things that make a climb hard."

"What are the things that do?" I asked.

"The lack of holds," he said simply.

We had descended to the valley floor. In the late afternoon the trees seemed rich and green, the Merced River clear enough to see every pebble in its bed. Suddenly there loomed out of the dusk the top of a great, pale bulwark, like the blunt prow of an enormous ship facing not quite toward us. A thrill of recognition went through me, I had seen so many photographs: it was El Capitan. There was still a little light, and Robbins stopped the car, took a pair of binoculars from the glove compartment, and examined the face. There were several parties climbing, he commented, at least one on the Nose, and there was someone bivouacked above the Roof, a large overhang more than two thirds of the way up. Bivouacked meant attached to the face in a kind of hammock in which the climber would pass the night with 2,000 feet of empty air beneath him. A climb of El Cap by any of its routes takes several days, and sometimes longer, depending on the conditions and the ability of the climbers. It is extremely difficult and exposed, and to have some idea of scale one must imagine a wall more than twice as high as the Empire State Building.

A few days earlier we'd had dinner at Robbins's house in Modesto with another well-known climber, T. M. Herbert. It was a congenial occasion. Herbert is a schoolteacher in a small town near Merced and a man of great wit and vitality. He made what seemed to me a surprising confession: he said that as a boy he had been terrified of heights, and that the germ of that fear was still within him.

"T. M. never falls," Robbins said. "He puts in protection every three feet and sometimes goes down the rope to double-check what's already in."

The longest fall he'd ever taken was thirty feet, Herbert admitted. Robbins, on the other hand, has fallen frequently. Generally speaking, among serious climbers there is no such thing as not falling. It is inevitable. These falls are protected by a belay rope, but they can be dangerous.

"Have you ever fallen when you didn't more or less anticipate it?" I once asked Robbins.

"No," he said. "Once, when I first began climbing, I leaned back on a piton I'd just put in and it pulled out. I fell thirty feet and broke my arm."

It had been what climbers call a "ground fall," meaning that one hits the ground. Thirty feet is a considerable distance—men have been killed falling from stepladders—but I had already heard of 150- and even 200-foot ground falls where the climber not only had lived but had gone back to climbing.

It's disturbing, perhaps, to think of Robbins, one of the greatest climbers alive, as losing his hold and falling—after all, if he falls, then what about me?—but the reason has nothing to do with lack of ability. Robbins falls when he attempts something that is at the very limit of his powers, and it is his nature always to extend these limits. He expects a fall and is prepared for it.

Herbert and his wife were on their way to Yosemite the night they spent at the Robbinses'. Close to forty, Herbert was as passionate as ever about climbing. Earlier he had spent an hour by himself doing exercises in the living room. He was climbing as well as he ever had, he told Robbins. He was going to Yosemite every weekend. He was still in there. Climbing had changed, of course, he admitted. A new generation had appeared.

"All climbers are on dope now," he said somewhat resignedly. "They're smoking during ascents, even dropping acid."

Robbins said nothing. He and Herbert have known each other

for more than twenty years. When he was first starting to climb, Robbins told me, one of the things that impressed him was the sort of men he met. They were men he admired, who were superior to anyone he knew "down there" in the city. It was one of the things that made him decide to choose climbing as his life. Marijuana as a necessity for Yosemite bivouacs was obviously something foreign to him.

"How many times have you climbed El Cap?" Robbins asked at one point.

"Hundreds of times," Herbert said.

"I don't mean in your imagination."

"Three," Herbert said.

Light had come in Yosemite. We ate in the large restaurant in the lodge, Robbins, his wife, Liz, their young daughter, and I, together with hundreds of visitors: old couples, campers, sightseers, and, of course, a sprinkling of climbers whose very appearance set them apart. They were indifferently, even poorly, dressed: plaid shirts, old sweaters, beards, and the filthiest of pants. As they ate or sat afterward in the bar with their girlfriends, one leg was often tapping nervously up and down. It was characteristic, Robbins said.

I climbed with Robbins the following day, a short route in an area called the Manure Pile. He had picked a climb called "After Six"; according to the Sierra Club Guidebook, it is a Grade II Class 5.7 route first climbed by Yvon Chouinard and Ruth Schneider in 1965. There are a number of systems to classify the difficulty of routes. The Yosemite system uses a Roman numeral to give the overall length and difficulty—Grade I takes a few hours, Grade III most of a day, etc.—and the Arabic number gives the level of the most demanding section. "After Six" is a moderate climb that might take two or three hours.

We roped up near the bottom of the first pitch, which happens to be the most difficult. Two husky girls were engaged in climbing it. Liz talked to them later. They were from Wyoming: this was their first climb in Yosemite, and they were just warming up. Rather than wait, we moved twenty feet or so to the right, where there is a variant, and began there. Climbers who are equals take turns leading, but of course we did not do this. Robbins went first, wearing corduroy trousers, a shirt and sweater, and a sort of white, old-fashioned golfer's hat. Over one shoulder he had slung the nylon loops with aluminum wedges that are often used instead of pitons in Yosemite and elsewhere. These come in a great variety of shapes; they are placed in a crack where it narrows or is irregular and jam there. They serve the same purpose as pitons, which are a kind of flat steel spike with a ring at the blunt end to attach the climbing rope to the mountain, either firmly or so it can run freely. With wedges, however, the rock is preserved from all the damage of "nailing," as climbers call piton placement.

From the ground, Robbins seemed to move up the rock with ease, using the toe of his shoe in a crack that was about an inch and a half wide and finding occasional holds off to the side.

"The thing is," Liz, who was standing beside me, commented, "you can't tell whether it's easy or hard from watching him. It all looks the same when he climbs it." She's made many climbs with her husband, including a repeat of the sensational face of Half Dome. She described the long, exposed ledge near the top to me—the wall slowly pressing her off it until she finished on one knee with the other leg dangling in space. She also climbed partway up the Nose of El Cap with him—"The most thrilling thing I've ever done," she said.

"Off belay," a voice called down. It was Robbins, eighty feet or so above. He had finished his lead. It was my turn.

Almost from the first moment, certainly from the time you are eight or ten feet off the ground, there is the feeling of being in another element, as distinct as diving into the sea. Robbins was in a position where he could watch me as I struggled. I had seen more or less clearly what he had done when he was on the lower portion, and I attempted to do the same thing, but before long I was moving on my own and completely involved in trying to find a way to climb it. To my inexperienced eye, there seemed to be a number of possibilities, or what could be possibilities, for holds. Most of these quickly proved inadequate. Others led to impasses. There comes the moment when one must gather oneself and try. I had done some climbing, not very much. I knew certain basic things, but sometimes, even on this easy route, it seemed as if he had taken the secret of his ascent with him. From time to time a bit of advice would be called down to me when I had come to a standstill—"Try pressing down on that place over to the right," or "Try and get your left foot there and use your right on that little hold." I was hand-jamming and fist-jamming; there was a period when it seemed I was clinging, legs beginning to tremble, for fully five minutes, unable to find any way of continuing until finally the smallest hold that I had first rejected, then come back to, and then rejected again, became the right one.

I had no fear. With him belaying, I would fall a few feet at the most if, as it seemed would happen any moment, a foot slipped and my fingers slid from whatever they held to. But I did have the anguish, the intense anguish of not knowing if I could make it. That, Robbins told me, never changes—it was still the same for him as it had been in his first climbing days. Sometimes he had remained in one spot for more than an hour trying to find some way to move, trying to solve the rock as if it were the door of a bank vault.

It took us about three hours to do "After Six." The wind had picked up and was blowing strongly toward the end. We stood on top for a minute or two, coiled the rope, and then started down a path off to the side. In twenty minutes we were back at the bottom. There had been times when he had gone out of sight above me and I couldn't hear his call but waited for a signal on the rope to begin—I had been alone. I was tired but happy. Robbins had the appearance of a man who has been on a leisurely stroll.

That night we had dinner at the Ahwahnee. Outside it had begun to snow. In the great dining room, filled with people and the warmth of conversation, we sat near one of the windows while the snow went through the darkness at a flat, wintery angle. Robbins mentioned the climbers we had seen on El Cap, probably a little cold and frightened, he said; they hadn't counted on a snowstorm in May. Many of them started big climbs surprisingly ill-equipped. There was a touch of disapproval in his comment. As we were to find out, there was considerable foresight as well.

Fine meals in expensive hotels have not always been part of his life. He was born in Point Pleasant, West Virginia, on February 3, 1935. His parents were divorced by the time he was six. His mother moved with him to California and remarried; they lived in Redondo Beach and then Hollywood. After the war she divorced again. She worked as a cosmetics expert in a drugstore and they lived with relatives to cut down expenses.

He had his first taste of the mountains with the Boy Scouts on a trip to the High Sierra sponsored by a local radio station, KFI. They climbed Fin Dome, a mountain near the Rae Lakes. "We used ropes. I remember it was fabulously easy for me. The others had trouble. I had none. I just wanted to climb and climb and climb. I was intoxicated with it." When he quit school in the tenth grade—he was getting poor marks, learning nothing—he had a feeling of inferiority; he wasn't good at sports, he wasn't good at anything. And yet at the same time, he says, "I knew I wanted to excel. I felt different from other people. I felt either inferior or superior. I wanted to do something heroic, great." He was going to the mountains to climb as much as he could, often alone. "I always had trouble recruiting partners." His first appearance at a climb of the Sierra Club established his reputation. He had a cast on one arm—it was two weeks to the day from the fall he had taken when the piton pulled free—but he climbed anyway. He was soon excelling at boulder problems and nervily applying the moves from these to the airy heights of Tahquitz Rock, a favorite location not far from Palm Springs. He was the outstanding young climber in the area, and his ascent of "Open

Book," a 200-foot inner corner at Tahquitz, was the first 5.9 climb in the country. The route had been done before, but Robbins made it "go free"—that is, he climbed it without using pitons for direct support. It was 1952. He was seventeen.

The first of his big routes was a second ascent of the north face of Sentinel in Yosemite. It had taken the original party four and a half days. Robbins and his companions did it in two. Climbing it again and again over the years, he eventually reduced the time to just over three hours. It's now been done in two.

By 1958, the ascent of Half Dome behind him, he was in the army, a clerk in Officers Records at Fort Bliss, Texas. For a year and a half he forged passes and caught an airplane ride north almost every weekend to climb in one place or another, hitchhiking back on Sunday, sometimes arriving only in time to shave, change clothes, and report to work. It was during this period that Tom Frost, an aeronautical engineer who had taken up climbing and was later to accompany Robbins on three of his major ascents, met his future companion. Frost was working at North American Aviation and had fallen in with a group of Los Angeles climbers.

"We'd go out to Tahquitz all the time," Frost says. "I heard frequent mention of Royal, Royal, Royal who did this, who said that. It turned out he was a friend of theirs in the army. One time we were climbing at Mount Pacifico; they were small rock cliffs, about twenty feet high. Someone pointed out a thin, diagonal crack big enough only for your fingers in places, with thin footholds and the wall overhanging slightly. It was called the 'Robbins Eliminate.' It had only been climbed twice, by Robbins and someone else. Well, I figured out a way, but couldn't do it. I went back to Los Angeles and dieted for a month and exercised. On our next trip to Pacifico, Robbins happened to be there. I tried the lower part, then asked for a belay and climbed it. Robbins was sitting there on a rock. He didn't say anything."

The next time they met, however, Robbins took Frost aside and confided his plans for an ascent of the Nose of El Cap—in Frost's words, "an exceptionally serious undertaking." Warren Harding, a famous siege climber, had taken a total of forty-five inconsecutive days and thirty nights to do it the first time, two years earlier. Harding used methods that opened a debate which still continues. The climb was up such blank rock that he pounded holes in it with a drill and then fixed small expansion bolts in these holes, hanging from them as he proceeded upward, step by step. Bolts had been known since before the war, but the excessive use of them went against the feelings of many, Robbins among them. Robbins's plan was to do it in one push, without coming down and going back up again on fixed ropes. Frost thinks that he had been asked to go along because more qualified climbers had turned it down, not believing it could be done. "They thought they would perish," he says.

The climb was made in September 1960. Robbins, Frost, Chuck Pratt, and Joe Fitschen made up the team. "Robbins had tremendous confidence," Frost says. "He's an exceptional leader. At bivouacs he'd cut off an inch of salami and pass it over, an inch of cheese and pass it over, an inch of bread, let you have three swigs out of the water bottle, and then go to sleep. He's a very strict disciplinarian. One of his great assets as a climber is the control he has over himself, his mind and his body. You didn't have to worry about anything when you were climbing with him. If you did what he said, you'd be all right."

They had taken enough water for ten days, one quart per man per day. They made it to the top in seven.

The following spring Robbins and Frost were gazing dreamily at the unclimbed southwestern, the left-hand, face of El Cap. The face had a number of weaknesses but there had never seemed a way to link them. Suddenly they saw a possibility, roundabout, but it might go: it was what became known as the Salathé Wall, for a great Yosemite figure of the '40s, and it is now considered the finest rock climb in the world.

There were thirty-four leads, or rope lengths, on the climb, many

5.8 or 5.9 with A3 and A4 nailing. Artificial climbing—hanging directly from pitons, bolts, or whatever—is designated A1 through A5 in order of difficulty. Much of Yosemite big-wall climbing is artificial—on this climb more than half.

Robbins himself concedes it was his drive and determination that were the reason for his success. Many people surpassed him in talent, he says. "I did the first 5.9, but Pratt did the first 5.10. If I'd had Pratt's talent and he had my drive . . ." His voice trails off. One thing he has always gotten from climbing is battle. Not just challenge—he needs to strive. It is so much a part of him that in games, of which he is fond, if he cannot find someone to play against, he will play against himself. For more than twenty years the greatest influence on his life has been Ralph Waldo Emerson, whose "Self-Reliance" I reread when I learned this. It begins with a verse of Beaumont and Fletcher:

Man is his own star, and the soul that can
Render an honest and a perfect man,
Commands all light, all influence, all fate . . .

But of all that is in the essay, one sentence struck me: "The force of character is cumulative." It seemed to me that this helped to explain the particular course Robbins's climbing has taken in the last eight or nine years. Following other climbs of major importance, both in Yosemite and in the Alps in the years 1962–67, Robbins climbed El Cap solo in 1968. He was on it for ten days. We already have some idea of the difficulties of such an attempt under normal circumstances; to do it alone implies an exceptional person.

Solo climbing has a long history. Hermann Buhl went to the top of Nanga Parbat alone, and Darbellay did the north face of the Eiger by himself, but "for me," Robbins says, "Bonatti is the great example. His solo of the Dru [a 3,000-foot granite pinnacle near Chamonix that Robbins put up two routes on himself] is one of the great achievements in mountaineering. It took six days. Escape was very difficult."

To climb dangerous faces alone takes an immense amount of inner strength. Even Bonatti felt that eventually the solo climber must run out of luck. I asked Robbins about this, and what there was to insure his safety under such conditions.

"Externally, nothing," he said. His protection came from within, from not committing himself to a move unless he was certain of three out of four points of support, so that if anything slipped, a foot for instance, he would still have the other foot and two hands. "There have been times," he added, "when my life was absolutely in the balance."

The El Cap climb, he admits, was "a bit inspired, separate from what others were doing. It required a bit of vision and an aptitude for climbing alone."

He has done a great amount of solo climbing since, mostly "free" solos where he carries absolutely nothing except for a rope if he is going to rappel down, which is the normal method of descending a face—the rope is doubled through a piton or around an outcropping, and the climber walks down backward, feet against the rock, the rope supporting him and being played out as he goes. Of this recent climbing he has said very little. He has mixed feelings about it as well as a long-established disdain for publicity, that of a man who is famous despite attempts to elude fame, as if the exposure of things somehow diminished their value, or, as Emerson said, "My life is for itself and not for a spectacle."

One of his best-known acts took place in 1970. Harding had put up another route on El Cap, spending twenty-seven straight days and nights on the wall, the longest ever in this country, and placing more than 300 bolts in the process. In the middle of winter Robbins and Don Lauria made the second ascent, cutting off Harding's bolts as they went, as if they were blemishes on the sport. They cut some forty before having second thoughts, but the controversy that resulted was intense.

Robbins and Liz were married in 1963. After several seasons teaching climbing and skiing in Europe, they moved to Modesto, a prosperous agricultural town about halfway between San Francisco and Yosemite, which had been her home. Her father owned a paint and wallpaper store there and for almost a year Robbins tried to become a paint salesman, with an eye to one day taking over the business, but it didn't work out. Instead, he and Liz began selling climbing boots in their spare time, at first shipping them from their kitchen table. They were imported boots, French-made Galibiers, and they became the backbone of what has turned into a success- ful outdoor equipment company. They have two shops, each called Robbins' Mountain Shop, one in Modesto and the other in Fresno, and a substantial wholesale business. "The Merchant of Modesto," he says of himself mockingly. Still, there is the unquenchable in him. He and Liz went to the 1974 meeting of the American Alpine Club by stealing into the Oakland yards and hopping a freight to Portland, twenty-four hours through a blizzard, then taking a cab from the Portland yards to the motel.

In Yosemite, the snowstorm continued through the night. The next morning we walked to the base of El Cap; I wanted to see what the beginning of the big routes looked like. It was a little after nine. As we approached, El Cap towering above us through the trees, we began to hear faint shouting. Someone on the face was calling, one word repeated over and over: "Help!" Robbins stopped. He listened, then cupped his hands to his mouth.

"Where are you?" he called.

"Help!" the voice cried.

We began to walk more quickly, joined by two other climbers, while from above us the cries continued. Soon we were hurrying over the rubble at the very foot of El Cap. The granite, an immense apron, rose at a steep angle. We finally located the climbers. They were up on a place called the Ledge and visible through Robbins's binoculars. A rope was hanging down to the left of them, a strangely idle and useless rope. It was possible to shout up from here and be heard. We lay on our backs and looked up about 700 or 800 feet. They were above a large, indented arch and could not see the wall beneath it. If they rappelled down, they thought, they would not be able to touch the face and would end up hanging in midair.

Robbins shouted up and told them to come down anyway, it was not as bad as it looked, they would find a place to set up another rappel. "Tie a big knot in the end of the rope!" he warned.

It was on this face, Robbins had told me, that Jim Madsen, an exceptionally strong climber, had rappelled down to check on two other climbers who were making slow progress. It was a sort of tentative rescue. His shoulders laden with extra coils of rope, Madsen had started down from the very top and somehow, no one will ever know exactly, had rappelled off the end of the rope and fallen to his death not far from where we were. The immense length of that fall and the helplessness of the climber, falling, remain in my imagination.

After a while a blue-clad figure began to make a very cautious descent. At the end of the rope a huge knot, clearly visible through the binoculars, was tied so it would not slip through the rappel brake. In addition, he had a separate belay line in case anything went wrong. The snow had begun again. It was swirling across the granite like the snow in a glass paperweight.

"An overhang can really spook you when it's beneath," Robbins commented. "These fellows were demoralized, ready to come down. Every foot you come makes you feel better," he added. "It's a lot better to fall from one hundred feet than seven hundred. The result is the same, but why go through all that anguish?"

An hour later, the two had made it safely down one rope length and were preparing to do the next. They would make it, Robbins said. We left them under the supervision of the two climbers who were sitting beside us, one of whom had climbed the route.

"Are your anchors OK?" he shouted up to them. "What are they?"

"One bolt and two fixed pins [pitons]!" was the reply. He sat back and relaxed.

There are young climbers, relatively inexperienced, who attempt and often do the toughest routes in Yosemite. There are climbers who flash across the scene like a comet—"three-year men," Robbins calls them—and disappear. And there are climbers who own only shoes and a swami belt, everything else belonging to whomever they're climbing with. This picture of a sport that can welcome its poorest adherent is an appealing one. Climbing, unlike most other things, has beneath it a great and inescapable danger, and it is this danger that purifies it and gives it its rank. Robbins has given his life to it, and what I think he objects to are those who face this danger in ignorance or afterward turn away, renounce it as if it had not really counted.

"He always wanted to do things in a better way, a superior way, purer," Frost says. "He was always raising the standard. When I climbed with Royal, I always had great experiences that I wouldn't have had otherwise. He was at the frontier of the sport. It wasn't just that he was a leader. He stood for something right. For the most incredible length of time, Royal was keeping up competitively with every climber there was. Everyone has his specialties—cracks, chimneys, whatever. But nobody could put up a harder route, nobody could do a harder boulder problem. He kept that up for a long time. If a younger climber comes along who can do something better than I can, I don't care, but Royal had to do it better."

We will all die and be forgotten, but there is in climbing a mythic element that draws one on. Half Dome, El Capitan, the Dru: these are names we have given to things that will be here almost as long as the earth itself.

Quest
March–April 1978

The Rock and the Hard Place

Racing for the Cup

At seven thirty in the morning, the loudspeakers begin announcing in German. It is the dead of winter. The mountains are barely visible. Lights are just beginning to come on in hotel windows. The first lone figures trudge toward the cable car station. In a little while the racers will be going up. All morning as they free ski, or in the words of a coach, do frisky runs, the crowd is gathering, building up along the sides of the course like a kind of dark debris clinging to the edge of a stream. The racers are cruising, making graceful turns, getting in tune with their skis.

"I always try and tell myself I'm doing great," Steve Podborski says of this phase. He is a graceful little Canadian, a coming champion. The crowd follows him around like a star.

About an hour before the start, in a nearby restaurant or hotel, the racers change into sleek one-piece suits that cling like silk stockings. Beneath them they wear nothing, not even an aluminum cup, just briefs. Races are won and lost in hundredths of a second. At high speeds, sixty miles per hour and up, it is wind resistance that causes most of the drag; anything that diminishes it is important. Having dressed, they enter the fenced-off area, separated from the crowd.

155

A World Cup race. On screens all over Europe, the prelude begins. It is always the same: helicopter views of the course that evoke disaster coverage, discussion of the key sections, standing of the racers, clouds, steep snowy mountains, the crowd. Finally there are the participants, like toreros in their suits of lights, distant, unamiable, and at the moment of their task immensely potent. The excitement is mounting. The starting clock is running, something begins to beep. The racer is living on nerve, the starter is counting. Go!

Down the course gathering speed, the scraping of edges, the blue of the snow, the sudden, terrifying liftoffs and plunging flight. Past trees, blurred faces, mountain huts they fly: harrowing turns, stunning recoveries from certain disaster. The crowds are thickest at the dangerous places. You can hear the racers pass; they are whistling like projectiles. And then there is the last schuss to the finish.

Skidding to a stop with a spray of snow, they look back immediately to see their time, unhappiness crossing their faces or the joy of triumph, white teeth shining.

There are other races, but none like this. "The giant slalom isn't interesting," Podborski says calmly. "A lot of big turns. The slalom isn't interesting either. But the downhill anyone can understand."

The season begins in December with a men's downhill in Laax, Switzerland, and then with the traditional opening in Val-d'Isere, France. Through March, moving from country to country, there are races, more than sixty altogether, counting toward the great crystal trophy called the World Cup. There have been years when it was so close that the winner was determined on the final day, but one of the big thrills is in January, when, as they do every year, the racers and their large retinues come to a 700-year-old town in the Tyrol. In addition to the ancient churches around which it is clustered, the expensive hotels, the snug pensions lost in the snow, the dark firs, the restaurants and gorgeous air, the town possesses one other attribute: it is home to the most famous downhill of all, one of the two so-called classics. The town is Kitzbühel. The course is the Hahnenkamm.

"When a racer comes to Europe," says Mike Farny, a member of the U.S. team, "all he hears about is the Hahnenkamm, how tough it is, who got wrecked on it. Some of them are so nervous the first time they can't eat breakfast."

"Unquestionably the toughest downhill," Bob Beattie agrees. He is a former U.S. coach who now does coverage for ABC. "It has dramatic changes of terrain, cross-hill traverses, and fall-away turns that are like turning on a tennis ball. Technically very difficult," he says coolly. He is never awed. When he was a boy wonder at the 1964 Olympics, his racers, Billy Kidd and Jimmy Heuga, won the first U.S. men's medals ever, silver and bronze. No American man has yet won an Olympic gold.

Austria is a small country, much of it mountainous. Kitzbühel, which is one in a necklace of snowy Alpine towns such as St. Anton, Gstaad, and St. Moritz, rose to the list of fashionable places after a visit by the Prince of Wales in 1928. But it is famous, too, for its great skiers—the wonder team of the 1950s: Pravda, Hinterseer, Molterer, and Sailer. Their photographs can still be seen displayed in shops: young men, the sun in their faces, leaning on their ski poles with the insouciance of champions. It was Toni Sailer who went through the roof, sweeping all three golds at Cortina, Italy, in 1956 (a feat that only Jean-Claude Killy has duplicated) and winning two more at the world championships two years later. He lost the slalom. In gratitude, Kitzbühel gave him and Molterer plots of land. Sailer built a small hotel on his.

"There used to be a lot of champions, but now it's too chichi," the press chief for the Hahnenkamm, Michael von Horn, says of the town. "The hard element is gone. There are too many other things; they go into business. Nowadays the champions come from backwoods places like Mooswald."

There are stunning faces from Munich and Vienna in the Landhäusl every night, or up at the Romerhof; insolent faces without problems or cares. St. Moritz is classier but also more formal and far more expensive. Here there is a hint of scandal, new money, of reputations that aren't quite right. The town is crowded. The casino is filled. People even come by taxi from Munich, about $120, not much when split several ways; the hotel will send one for you. The various bars and dance halls are either jammed because they are in vogue or mysteriously empty, with orchestras playing to nearly vacant floors.

The bar of the Goldener Greif is a gathering place. Late in the day everyone comes by, coaches, racers, journalists. Originally a gasthaus where farmers stopped for a drink on the way home from market, the hotel belongs to three brothers named Harisch and is extremely well run. The Harisches have been innkeepers for generations. Their mother cooked English dishes for Edward VIII when he was prince. The duke of Kent stayed here, and the Kennedys. Chaliapin sang in the bar.

At another of their hotels, the Munichau, a fortress-like outpost several miles from town, the American team is housed. In a small dining room they sit looking at videotape of their practice runs. Courage, technique, finesse, strength, and stamina—these are the qualities Killy mentioned when asked what was demanded by the course. On the tape are mistakes, bad runs, crashes. "Oh, daddyo," someone murmurs as a racer goes out of control. Another splatters. "ABC'll put you on TV for that one." The upper part of the course is extremely steep. The speed gained in the first thirty seconds carries the racer through the slower middle section.

Andreas Rauch, the U.S. downhill coach, is twenty-nine, quiet, and well-spoken. He is Austrian, with the prestige of having coached for four years on the Austrian team. Now he is trying to build a racing squad almost from scratch. He is very meticulous. He attends to every detail himself except for the video pictures; his girlfriend does that. Rauch knows the litany of disasters—he has been to Kitzbühel before. "Erwin Strickler, he was Italian, finished his career here in the Hausberg compression," he recalls. "Antonioli crashed in the same spot—also out for his career. Hans Enn crashed in the final compression, where you have the fastest speed. Last year Farny was out for three races after falling here. In 1979, eight of the first fifteen racers fell."

The falls are brutal. Instantaneously, what amounts to a racer's existence explodes. It takes time to regain confidence and get over that, sometimes two or three races. And this year the course is incredibly fast. It's difficult to compare years; in the 1930s, the record was around three minutes. The length of the course, however, has changed slightly over the years; sections have been widened, bumps removed, there are fewer or more gates. The weather is always different, the snow, the light. More important, equipment has changed. There is no absolute standard, but by the 1950s the time was down to two and a half minutes, and in the 1960s, less. At the start of the season, the record belongs to Franz Klammer, who streaked down in 2:03.22 in 1975.

Now something else is happening. In training runs they are breaking two minutes. Fantastic, everyone is saying.

"The top was fast," Beattie explains. "Usually it has ripples, but today it was absolutely smooth." It is so fast that if you touch the snow to keep from falling, as one U.S. team member did, you will burn a hole in your glove.

It's hard to figure the race from the training runs, although the early finishing order is always watched carefully, and certain racers are singled out. "Guys that are in front in training are almost always in front in the race," in Rauch's opinion. "They have to go full speed in training because there are so few runs—the maximum you can get before the race is four, and usually you get only three or less." Most of the time they go all-out and then slow down at the end of the course so as not to give themselves away. The best ones do this, Rauch says. To circumvent it, rival coaches end their timing a hundred meters from the finish.

The evening before the race, starting positions are decided. The racers are ranked according to their past performance in seeds of fifteen, but the order within the seed is determined by a draw. Position is important. In the downhill it's usually better to go in the second half of the first seed, when the snow has iced a bit and is faster. But weather can change this. It might be snowing, making the course slower.

At night the lights are on everywhere. The restaurants are crowded. There are five hundred newspaper, radio, and TV people in town, *Corriere della Sera*, *Stern*, *Asahi Shimbun*, the London *Times*. There are sixty-six reporters from Austria alone. The talk is entirely of racing, past champions, the poetry of names. Innsbruck, six years ago, was where the Canadians began coming on. Klammer won there.

"And in 1980?"

"Lake Placid. The winner was Leonhard Stock."

"Of course. That's right. Who was second?"

Silence.

"You know, that's the thing," someone says. "You never remember who came in second."

On Friday there is a race to make up for one canceled at Morzine earlier in the month. First place goes to Austrian Harti Weirather, second to Podborski, third to another Canadian, Ken Read. Klammer, the veteran from Mooswald, is eleventh. In a silver suit marked USA, Phil Mahre finishes thirty-seventh. The downhill is not his scene. They are expecting 30,000 people tomorrow, especially with an Austrian win today, which usually, they say, brings 10,000 more.

Saturday morning is cold and clear. By nine o'clock, crowds are flowing toward the mountain. A band is playing. Helicopters clatter overhead. People have come for the day by car and train. Kitzbühel lies in a loop made by the railroad, and there are tunnels under the track. A friend of mine ended his skiing because of this. Elated after a magnificent day, he decided to ski through a tunnel and right into town. At the last moment, he says, he discovered he had forgotten one thing—it doesn't snow in tunnels.

The prerace show is ending. Ski instructors are coming down in close formation, some carrying flags. Hang gliders with advertising on their wings float above the crowd. A group of Americans stand on a snow-covered rooftop waving an American flag.

The forerunners are arriving. It is impossible to see all of the race—it covers the entire side of a mountain. Nevertheless, it has begun. From the starting gate it is a steep, narrow descent to a sharp left turn. Then a plunge into an even steeper chute called the Maus-falle—the Mousetrap—down which racers go most of the way in the air. In a race, they are not trying to survive this first icy pitch. Instead they are skating, poling, accelerating down it. Every scrap of speed is important. They are on the best of their eight or ten pairs of skis, the ones with the right base, the right grind, the right wax. At the bottom is the first compression—the sudden flattening out that drives the body down on the legs with great force—and the three turns into the Steilhang.

Weirather has the number-two position; because of that, per-haps, he's not particularly fast. The Russian who comes next crashes on the Steilhang. Now Klammer. The crowd is expecting something. A roar goes up! Best intermediate time! They are waiting for him and beginning to shout, "Hopp! Hopp! Hopp!" Suddenly, a black speck, he appears. Down he drops, crossing the finish amid cheers. 1:57.78. A roar. He's in first! He stays there, racer after racer. Pod-borski is number fourteen. He never goes wide open on the training runs, he says. "In the past I did. I would have the best time, and in the race I fell because I was trying to do a little more. So I finally fig-ured that out. Now I leave myself that little bit of room I can move into for the race." The fact is, you must ski beyond your ability. You have to have something extraordinary motivating you. Podborski demolishes the upper section. He is doing all right in the middle. His skis are right, so is the wax.

It is a matter of hundredths. In his canary-yellow suit and black helmet, fairly flying, he hits the last pitch, the Hausberg, bottoms, turns. Hundredths are streaming off like ions. The final stretch, into the finish pen, spraying snow: 1:57.24. He has won for the second straight year. Ken Read is third; Phil Mahre finishes fourteenth, about 1.7 seconds behind Podborski. The first sixteen places are separated by only two seconds.

That night there's a party for the racers and their guests at the Londoner, a popular bar. The phone at the hotel rings all the time for the Canadian team, but the calls are switched to the coach. "Otherwise we'd be doing nothing but answering the phone," Podborski says. They even call in Toronto. He has a recording machine there. They call him from West Germany and say, "Oh, Steve, I love you," and hang up.

"I'm not here to chase girls," he says. "I'm here to ski."

Nevertheless, on the snowy street two beautiful girls with black-rimmed eyes roll down the window of their car and ask impatiently, "Which way is the Jagerwirt?" That's the hotel the Canadians are staying at. "Yes," they cry, "but where is it, which street?"

Sunday is the slalom. It is a different kind of excitement, trickier, like watching a gymnastics match. One after another they shoot down, banging the poles out of the way with their shoulders, knees pumping as the crowd chants and rings cowbells.

Ingemar Stenmark, from Sweden, is the attraction here. He is a phenomenon, the sort that appears only once or twice in a generation. Tall, intelligent, aloof, like a great reddish dog, he reportedly earns well over half a million dollars a year. He has been at the top since winning the World Cup in 1976, 1977, and 1978, when they changed the rules to keep him from making it boring. He is twenty-six. He may not be back. "You can be in the top ten for ten years," he says, "no more, and I have eight. I don't think you get physically tired, but mentally you're spent."

As he competes now in these final months against Phil Mahre and his twin brother, Steve, there is really no one like him. He has that best-loved element of greatness: an unmistakable style. The possibilities in the event are limited—there is a steep hill with sixty gates the racer must flash through faster than the others; that's all there is to it. Nevertheless, Stenmark makes himself different. Immensely smooth and powerful, he is whacking the hinged poles aside as if he

were batting balls, this confident champion who disdains the downhill and the "paper" World Cup points he might win by entering it
and is content to be absolute king of his domain (though Phil Mahre
will surpass him in both of his specialties before the season is over).
He is skiing with unforgettable authority, not sitting on the comfortable lead of his first run but risking everything anew on the second,
courting disaster. Across the finish line and the time flashes on the
scoreboard, almost two seconds faster than Mahre. A slight smile—
less than a smile, something within—crosses his fine features as he
looks up and sees it. The day is his. His long-limbed Swedish fiancée
is smiling. This is probably his final season. The crowd has a last
glimpse of him there in the winter sunlight. A line of Auden drifts
through the head. *The white Alps glittered. He was very great.*

Geo
December 1982

Getting High

Far up, on top, there is still some sun. The canyon is almost empty. Swallows are darting across it in the dusk. A lone figure wearing a pair of loose white pants walks to the Bastille, a rock that rises almost vertically from the road, touches it with both hands as if it were the side of a horse, and after a moment begins to climb. It seems a frivolous attempt, an act that will shortly be abandoned. There is no way up. There are some irregularities, a crack, a niche or two, nothing more. The climber moves smoothly, almost mysteriously. He pauses only to look, deduce, and continue upward. He has neither rope nor equipment. He appears to be, he is, in another world. Never glancing down, he sometimes stops to shake out his hand, then climbs on. Higher and higher. The rock is even more sheer. He is climbing toward the sun, the last touch of which lingers far above.

Boulder is a city of 83,000 at the foot of the Rockies. It is the kind of provincial city that foreigners would love—handsome inhabitants, beautiful streets, and a marvelous old relic of a hotel in the middle of town. The hotel is the Boulderado, built in 1906. It has three lively bars, two restaurants, and a lobby from mining days, where young men in Levis indolently polish the brass. There are 20,000 students at the University of Colorado, and the median age in the city is only twenty-four. To the east side of town are large shopping centers and motels. To the west are the mountains. Boulder is the last city of the plains.

It is also the capital of American climbing, if a capital must have theaters and paved streets. No climber on the way from the East to Yosemite would pass up Boulder and a try at Eldorado Canyon or the East Face of Longs Peak. The Gunks (the Shawangunks in New York), they say, are roofs; Yosemite is cracks; Colorado is steep, hard, face climbs.

No one knows how many climbers there are in Boulder, probably thousands—students, doctors, university professors. Though long popular in Europe, climbing until recently had few enthusiasts in the U.S. In the past decade there has been a tremendous surge of interest. Now it is on television, there are magazines devoted to it, and soon there may even be speed competitions—climbing races. The Russians have had them for years.

For those who live far from the mountains, the whole idea of rock climbing must seem special and exotic. One must be near the mountains to understand it, one must be thrilled by them. The perils of climbing are overrated, but they have at their core one of the deepest of human fears, that of great heights and falling. For some climbers these fears are insignificant. For others they are something to be overcome.

Turn off the main highway south of Boulder and head west. Open country. There are houses scattered along the road, distant foothills with patches of forest, excavations, horses grazing in the fields. After a mile or two the entrance to a canyon appears, guarded by a buttress of rock. There is a shantytown of summer houses, shacks, and trailers strewn along the creek—Eldorado Springs, population about 225, climbers, car guys, and old-timers. It used to be a resort on land bought from the Union Pacific Railroad: "Finest natural warm springs in the state." There is still a swimming pool; there were once stables, a big hotel, and a dance hall. A stairway of 1,350 steps went up one side of the canyon, and a wire-walker named Ivy Baldwin thrilled the crowds by crossing 600 feet in the air. Eisenhower spent his honeymoon here in 1916. Excursion trains ran from Denver. The steep canyon walls that seem ageless were objects of natural beauty, nothing more. In fifty years they were to bring Eldorado Springs to life again.

The cliffs are formed of an extremely hard sandstone with surface irregularities, which provide holds. These are often very small. In the most difficult climbing there are holds no thicker than the edge of a shirt button. Farther north, in Boulder Canyon and Rocky Mountain National Park, the rock is mainly granite marked by vertical cracks. This is the same rock found in Yosemite. Climbers usually excel at crack climbing or face climbing, one or the other. A few are equally adept at both.

Hard Times, Trail's End, Romeo—the houses in Eldorado all have names. In the middle of town is a green cottage with a sign: International Alpine School. Some of its letters are missing. A flight of stairs leads up to the door. The porch is a small office—some photos on the wall, a desk, typewriter, and a box in the corner marked "Inactive Files." In the main room hang coils of rope and slings of climbing hardware. In back are a small pantry and toilet. The water comes from an irrigation ditch, the heat from a stove. There is no insulation. The rent is $70 a month. There are two lofts, one filled with sleeping bags, the other with a mattress. In this kingdom reigns Kevin Donald, director of the school. He is thirty-one, tall, slim, naked to the waist. He knows every person and every dog in town, "Hi, Czar. Hi, Chinook. Hi, P.P." That last stands for Perpetual Pup, he explains. He knows many of the visitors as well. He's taught a lot of them to climb.

There are at least four climbing schools in Boulder plus the underground. At the International Alpine School, for around $400 in the summer and $500 in the winter, you can spend up to seven days learning to climb. Food, tentage, and equipment are included. Kevin also hires out as a private guide for $100 a day.

Rock climbing has a scale by which it is graded, a decimal scale starting with 5. A climb of 5.1 or 5.2 is easy. 5.6 can give pause. It was intended that 5.9 be the ultimate, but things have gone so far past the earlier limits that there are now grades of 5.11 and 5.12. Kevin is a solid 5.11 climber. In practical terms this means he can climb almost anything, including buildings, a tradition at the University of Colorado, where the library and Macky Auditorium, especially the latter, are among the favorites. There is a basement entrance to Macky with a large wall where stones protrude slightly from the mortar. They are covered with chalk marks—gymnast's chalk is used to give climbers a better grip—and students, as well as ex-students and some who have never even registered, can be found clinging to the stones like lizards. Sometimes in the late afternoon the organ is playing inside the auditorium and great, Wagnerian chords flow over the figures working their way upward.

There are climbs off campus as well. There's a well-known lay-back on the Colorado Bookstore and good hand jams on the Public Service Building. "They're about 5.9," Kevin estimates. Climbers also practice on large rocks and the lower parts of the faces themselves. This is called bouldering and is a separate art. In the canyon many of the boulder problems are named: Green Hornet, Slap in the Face, Turok's Mantle. Kevin, who studied modern dance to give himself more grace in his climbing movements, is a resident expert.

"There are some real nice moves," he comments genially to a couple of visiting climbers. He is barefoot and wearing his white pants. "You guys are strong, you'll be able to do this without any trouble."

He's sandbagging. The nice moves turn out to be excruciatingly difficult: two finger pull-ups to reach an overhang, horizontal levers, abrupt swings from one half-inch hold to another like an orangutan.

"Hey, neat! You almost got it," Kevin cries. "Now bend back more."

The visitors are barely holding on. "Your weight is entirely on your right leg, see?"

They can't do it. They drop off like dead flies.

"Aren't there any good finger cracks?" one of the climbers keeps moaning.

Extreme, acrobatic moves are not the sort of thing one does on a real climb—they're too risky. There is a radical school that believes in the concept "No shoot, no loot," that is, if you don't take chances, you don't win, and its adepts are willing to take ten or twenty short falls in a row, hundreds of feet up, attempting something hard. Of course, they are protected by the rope, but there is something impure about these repeated attempts, at least in the view of many climbers.

Technical climbing is done with a rope. The theory is faultless. One climber secures himself to the rock. The other climbs, protected against too long a fall by the rope, which is paid out to him as he goes and which, further, passes through carabiners clipped to loops on pieces of metal, called nuts, that are wedged into small cracks. The rope will not break. The danger usually occurs when the belayer is not well enough situated to hold a fall, when he has been obliged to stay in a place that is unsuitable. "If you come off now, we're both going," is a chilling warning. Accidents also take place during the descent when the danger seems past. Rappels are particularly risky. There are the dangers of "easy" places where one doesn't bother with regular procedures. Finally there are the so-called objective dangers of rockfall, avalanche, and the like. In the U.S. last year there were forty-two climbing fatalities.

Kevin doesn't take falls. He has fallen forty or fifty times, but that was over a sixteen-year period. Usually he expects it—when he's overextending himself or trying for something too difficult. If he thinks he may fall, he goes down and comes back another time. The big change that has taken place during the time he's been climbing has been the freeing of routes. Many of the climbs in the canyon and elsewhere were first done with what is called aid—pitons were driven into cracks in the rock and climbers clipped into them and stood in a kind of nylon sling. Gradually the idea became to do the climbs without aid, to do them free. The climber may use only his hands and feet, even when the rock is past vertical. To so much as hook a finger through a piton already in place is forbidden.

One of the main figures in making routes go free was Jim Erickson, a contemporary of Kevin's. There is one particularly intimidating climb called the Naked Edge, located in what the guidebook describes as a superb position, 400 feet up on Redgarden Wall. It is a long, exterior corner high in the air and at one point must be crossed where it is said that a fall will cut the rope. It was Erickson who first climbed the Naked Edge free. A purist, he has never gone back to do it again. The climb is 5.11 and is now a classic. Kevin had been away from climbing for several years. As soon as he arrived back in Boulder, he called a friend.

"Hi, Ron, this is Kevin."

The reply was simple. It bridged a decade. "The Naked Edge went free."

It was a turning point in his life, Kevin says. "I couldn't believe it. I was just blown away."

He can do forty-five chins. Erickson can do fifty. Kevin is the more natural climber of the two, with the torso and thin legs of a gymnast. Erickson is shorter and chunkier—he has more of a mountaineer's build. He had to work harder to become a climber and it was this extra effort, Kevin believes, that made him great. Climbing is superb exercise but it is not like other sports, not even boxing. There is more at stake. Kevin used to box—he was knocked down three times in the first round by Sandy Cisneros.

"Finally I just decided to stay down. It was all over. You can't do that in climbing. You've got to go to the end. You can't walk away from it when you're up there. You're responsible for yourself and you've got to do it."

There is always something you cannot or are afraid you cannot do. Like everyone else, there is a point at which Kevin feels the anguish. It is usually on difficult climbs when the point of no return is passed and the only way remaining is up. Not all climbs have this, of course, but when they do he can feel it, the voltage, the adrenaline rush. It's the adrenaline that makes your legs tremble. Too big a rush finishes you, you can't go on.

"The thing is not to burn out, to control it. Don't freak out, keep your head. You have to save your strength to the end." The psychological element in the sport is immense. The space beneath one, the implacability of the rock, the move that must be made. Somehow you do it: on top at last. On top of Psycho with its frightening overhang, Rosy Crucifixion, or the Grand Giraffe. Across the way the Bastille is dotted with climbers. To the east as far as one can see are the plains. The scene is ravishing, the feeling of comradeship and victory, supreme.

Steve Komito has a climbing boot shop in the town of Estes Park. From his porch the summit of Longs Peak is visible. Komito is thirty-eight years old, short, and good-natured. He is, he says, the classic bad-luck guy, the victim. His father was in the furniture business in Fort Wayne, Indiana, and Komito had never so much as seen a mountain when he came upon a copy of *Annapurna* by Maurice Herzog. He read it and was overwhelmed. For the first time in his life he was in the presence of something that really took hold of his spirit. He began to devour books about climbing, and in the last year of high school went on a YMCA trip to Wyoming. The group spent one day in climbing school and then climbed Grand Teton. He was hooked.

His parents wanted him to live in Florida so he would be there when they retired, but he left the University of Miami and moved to Colorado. That was in 1960. Soon after he fell in with a legendary figure of the era, a six-foot-five giant named Layton Kor, a man of demonic energy who sped from one climb to another in a bald-tired

Ford. For a decade Kor was the leading climber in Colorado and constantly in search of new partners. One night he ran into Komito at a party and immediately latched onto him. They went on their first climb the next morning at dawn. It was an ascent of something called Outer Space. It was 5.8 with aid, a high rating for those days.

"Don't worry, Komito," Kor was fond of saying as they clung to a face. "The worst that can happen to us is we'll fall off and get killed."

"He got me doing hard climbs," Komito says. "I'm not athletic. I'm not brave. To me every accomplishment is a major break-through, and every failure I've expected anyway. With Kor I was afraid all the time, but it gave me what I needed. It was something I could do and be proud of. And I had the friendship of someone I respected. What it gave me was a breakthrough to something many of my contemporaries don't acknowledge: manhood."

By his own admission Komito is a perpetually mediocre climber. He climbs twenty or twenty-five times a year. He still has certain ambitions, however: the principal one is to continue climbing to a very old age. On trips to Europe he has been moved by the sight, which is common, of men and women in their sixties and seventies hiking and sometimes climbing in the mountains. They represent to him something admirable in a society that has become more and more artificial and throwaway.

Fifteen miles from the shop is the great, glacier-shattered East Face of Longs. It is 2,000 feet of vertical and more-than-vertical rock interrupted only by one wide ledge. The top portion because of its shape is called the Diamond. By any standard it is a great wall climb with the traditional hazards of storm and rockfall. The Diamond was first climbed in 1960. The first winter ascent was in 1967 (by Layton Kor). A first solo ascent came three years later.

There is a hiker's route that goes up the back. It's a long trek of ten or eleven hours up and down, but it is very popular during the summer and has been for nearly a century. From the top one can see a hundred miles—to Pikes Peak, the Mountain of the Holy Cross, as far as the Medicine Bows in Wyoming. Little children have made the climb, people on crutches, and even an eighty-five-year-old minister, an example to warm Komito's heart. Longs Peak is 14,255 feet, well up among the fifty-three mountains in the state that are over 14,000. All of the Fourteeners, as they are called, can be climbed without a rope, and a surprising number of people have climbed them all. Some are members of the Colorado Mountain Club and send in notices of their having completed the circuit to the club's magazine. Colorado governor Dick Lamm has climbed fourteen of the mountains, including Pikes Peak on New Year's Eve, probably one of the safest ways of spending it.

In Boulder anyone can turn out to be a climber. The waitress at the Goode Taste Crepe Shoppe is a pretty girl in a long dress. She hands us some menus.

"Were you up climbing today, Jennifer?"

"Yeah, it was great."

"Where'd you go?"

"We did the Great Zot."

"Out of sight."

Many women are climbing in Eldorado these days and at least three of them are outstanding. Women tend to have less upper-body strength than men, but climbing is done mainly with the legs, and balance, intelligence, and deftness of footwork are extremely important.

Molly Higgins is a lab technician in a hospital. She has blond hair and the decent, American face of a girl in the emergency room who is there when your eyes open and you love her from then on. She is very together. She has climbed the Diamond and Yosemite's El Capitan. She comes from a town near Philadelphia, on the Main Line. Her mother works in a bookstore—her father died when she was thirteen.

Molly was always attracted by mountains. One day her mother brought home some literature from Colorado College, tossed it on the table, and said, "How'd you like to go there?" A pamphlet from the college mountain club was pinned up in her room all that summer.

Two weeks after she arrived in the fall of 1968 she was climbing in the Garden of the Gods. She loved it, but the club was as much social as athletic and she liked the hiking even more. One day she and a boyfriend found a rope on the floor of a storage room and went out to try a climb. It was sixty feet high. For two hours she watched while her boyfriend attempted to do it. Finally she asked to try. She was wearing lug-soled boots and after a fearful struggle managed to get to the top. She was so grateful that she fell on her knees and kissed it. The boyfriend never did follow. "It really turned me on," she says. "I could feel things in myself I couldn't feel other places. I was frightened, but on reaching the top and overcoming that fear I felt an incredible self-esteem."

By the following year she was climbing in Eldorado Canyon. She did the Bastille Crack, Ruper, the Grand Giraffe. She didn't realize that her ability to protect—to put in pitons at the proper places—was very poor. One day, reaching up with the rope held in her mouth, she slipped and took a thirty-foot fall. She nearly lost four teeth. She was badly scared but somehow brushed it off. At Longs Peak that autumn it happened again, this time more seriously. She was climbing Stettners Ledges, a classic route on the lower East Face. The smooth, glacial granite, the altitude, the exposure. "I was scared out of my tree," she remembers.

Just below the crux pitch she fell. She hadn't been putting in enough protection—down she went for eighty-five feet, hitting various ledges. Fortunately she was wearing a helmet. It was a terrifying fall. The boyfriend with whom she was climbing was so unnerved that he gave up the sport, and because he was her only partner, she had to give it up too. It was three years before she tried again.

In the summer of 1973 she was working for Outward Bound near Gunnison and one day she grabbed a girlfriend and went up to climb.

"I started all over again. We began on 5.0s. Nuts had come out then and we were using them for protection. There was no one to rely on but ourselves—I'd always leaned on a man, depended on him completely, but the minute we began this I was suddenly a different kind of climber. I could climb my own way. It was very significant."

The following spring she went to Yosemite and that summer to the Pamirs in the U.S.S.R. as part of the American contingent of an international gathering. This was the summer when eight Russian women were caught in a fierce storm as they were attempting to traverse Lenin Peak. There was no chance of rescue. They died one by one, in radio contact with the base camp until the end. "Please forgive us. We love you. Goodbye."

Molly herself survived an avalanche, high altitude, snow, and ice. She had been unhappy all during the expedition, desperately lonely, and when she came back to the States extremely depressed, she turned to a friend for advice. He was a climber, a real heavy, in her words. What he told her was simple. "If there's something you really want to do, do it, and do it as well as you possibly can. You need no other justification. If you want to climb well, spend every spring and fall in Yosemite."

Her partner in Yosemite has usually been another woman, Barbara Eastman. In 1977 they climbed the 3,000-foot Nose of El Capitan together. The Nose is 5.10 and A3, which refers to the difficulty of placing aid where it is called for.

"It was a magnificent climb," Molly says. "We were so close by then, we were good buddies. We knew each other's weaknesses. We knew when the other got scared and how to nurse her. We didn't get scared on the Nose, though." Molly's not bothered by the height. If she has a good anchor, she likes to look down. She's happy there. "We were very sisterly. I'd be tired and have to do a hard pitch and begin to whimper. And she'd just clean my glasses and say. 'Go ahead, Molly, you can do it.'"

Other women climbers she rates with herself include Beth Bennett and Coral Bowman, her Boulder rivals. They're both better face climbers, she concedes—she gives them Eldorado. They're slimmer than she is, stronger. Coral, who is a schoolteacher, last year had the start of what would have been a legendary fall. She was on the Naked Edge. At the top of the second pitch, perhaps 500 feet in the air, she had to rappel down to free a haul rope that had gotten fouled. She untied from her partner, Sue Giller, made a figure eight knot in the rope, and clipped into a carabiner. Then she leaned out over nothing and started down. Somehow the carabiner was forced sideways, oddly tilted. The gate opened and the rope came out. She was falling. For a horrified moment her eyes met Sue's. "I knew I was going to die and I didn't want to die." She had gone about twenty feet when with incredible alertness she managed to reach out and grab the haul rope. She knew she wouldn't be able to hold on but somehow she did, getting third-degree burns as the rope sang through her hands and gradually slowed her. She came to a stop and found a foothold. "Sue! Help me!" she called.

Her hands were in a cast for five days. Three weeks later she was climbing again.

In the 1950s there were a few, isolated climbers in the area, perhaps twenty altogether. Now they are everywhere. The bulletin boards at Boulder Mountaineer and Neptune Mountaineering are filled with notices of skis, sleeping bags, and bicycle parts for sale and also requests for climbing partners (*Lead 5.9. Will need warm-up as it's spring. Leave number. I live in a van*).

Climbing is more than a sport. It is entry into myth. For those irresistibly drawn to it, it becomes a life, and there is always a pack of dazzling new climbers biting at the tails of those who have gone before. The important routes have all been climbed. Many of them have now been climbed free; in some cases they are being done solo. Charlie Fowler, who is celebrated for being so far out that what he does is almost unimaginable, last year soloed the Diamond, eight vertical pitches in an hour and a half, without a rope. This doesn't discourage young climbers, rather it seems to draw them on. Only a few, in any case, will have the talent and intensity to make themselves known. For most of them there is joy enough in the feeling of working their way upward.

Jim Erickson, on the other hand, has seen the darkness that lies at the end of ambition satisfied. He works as the manager of a small factory and climbs occasionally. He studied music and is married to a violinist. They have a son. Erickson's name, together with a few others like Pat Ament's and Roger Briggs's, will always be linked with a certain period of Colorado climbing, but for the veterans, those who have given everything, there is an emptiness afterward. Life is not the same.

Climbing has no referees, no arena, no titles. It has a certain ethic that, in recent years, has been veering toward the extreme. The hard climbs in Eldorado are visible because of the chalk marks on them, evidence of where crucial handholds are. Erickson will not use chalk—the white bag of courage, it has been called. Further, he will not continue a first ascent on which he takes a fall. If that happens, he goes down and abandons the attempt permanently. His feeling is that no climb should be done in a way that differs from how it would be done solo without a rope. Even the retreat, if one must be made, can have nothing artificial about it such as lowering off a piece of protection.

Not everyone conforms to such standards, of course—not everyone can. Climbing has its champions, and they are chosen in what is perhaps the only way. They are singled out in the hearts of others in a confusion of envy and love. They are champions for reasons that are in part clear—their accomplishments, their personalities—but also for things that are not so easy to define. A brilliant climb in itself is not enough to elevate someone into the pantheon. Mountains cannot be assassinated nor the heights won in a single day. The glory belongs only to those who have earned it and usually over a period of time. In this regard, the morality is absolute. There are no upsets, no undeserved triumphs. In one sense, there is no luck. This severity gives the sport its strength. There is a paradise and a final judgment. Above all, climbing is honest. Honor is its essence.

Still, at the end, there may be a question. "People like to do climbs with big numbers on them," Erickson says. It's like a drug. For many this means doses of increasing strength until even these begin to lose their effect. "The thing about it is that it is self-indulgent, it has no purpose. It accomplishes nothing except for personal pleasure." Sometimes, he says, he's ashamed to admit that he is still climbing at his age. He is thirty.

Logan Construction is on the second floor of a small shopping center. There are two rooms, some drafting tables, plans tacked on the wall and a blackboard with "I love you Daddy" scrawled near the bottom. Jim Logan is divorced. He has twin boys. "I raise them half the time," he says. "I have them every Wednesday through Saturday."

Logan is slight, with light brown hair and a reddish beard. He's thirty-two, wears glasses, and has a quiet, easy manner. A few years ago he went out and taught himself to ice climb. That summer he did the North Face of the Eiger. It was his first real ice climb and one of the few American ascents. "I put my first ice screw in on the Eiger," he says. "The mountains have always interested me. I was a good climber when I was a little kid. My mother says I could always climb trees and buildings better than anyone. I liked being up in the air."

Born in Texas, he came to prep school in Colorado when he was sixteen and entered the university two years later. He was already a fair climber. One day in Boulder Canyon he saw two young men— one of them was Ament—struggling to do a climb called Final Exam. They weren't getting very far. Logan walked up in his cowboy boots and asked if he could try. They laughed but he changed shoes and did it first crack. The next day Ament introduced him to his friends in the college cafeteria, "This is Jim Logan and he's a 5.10 climber."

He stayed in the background, however: he did very few first ascents. The big shots then were Kor, Ament, Larry Dalke, Bob Culp, Wayne Goss—he was in awe of them, he didn't think he was in their class. Nevertheless he entered the world of climbing. He dropped out of school and went to Yosemite. He climbed every chance he got. He found a job as an apprentice in a machine shop. His parents disapproved strongly. "You're going to grow up to be a ditch digger," his mother would say. He reached a certain high point in his life when he and Dalke climbed the Diamond in one day. That was in 1968. Then he was drafted.

Climbers as a group were opposed to the war and not ready to serve. The usual thing was to get a mental deferment. They went in for the examination stoned, incoherent, and unkempt. Logan was a Texan, he played it straight. He was sent to El Paso for basic training.

"I was devastated by it," he says. "I lost all sense of value as a human being. I was in the army for two years. I spent a year in Vietnam, at Camranh Bay. I was a personnel clerk attached to Headquarters, U.S. Army Vietnam. I hated it. It was like being in prison.

"I used to go to a village and spend the night with a Vietnamese girl. She had two or three other boyfriends. I used to work the Ouija board for her friends, girls who had GI boyfriends who'd been killed. One guy had been killed by a tiger. They'd ask me questions. 'Are you still there? Do you still love me?'

"When I got out of the army I flew to San Francisco. Wayne Goss picked me up and we went to Yosemite. I couldn't climb. For the first time in my life I was afraid. I was a physical and mental wreck. In the army they destroy your self-confidence and then give it back to you a little at a time. In climbing, self-confidence is very important, knowing the next move is going to go, the next pitch is going to go. I'd fought on the wrong side in the war. I was very bitter."

Logan got married, bought some land in Boulder with the money he had saved in Vietnam, and built a house. He learned carpentry and became a small contractor. He and his two partners design and build three or four houses a year.

Slowly he returned to climbing. He went every couple of weeks or so. By 1974 he was more or less back to normal. He was climbing 5.11. The next summer he spread his wings and climbed the Diamond free with his friend Wayne Goss. It was the first free ascent of any route on the Diamond. It crushed Roger Briggs, he remarks innocently. "Roger really wanted to do it."

There is a pleasure in outdistancing one's companions. It would be a saintly nature that did not feel this. Logan, like others, began to feel that the future was the big mountains—that was where climbing had to go. The days of significant achievement in rock climbing were over. The need for something conceptually interesting took him to what has been called the most difficult climb on the continent. In 1978 he did the Emperor Face of Mt. Robson in Canada.

"It was something everybody wanted to climb," he says. "Yvon Chouinard wanted to do it—he said it was the hardest climb there was. And Jeff Lowe—it was his life's ambition." Logan says it without malice. He did it, they didn't—it could have been the other way around. He's like a great jockey who explains matter-of-factly that he merely had the best horse. It was some horse. Five or six thousand feet of extreme climbing. The last pitch alone, at the top, took them eight hours.

His business requires only eight months a year; the rest of the time he can do as he likes. "I feel like I'm on top again of the world of climbing. I'm very excited that there's an activity I can be on the leading edge and push the limits of—that's very appealing to me.

"There was a time." Logan says, "when I climbed in Eldorado and knew every car that drove in, when every good climber in the country knew every other good climber. I can remember when I went into the Hiking Club looking for a partner, I was leading 5.7s and 5.8s, even some 5.9s. They said, 'Get out of here, kid. If you could climb that well, we'd have heard of you.'"

He sits silent for a while.

"Wayne Goss is a commodities broker in Chicago now. Dalke is a drapery hanger in Boulder. Layton Kor is a bricklayer and a Jehovah's Witness." He pauses. "All of them finished with climbing," he says.

Life
August 1979

The Alps

The great Alps link one in some way to one's immortality.
—Hilaire Belloc

I once spent a night sleeping, more or less, beneath a huge boulder that formed a kind of cave in the mountains above Chamonix. It was at the base of the Dru, a legendary towering granite spire 1,500 feet high. I was alone, paying tribute. Sometime after midnight there was a distant sound: thunder. Slowly it grew closer and soon a tremendous storm began. The very rock above me seemed to tremble in the thunderclaps. I almost imagined it would be split by a bolt of lightning to reveal me, insectlike, at the foot of a towering, angry mountain god. The storm finally passed, but I lay awake until dawn. The Alps are famous for swift changes of weather. In the middle of summer climbers can be caught in blizzards, occasionally with tragic results.

It was in Chamonix that I first climbed, and learned to ski in St. Anton, famed places both, one in France and the other in Austria but each in the Alps, the great upper story of Europe. From the mountains, in all directions, flow mighty rivers, the Rhine, Rhône, Po, and Danube; a necklace of immortal cities lies in the surrounding foothills and plains: Nice, Grenoble, Geneva, Turin, Milan, Munich, Salzburg, Vienna, and, stretching a bit, Venice. You are simultaneously in the center of civilization and the most majestic, thrilling wilderness.

It is essentially a geologic wilderness: fierce, jagged peaks in parallel series. The timberline is relatively low; above the trees typically are meadows that for centuries have been used for summer grazing. There are few wild animals.

The civilization of this rugged area is found in the many towns and mountain inns and huts. In the Alps, as in most of Europe, you eat well—it is part of the culture. Bread is still handmade, the butter is fresh, many things come from farms nearby.

Much has changed in this tumultuous century—the population has flowed into cities, with their hectic and somewhat artificial life—removed from the forests, streams, silence. But like a great island the mountains stand, safe from development, useless in the most noble sense.

These are the Alps. High up, near the sky. Walking a path far from anything made by man, the sudden sound one hears is that of a cowbell. A farmer's small herd, here in the clouds, is just beyond the bend.

National Geographic Traveler
October 1999

Offering Oneself to the Fat Boys

I can't remember when I started to ski powder—when I had to, probably. Like all hard lessons it left its imprint, a word that is a symbol, since the track of skis in untouched snow, their pure, solitary signature, is not the least of pleasures.

Among innumerable times, one that stands out in memory was when a doctor I knew from New York came out for a week to ski and said, Why don't we meet on the top in the morning? That night it snowed. In the morning there was at least a foot and a half of fresh powder covering everything. The ride up was cold. Snow was blowing from the crest.

The doctor had an instructor, Dennis, lean and good-natured. The three of us stood on the Shoulder of Bell in Aspen. The run dropped like a stone through the trees below. Dennis smiled. It looked great, he said. He offered some advice, "Always start with your skis pointing straight down," and pushed off.

They say that all men are subject to feelings of doubt at one time or another, but I remember thinking, Is he? He was going down like a leaf in a stream, bouncing from side to side over bumps, stumps,

who knew what, snow flying from his legs. There's no choice: he
goes, you go. It was one of the runs of my life.

That was with regular skis, of course. In those days expert opinion was that black Heads were the best for powder if you happened
to own a pair, but if you were good you could ski on anything. I
once heard of a hero in Jackson Hole who skied in a race on a pair
of seven-foot two-by-fours straight from the lumberyard with the
front ends shaved up and bindings mounted on them.

Times change. There arrives a long box with nothing on the outside to indicate New Era. Within is a strange pair of skis, unnatu-
rally wide, almost five inches, and looking like a softball does when
you are used to a baseball. They are Atomics, Powder Plus, and in
a yellow slash near the middle is written "Fat Boy." They've been
around for several years, I know, and I also know they make a huge
difference—you stay right on the surface of the powder, float on it.
The idea makes sense.

As I look at these broad, round-tipped skis there rises in me
the familiar conflict, complexity versus simplicity. The fully out-
fitted skier now possesses, besides expensive clothes, two kinds of
cross-country skis, downhill and slalom skis, telemarks, randonnees,
and now powder skis, and there are at least three types of those,
fats, chubbs, and bow ties, never mind the distinction. This is not to
mention snowshoes and snowboard. It used to be easier.

I think of a story Mike Burns, a producer I know, told me of
going out to play golf with his stepfather. At the first tee a stranger
came up wearing old pants and work shoes and carrying a canvas
golf bag with three clubs in it. Would they mind if he joined them
for a round, he asked?

Mike's stepfather teed off, sliced one across the road, and then
topped his second drive, which bounced down the fairway. Mike
stepped up and did about the same. The fellow with the canvas bag
took out a worn three wood and hit a ball 200 yards or more, straight
as a city block. I liked him in the story and in life as well—it was Ned
Vare, a wonderful golfer who used to live in Aspen years ago.

Be with me, beauty, for the fire is dying . . .

I don't know if I'll be on the Shoulder of Bell after a storm any-more, but you never lose the taste for powder. I would like to ski it and cut through the crud the way Ned Vare played golf, but I'm probably going to have to use a pair of Fat Boys to do it. I have plenty of company, and not many people have ever heard about the guy on the two-by-fours.

Outside
December 1995

The Life

Passionate Falsehoods

I was sitting in the compartment of a train as it swept through bleak German countryside, going from Bremerhaven to Frankfurt. Points of rain appeared on the window. In the bluish issue of a women's magazine—the models, maddeningly prim, wore little hats and white gloves—there was an article that caught my eye. It was a tribute to a plump Welsh poet, with a beguiling photograph taken outside the door of his studio in a seaside town, a manuscript stuck in the pocket of his jacket. The poet was Dylan Thomas, and the tribute, written by John Malcolm Brinnin, had somehow ended up in *Mademoiselle*. Brinnin's lyrical description of the poet's seedy, romantic life was an introduction to the poem that followed. It was "Under Milk Wood," roguish, prancing, with its blazing characters and lines. The words dizzied me, their grandeur, their wit. The drops of rain became streaks as in the soft, clicking comfort of the train the voices spoke: housewives, shopkeepers, shrews, Captain Cat— the blind retired sea captain dreaming of a strumpet, Rosie Probert ("Come on up, boys, I'm dead").

I was at the time an officer in the United States Air Force. With me in that Bundesbahn car, which had, I suppose, survived the war—within me—was a certain grain of discontentment. I had never made anything as sacred or beautiful as the poem I had read, and the longing to do so rose up in me. I gazed out the window. It was 1954, winter. Could I?

The war *I* had survived was the Korean War. I had returned from it two years before, rich with memories of flying as a fighter pilot. I had kept a journal. I had written before: stories and poems as a schoolboy, and later, in the Air Force, a novel, which was sent to a publisher and turned down. The fateful letter, however, offered encouragement. If I wrote another book, the publishers would like to see it. And so, on an iron cot in a Georgia barracks one afternoon, seemingly without effort, I wrote the outline of a novel, and on weekends and at night over the next two or three years completed the book. It was called *The Hunters* and was immediately accepted. That was 1957.

The hour had come. I resigned from the Air Force, probably the single most difficult act I had ever performed, with the idea of becoming a writer. I had been in the military for twelve years. I had a wife and two small children. Thinking every day of the life I had left, unable to believe in myself apart from it, I sat down in despair and tried to write. A few years later, a second novel was published. It was more ambitious but also more derivative, and it disappeared without a trace. But I was, despite that, a writer, and could be introduced, at least for a while, as such. The problem was that I had no way to support myself. Then, almost as if on cue, a door opened to another world.

My entry was by way of a cluttered back room, toppling with papers. The room belonged to Howard Rayfiel, a junior member of the staff of two prominent New York theatrical lawyers. Rayfiel—large, soft, animated, the son of a lawyer and brother of a movie writer—was an impresario of a phantom company on his own time. The company had one other member, a theater director who had

had some limited success, and the two of them invited me to write a script. Flattered, needing money, bored by the loneliness of writing a new book—the usual circumstances—and also believing that I could put my hand to almost anything, I returned the brief smile the movies had just given me—it was an intoxicating moment—and began what turned out to be a long affair.

My script, called "Goodbye, Bear," was a sentimental bouquet laid at the feet of a certain type of young, irresistibly cynical New York girl, the flower of every generation. In this case, she was nurtured in such bygone hothouses as El Morocco and the Stork Club and was seen through the eyes of an infatuated but unforceful man. The story had no barb. It was merely a history and would have been better as a poem, but it possessed a kind of lovely dignity. It also produced an unexpected result, reminiscent of the Chinese fable of the mandarin who stood by the river fishing with a straight pin instead of a hook. When word of this curious behavior reached the emperor, he came to see. "What could anyone hope to catch with such a hook?" The answer was serene. "You, my emperor." The emperor, uncrowned then, was Robert Redford, just becoming known on the New York stage. Somehow, he had gotten hold of the script, and we met for lunch, two naïfs in the sunlit city.

There come back to me many memories of Redford when he was new and his image that of purest youth. One morning in London at the entrance of the Savoy, three or four women came up asking for an autograph. As he signed, he gave me a sort of embarrassed smile. "You *hired* them," I said to him afterward. He broke out in a wonderful laugh—no, no, he hadn't. The car that was driving us to the airport that day broke down in the tunnel just before Heathrow, and we got out and ran for the plane, carrying our bags. That was how easy and unattended his life was then.

Later, in 1968, we went together to the Winter Olympics and Grenoble, slept in corridors, since rooms were unavailable, and rode on buses. By then, I was the author of several scripts, although none had been made into movies, and had been hired to write "Downhill Racer," a ski film that Redford would star in. We travelled for weeks with the United States team.

At dinner one night, I remarked that I saw Billy Kidd as the model for the main character. Kidd was the dominant skier on the U.S. team and, in the manner of champions, was somewhat arrogant and aloof. He was tough—from a poor part of town, I imagined, honed by years on the icy runs of the East.

Redford shook his head. The racer he was interested in was at another table. Over there. I looked. Golden, unimpressible, a bit like Redford himself—which of course should have marked him from the first—sat a little-known team member named Spider Sabich. What there was of his reputation seemed to be based on his having broken his leg six or seven times.

"Him?" I said. "Sabich?"

Yes, Redford said; when he was that age he had been just like him—vain, savvy.

So easy, all of it, such play. Back in New York, when I went into restaurants with Redford, eyes turned to watch as we crossed the room—the glory seems to be yours as well. There was a dreamlike quality also, perhaps because Redford seemed to be just passing through, not really involved. It was washing over him, like a casual love affair. He wore black silk shirts and drove a Porsche, disliked being called Bobby by eager agents, and more than once said, "I hate being a movie star." Nevertheless, he became one, with the life of evasion that went with it, of trying not to be recognized, a life of friends only, of sitting at the very front of the plane, the last to board, like a wanted man.

Years later, at forty, he looked better than when we had first known one another. The handsome, somewhat shallow college boy had disappeared and a lean, perceptive man stood in his place. From a kind of unconcerned amusement and a natural caution he had made an astonishing success. His days had a form; he accomplished something during them. As if glancing at a menu, he was able to choose his life.

We drifted apart. I wrote another film for him, but it was never made. "My presence in something," I remember him saying, perhaps in apology, "is enough to give it an aura of artificiality." He knew his limitations.

I saw him last at a premiere. A mob was waiting. Inside the theater every seat was filled. Then in the bluish gloom a murmur went across the crowd. People began to stand. There was a virtual rain of light as flashbulbs went off everywhere, and, amid a small group moving down the aisle, the blond head of the star could be seen. I was far off—years, in fact—but felt a certain sickening pull. There came to me the part about Falstaff and the coronation. *I shall be sent for in private*, I thought, consoling myself. *I shall be sent for soon at night.*

As I think of early days, an inseparable part of them appears: the thrilling city—New York was that—and a kind of Athenian brilliance over everything, which might well have been the light coming through the tall glass archways of Lincoln Center, where, in the fall, the Film Festival was held. It drew what I felt to be the elite, the great European directors—Antonioni, Truffaut, Fellini, and Godard—presenting a new kind of film, more imaginative and penetrating than our own.

The city was leaping with films, schools of them, of every variety, daring films that were breaking into something vast and uncharted, as an icebreaker crushes its way to open sea.

I was living not in New York itself but thirty miles from it, with my wife and children, in a half-converted barn in Rockland County. By chance, I met a writer named Lane Slate—he had a place just down the road—and was drawn to him immediately. He was irreverent and well read, an expert on Joyce, on films, on painting—the very companion I had been longing for. Together we made a short documentary called *Team, Team, Team*, some twelve minutes long, about football, the sweat and dirt of practice. It was my first film. A few months later, to our astonishment, it won first prize at Venice.

On the strength of this initial success, Lane and I formed a company and made documentaries—ten or twelve of them, scraped together, some of them eloquent. We travelled over the country, flying, driving, checking into motels, the mindless joy of America, beer bottles lying by the roadside, empty cans tumbling like paper. It is his curious charm that I remember, and how quickly he could make himself liked.

Our final film was on American painters: Warhol before his real recognition, Rauschenberg, Stuart Davis, a dozen others. Then Lane's older son was hit by a car while riding a bicycle and died a few days afterward. We had already begun gradually to separate. Perhaps we had lost the power to amuse each other.

In 1963, about the time that Lane and I stopped working together, a friend introduced me to Peter Glenville, an Englishman who had directed *Rashomon* on the stage and the film *Becket*, and had an undeniable gift. I was invited to dinner—there were four of us, all men, in his New York town house—the meal served by a uniformed maid. Toward the end of the meal, Glenville asked if I would be interested in writing a script, a story he wanted to make in Italy. The mere proposal seemed a reward. He was showing his faith in me; he had tapped me, as it were.

I was sent a typewritten outline and felt, upon reading it, disappointment. It was trash: a young man in Rome, a lawyer, meets and falls in love with a beautiful girl who is strangely evasive about her personal life. She is either uncertain and innocent or—the evidence is flimsy, but his suspicions mount—a call girl. He marries her anyway, but incidents recur that are disturbing. I have forgotten the cliché climactic moment: Does she attempt suicide? Is there a final reconciliation amid the white sheets of the *ospedale*?

It was called "The Appointment." I told Glenville frankly that it would never possess the least merit. He understood my misgivings, but still the theme of jealousy was interesting and the locale . . .

The film's producer called from California. He had talked at length to Glenville. They were confident that I was the one to write the film. Forgetting everything, I inhaled.

I arrived in Rome with the name of a Count Crespi, Glenville had supplied it. The Count was cool on the telephone. I had to wait several days for an appointment.

He came out of his office to introduce himself, tan, handsome face, ears close to his head, shattering smile. "I am Crespi," he said, taking me into a small, plain room, where he sat down across from me.

I told him the story of the film, and he began without hesitation to suggest things. The girl, instead of being a model, which was rather commonplace, might work at *Vogue*, where his wife's former secretary, a very clever girl who spoke four or five languages . . . but *Vogue* is already a little too fancy, perhaps, he decided. A salesgirl in a boutique, he thought, or perhaps, yes, even better, a mannequin in one of the couture houses—Fourquet on Via dei Condotti, for example. "She may earn only eighty thousand lire a month, but it's interesting work, she meets people, a certain kind of person with money, taste. If she has something to attend, Fourquet will probably lend her one of his expensive dresses."

With heroic charm he began to describe the man in the film, the somewhat proper lawyer. He has a good car, he goes dancing, to the beach. He loves sport, like all Italians, though not as a participant, of course, and there is also something traditional about him—he still goes home every day at noon to eat with his mother.

Crespi's enthusiasm and his willingness to provide details increased my confidence. There might be a tone, I began to feel, a manner of presenting the film, that would redeem it. As we talked on, Crespi

began to shift his view, to see the lawyer as less sophisticated, not
from Fellini's Rome, where people had seen everything, but from a
place in a more provincial town, Piacenza or Verona. Yes, he said, he
saw it as a really romantic story.

At a dinner in the country a week or so later, I tried to follow the
conversation and the bursts of laughter at the table. It was all wicked
and in Italian. We were in a garden, grouped around an animated
woman named Laura Betti. She was a singer and an actress. Pasolini
and Moravia had written lyrics for her songs, and she performed all
the Kurt Weill–Bertolt Brecht repertory in Italian. She talked constantly, a cigarette between her fingers. Her laugh was irresistible.
Smoke poured from her mouth. She was blond, a bit heavy, perhaps
thirty years old, the sort of woman who proudly wore a sadness.

We were in the ancient world, it seemed, in the cool air, the
darkness beneath the vines. There were six or seven of us. They
were eating from one another's plates and talking about everyone:
about the famous actress who liked to make love in two ways at
the same time—you could always recognize such women, Laura
Betti said, by the way they looked over their shoulder with a knowing smile; or about the madwoman who walked the streets singing
about a little boy's dove that she had touched with her tongue. It
was all about love, or, more truly, desire. Rome was a village that
had no secrets. They knew everything, even the names of the four
countesses who had picked up an eleven-year-old Gypsy girl one
night and brought her to a noted journalist to watch him have his
pleasure with her.

The script I was writing, they asked, what was its nature? Though
feeling that it sounded naive, I described it. Perhaps it should not
take place in Rome, I suggested—someone had mentioned Piacenza.

"Bologna," Laura Betti said. "That's where it could take place. It
is famous for three things. Its learning—it has the oldest university
in Italy; its food; and, lastly, its . . ." Here she used the most common
word describing fellatio.

"It's a specialty," she said. "All the various forms are called by the names of pasta. Rigate, for instance, which is a pasta with thin, fluted marks. For that the girls gently use their teeth. When there used to be brothels, there was a Signorina Bolognese—that was her specialty."

But I remained in Rome. The heat bore down. Dark Sicilians rose at two in the afternoon. The Tiber was green and stagnant. On Sunday mornings, the highway to the sea was jammed with cars, the music from hundreds of radios beating the blue, exhausted air. Rome was a city of women: you saw them everywhere, women in expensive clothes at the Hassler or the Hotel de Ville; women travelling with their husbands and without; young women claiming to be actresses—who knows what became of them; pairs of women in restaurants reading the menu very carefully; women stripped of illusion but unable to say farewell; women who owned shops and went to Circeo in the summer; divorced women who had once had a life in Trastevere; girls who looked unbathed, sitting in skimpy dresses in the restaurants, with young white teeth; *principesse* born in Vienna, living in the solitude of vast apartments; and aging fashion editors who seldom strayed far from the Hilton.

Against them, the legions of men: the handsome scum; men whose marriages had never been annulled; men who would never marry; men of dubious occupation; men from the streets and bars, of *nullo*, nothing; men with good names and dark mouths; swarthy men from the South, polished and unalterable, the nail of their little finger an inch long.

One June evening I was introduced to a woman whose apartment might be for rent. She was small, well dressed, and untrusting—French-Canadian as I found out. Gaby was her name—Gabrielle, I suppose. She was seductive and at the same time disdainful; life had taught her hard lessons, among them, I sensed, to think always of money and to hate men. The result was a passionate interest in human frailty.

She rejoiced, somewhat bitterly, in the weaknesses and secret vices of those in the film and literary worlds: Moravia, Italy's most famous writer; Visconti; John Cheever (who had lived for a season or two in Rome); Pietro Germi, who left his wife for a young actress and was betrayed by her in the most humiliating way; Thyssen, the rich art collector; countless others.

She told me the story of a singer I'd met once. She had begun as an actress, a shy, sweet girl who was given a chance to sing in a revue. She had to sleep with the star of the show and afterward the producer. But they cut her part. She went to bed with the star's brother and, finally, the stage manager. He took her to a house, a large one, and into a room upstairs. It was dark. "Take off your clothes," he told her. When she had done this, he said, "Put these on," and handed her a pair of very high-heeled shoes. Then he had her get on her hands and knees on the bed. Suddenly the lights came on. There were other men in the room, all the previous ones, the star, the producer, the electrician, and they all came toward her laughing.

Gaby told the story of Corinne Luchaire, a prewar French star. "She was Göring's mistress."

I vaguely recalled a slender, beautiful blonde. "Göring's mistress? Not really?"

"Of course!" she hissed. "Don't you know anything?"

Corinne Luchaire, she said, had been arrested in her apartment in Paris by the French Resistance and kept there all night while forty-one men raped her. She spent three years in jail. At her trial, her lawyer read aloud the entire de Maupassant story of collaboration, "Boule de Suif"—about the whore who didn't know that the soldier who came to see her was German. "He was naked." I had never read the story, which was the first de Maupassant ever published, and even now I'm not sure if Gaby's version is correct, but it is the one I remember.

Gaby had been pursued, of course—that was one of the roots of her obsession. The Sicilian prince who, as they were dancing at a ball, took her hand and said, "Here. What do you think of it?" having placed his naked member in her hand. The lecherous journalists and lawyers. She rained images on me, some of them so intense they remained in my flesh like wounds.

She also introduced me to Fellini. She brought him stories. "Talk to me, talk to me": he wanted nothing in writing; he was inspired by listening, he said. It was often remarked that there were, at the time, only two real artists in all of Europe, Picasso and Fellini. Picasso, a god, was ancient and remote. Fellini was a man who sat in shirtsleeves: he resembled his photographs, rumpled, with black hair growing out of his ears, like an unsuccessful uncle.

I met him at the studio where he was working. The conversation began in Italian; he did not speak English, he apologized. I had recently been to the Vorkapich lectures at the Museum of Modern Art in New York. They were essentially a tribute to Slavko Vorkapich, the master of a kind of montage used in the nineteen thirties and forties: pages of a calendar falling away to indicate days or months passing; an ocean liner, then a train to show travel over great distances. The entire film world of the East Coast had attended the lectures, I said. It was difficult to obtain a seat, and of all the directors whose work had been chosen to illustrate concepts Fellini was the one most often used, with Eisenstein second. Fellini gave a modest nod. He seemed grateful, the honor. He had only one question. "Who is Vorkapich?" he wanted to know.

On a slip of paper he wrote his telephone numbers—if there was anything that might be of some help, he urged me to call him.

I was sitting one night in a restaurant, and two women sat down at the next table. One was American, older, with thin hands, and the other young, blond, with a striking figure. They had just been to Capri and were talking with animation about it. Soon they were sampling a dish I had ordered and I was tasting their wine. The younger one's glances were open and friendly. I could read palms, I told them—I found myself eager to touch her. "Tell me your name," I suggested.

"Ilena," she replied.

I examined her palm with feigned authority. "You will have three children," I said, pointing to some creases. "You are witty—it shows that here. I see money and fame." I felt her fingers pressing mine.

"You are an ass," she said gaily. "That means nice, no?"

Ilena may have been her name or it may have been simply the name she wore, like a silk dressing gown one longed to peel back. Warmth came off her in waves. She was twenty-three years old and weighed sixty-two kilos, the absence of any part of which would have been a grave loss. She was, I learned, a mistress of John Huston, who was in Rome directing a film. She had also been the companion of Farouk, the exiled king of Egypt. She had met him at the dentist's office. He was there with his lawyer, she said, a detail I felt no one could invent.

Farouk's days had started in the evening. Like a true playboy, he rose late. He liked fine cars—he had a Rolls and a Jaguar. He loved to eat. I thought of the large men I had known, many of them good dancers, graceful, even dainty. Was it true of him? "Darling, we never danced," she said.

It was clear that she had been fond of him. They had travelled to Monte Carlo together, to the *chemin de fer* tables, where, a prodigious gambler, he was known as the Locomotive. The night he collapsed and died in a restaurant on Via Cassia she was allowed to leave by the back door before the press arrived.

Whether or not she was an actress or ever became one, I do not know. Of course, she wanted to be—she had already played great roles.

We had a drink, the three of us, at the Blue Bar and a gelato on the Piazza Navona. On Via Veneto she stopped to talk with a group of elderly Italian businessmen. It was lovely to watch her. Her legs, the silk of her print dress, the smoothness of her cheeks, all of it shone like constellations, the sort that rule one's fate.

We dropped the American woman at her hotel, the Excelsior. Sitting in the car, I turned to Ilena and said simply, "I adore you. I have from the first moment."

In response she kissed me and said, "To the right." It was late; she had an appointment in the morning at Elizabeth Arden and wanted to go home.

"Are you married?" she asked as we drove.

"Yes."

"So am I."

It was to a man in his eighties, she explained. I recognized the story from the newspapers—she had married him to get a passport. He was in an old people's home, an *istituto*. She went to visit him there, she said.

We went on to the Parioli, where, in a somewhat dubious building on Via Archimede, Ilena lived. The apartment was small and drearily furnished, but on the wall was a large picture of John Huston that had appeared in *Life*. Lying on the floor were books that Huston had given her to read. He might just as well have given her a chemistry set or a microscope. "You must never stop learning," he told her—she could do him perfectly. I could hear the rich, rolling, faintly cynical voice that I knew from his documentary on the battle of San Pietro.

"Never stop learning," he repeated. "That's very important. Promise me that."

"Of course, John," she answered.

In an album were clippings of the two of them, Huston with a white, patriarchal beard. He was a *coccolone*—someone who likes to be babied—and very tight. "To get a thousand dollars from him is so difficult," she said. He was also lonely. He would call on the phone: "What are you up to, baby?"

"Nothing."

"Come right over. Right away."

He had no friends, she said, and hated to go out. He was living in a suite in the Grand Hotel on a diet of vodka and caviar. "John," she would ask him, "do you want some girls?"

"Bring them around," he said. "We'll have some fun."

She brought three, one of them eighteen years old—she liked

young, tender girls, she explained. The late afternoon was best. "Darling," she said to me after describing a scene that might have taken place at Roissy, "you're a writer, you should know these things."

Huston had fought at Cassino, she told me, as if in justification.

"No, he didn't."

"But he *did*. He's told me stories."

"He was a film director in the war. He never fought."

"Well, he *thinks* he did," she said. "That's the same thing."

I liked her generosity and lack of morals—they seemed close to an ideal condition of living—and also the way she looked at her teeth in the mirror as she talked. I liked the way she pronounced "cashmere," like the state in India, Kashmir. Her cosmetics bag was filled with prescriptions, just as the shelf in her closet was crammed with shoes. Once we passed a big Alfa Romeo that she recognized as belonging to a friend, the chief of detectives in Rome. She had made love with him, of course. "Darling," she said, "there's no other way. Otherwise there would have been terrible trouble about my passport. It would have been impossible." There was, I discovered, besides Huston, an Italian businessman supporting her.

There was a film festival in Taormina. She had looked forward to it for days, and when she finally went I languished in Rome. The week passed slowly. I heard her distant voice—I did not know where Taormina was, exactly—on the telephone. "Oh, darling," she cried, "it's so marvelous." She was going to have the same agent as Monica Vitti, she said excitedly. A director had promised her a part in a James Bond film. She was not staying at the San Domenico Palace; she was at the Excelsior. Tomorrow she would be at the Imperiale—I understood what all that meant—and on Sunday she was going to receive a prize.

"Which prize?"

"I don't know. Darling, I can't believe it," she said.

At last there was a telegram—I had felt that I might not see her again—"Coming Monday Rapido 5. Afternoon," and signed with her name. It was sent from Ljubljana—Yugoslavia.

I met the train. It was thrilling to see her coming along the platform, a porter behind her with her bags. Some things are only good the first time but seeing her was like the first time. I knew she would say "darling." I knew I would say, "I *adore* you."

The film festival had left a glow. At a reception there, among scores of faces, she had seen a young man in a silk foulard with a brilliant unwavering smile, a wide smile, "like a killer's." She was wearing a white beaded dress. Her arms were bare. Fifteen or twenty minutes later she saw him again. The second barrel, as the lawyers say, was fatal. She said only, "Let's leave." Without a word he offered her his arm.

I listened with some unhappiness but without anger. Faithfulness was not what I expected.

"You'll get to the top," I told her, almost reluctantly, "but you shouldn't . . ."

"What?"

"Nothing," I said. "I'll tell you later."

"If I don't become too much of a whore," she said.

We drove to Paris, coming up through the Rhône Valley. Past Dijon we were on a back road along a canal and came to a wide dam where fishermen's lines dropped forty or fifty feet into clear green water. The dark shapes of fish—I took them to be pike—were coasting lazily about. We watched the biggest ones approach, ignore the bait, and move off to lie motionless. "Like sultans," she commented. I felt she knew.

In some mysterious way that I accepted without wonder, the film I had been writing with little conviction went into production in 1968. At Cannes, the following year, its screening was less than a triumph. The audience, at a moment when it should have felt fulfillment, broke into loud laughter. On the terrace of the Carlton afterward, I could not help overhearing the acid remarks. There was some brief pleasure in having my doubts confirmed.

Movies are like passion, brilliant and definitive. They end and there is an emptiness. "The vulgar falsehoods of the cinema," as someone has put it. They are narcotic; they allow one to forget—to imagine and forget. Looking back, I suppose I have always rejected the idea of actors as heroes, and no intimacy with any of them has changed this. Actors are idols. Heroes are those with something at stake.

During the war, I remembered, we went to movies almost nightly. We laughed at them as the men and women in evening dress at Cannes had laughed at mine.

Nevertheless, filled with ambition, I had wanted to direct a film of my own. I had a story by Irwin Shaw, and a star—Charlotte Rampling—who had agreed to be in it. Then she changed her mind. At the last minute, after we flew all night to Rome, where she was shooting something else, she was persuaded to be in the film again. Visconti, she said—he was just then directing her—was a true genius. I tried not to be disheartened. I was judging her unfairly, by her conversation and personality, while there she was, flesh and blood and willing to perform. She refused dinner—to get back to a boyfriend, I was sure—and after twenty or thirty minutes raced off in a car. Her agreement to be in the film, however, enabled us to get the money to make it.

I was to learn many things about her: that she chewed wads of gum, had dirty hair, and, according to the costume woman, wore clothes that smelled. Also that she was frequently late, never apologized, and was short-tempered and mean. The boyfriend, a blond highwayman, was a vegetarian. He prescribed their food. "Meat," he murmured in a restaurant, looking at the menu. "That'll kill you." In the morning sometimes they danced maniacally in the street, like two people who had just had an enormous piece of luck. During the day, after every scene, she flew into his arms like a child while he kissed and consoled her.

Midway through shooting—we were near Avignon—she refused to continue unless her salary was doubled and her boyfriend took over as director. She got the money, but the producer refused to back the mutiny. When I heard what had happened, I found it hard to suppress my loathing, although in retrospect I wonder if it might not have been a good thing. The boyfriend might have gotten some unimagined quality from her and made of the well-behaved film something crude but poignant—something compelling.

The truth is, the temperament and impossible behavior of stars are part of the appeal. Their outrages please us. The gods themselves had passions and frailties—these are the stuff of the myths. Modern deities should be no different.

In the end the film we made, *Three*, was decorous and mildly attractive. It was popular at Cannes and had some flattering reviews in America. A young women's magazine voted it the selection of the month and critics had it on their ten-best lists, but they were alone in this. Audiences thought otherwise.

There were opportunities to direct again, but I remembered lying on the stone beach at Nice late one day, when we were close to finishing, wearing a pair of Battistoni shoes, and feeling utterly spent. I felt like an alcoholic, like Malcolm Lowry. It seemed the morning after. I looked down and saw the white legs of my father. All of it had demanded more than I was willing to give again.

For its real adherents the life never ended. I liked the stories of producers driving down to Cap d'Antibes in convertibles with two or three carefree girls. I had had notes placed in my hand by the wives of leading men, bored and unattended to, that said in one way or another, "Call me," and had seen actors emerging from the Danieli in Venice, wrapped against the fall weather in expensive coats, fur-lined within and cloth without. The fur was the luxury in which they lived, the cloth a symbol of the ordinary world from which they were removed. Off to Torcello for lunch, jolting across the wide lagoon, the wind blowing the dark green water to whiteness, past San Michele with its brick walls, the island on which Stravinsky and Diaghilev lay buried—the real and the false glory, one moving past the other, though there are times when one cannot tell which is which.

•

The best scripts are not always made. There are so many factors: timing, impulse, frivolity, accident. The films that are made are like menhirs, standing amid the rubble of everything broken or lost, the marvelous lines, scenes, the great effort lavished like milt over roe. The agents and stars kick through it idly. Perhaps it is this waste, this vast debris, which nourishes the glory.

I was *a poule* for ten years, fifteen. I might easily have gone on longer. There was wreckage all around, but it was like the refuse piled behind restaurants: I did not consider it—in front they were bowing and showing me to a table.

In Toronto, under amiable conditions, the last of the films I wrote was made. It was called *Threshold*, prophetically for me. Although I wrote other scripts, I had a deserter's furtive thoughts.

The movie was about a cardiac surgeon and the first artificial heart. The writing, as one sees often in retrospect, was imperfect, but I could not at the time imagine how to improve it. The budget was too small and the actors were not all ones we wanted. Some of the best scenes were dropped or awkwardly played as a result. When I finally saw the movie, feeling as always naked in the audience, I saw mostly the flaws, quite a few of them my own fault.

Years later, I wrote one (I thought) final script—overwrote, I should say. Again, only the seed of a story was provided: a reclusive star of the first magnitude who has not permitted an interview for years grants one to a very private, literary writer, one of whose books she happens to like. She has everything, he has almost nothing other than familiarity with the great dead and the world they define. Somehow it enthralls her, and for an hour or a week they fall in love.

Perhaps I dreamed that I was the writer, and the irresistible woman who had not had the least whim denied her was a symbol for film itself.

There was another final script, which in fact ascended a bit before

crashing, as the result of a director's unreasonable demands, and I
suppose there might have been another and another, but at a certain
point one stands on the isthmus and sees clearly the Atlantic and the
Pacific of life. There is the destiny of going one way or the other and
you must choose.

And so the phantom, which in truth I was, passed from sight.

I have forgotten the names of the concierges at the Inghilterra and
the Baur au Lac. Images, though, remain, innominate but clear.
Driving the roads of Southern France: Béziers, Agde—the ancient
countryside, husbanded for ages. The Romans planted quince trees
to mark the corners of their fields; sinewy descendants still grow
there. A woman, burnished by sun, walked down the street in the
early morning carrying an eel. Many times I have written of this
eel, smooth and dying, dark with the mystery of shadowy banks
and covered with bits of gravel. This eel is a saint to me, oblivious,
already in another world.

To write of people thoroughly is to destroy them, use them up. I
suppose this is true of experience as well—in describing a world, you
extinguish it and in any recollection much is reduced to ruin. Things
are captured and at the same time drained of life, never to shimmer
or give back light again.

There remains, though, in the case of those years in the movies, a
kind of silky pollen that clings to the fingertips and brings back what
was once pleasurable, too pleasurable, perhaps—the lights dancing
on dark water, as in the old prints, the sound of voices, laughter,
music, all faint, alluring, far off.

The New Yorker
August 4, 1997

The First Women Graduate

"Fennessy!" the first classman at the head of the table called. It was in the dining hall with its six great wings. "Look up here."

Fennessy raised her eyes.

"Do you notice anything about my hands?" He was holding them up.

"No, sir."

"I'm not wearing my class ring." The heavy, gold ring that is a kind of passport and instantly recognized in the Army was missing. "I'm not going to wear it again as long as there are cheaters here."

"Yes, sir."

"And I'm taking it off forever if there's ever a woman first captain. What do you think of that?"

"I think it would be a waste of a good ring, sir," Fennessy replied.

That was in 1976, just after the worst cheating scandal in the history of West Point. Robin Fennessy was a plebe. She was twenty-one years old and had completed three years at the University of Colorado, where she studied molecular biology on an ROTC scholarship. When the chance came to go to West Point with the first group

of women, she said, why not? This month she is due to graduate—
one of 61 women out of the 119 who entered originally.

The most famous military school in the world sits on majestic ground
overlooking the Hudson. It is fifty miles upriver from New York
City but the distance cannot be measured in miles; it is really fifty
years upriver. The drive goes north on graceful parkways, through
the woods of the Palisades, tract towns, and into country that has
existed almost unchanged since Revolutionary days. West Point was
a fortress then.

It is still a kind of fortress, vast and serene, far from the megacity
with its crowds, its glittering energy and broken streets. West Point
is the chapel of the Army, a "holy place" in Patton's solemn words.
It is also college, country club, and Forest Lawn. It is a separate
world in which the great constellations are Bradley and Eisenhower,
a world of order and old brick quarters where anyone of greater age
or rank is still called sir.

There are some 10,500 West Pointers on active duty in the Army,
about one officer in eight (in the expanded Army of World War II
it was one in a hundred), but they possess an influence out of proportion to their number and have always been heavily represented
among the generals. Their distinction has been so well confirmed
that, as one non-graduate put it, "If I knew nothing about West
Point and one was coming into my unit, I would expect him to be
everything on the basis of reputation alone." All of its graduates,
in service or out, together form an exceedingly loyal and cohesive
body. Their cadet experiences unite them with a powerful nostalgia.
They have taken the voyage together. The school, for all its solid,
terrestrial image, is like a cherished ship, a ship that does not love
in return.

In recent years it has been battered. The defeat in Vietnam,
humiliating to the Army, was especially stinging to those who pro-

vided the ethos for it, led it, and were its most devoted and ambitious servants. The demoralization came to a climax in 1970 when the then superintendent, General Koster, stood on a stone balcony in the mess hall and announced his resignation. He had been implicated in the cover-up after My Lai. Koster was never tried but his career was ruined.

The corps of cadets had gradually been increased in size from 2,500 to 4,400, and commensurate with these larger numbers, in 1976 came the greatest cheating scandal ever. One hundred and fifty-two cadets were found guilty of collaboration on a take-home problem in electrical engineering and dismissed—ninety-eight were later allowed to return—and cheating, it was agreed, had been far more widespread. In the same year, over strenuous and deeply felt objections, women were admitted for the first time. In 1977 a highly critical report mentioned among other things West Point's negative attitudes and resistance to change. Added to all this, the football team was moribund. It could not beat Navy and had not been of national prominence for almost twenty years.

The problems West Point was facing seemed to call for something other than the stewardship of another career-minded general. As it had in 1919 when MacArthur was sent in to straighten out things after the war and made a dazzling, unmilitary entrance in grommetless cap and worn puttees, the Army reached far, this time to the retired list. The man chosen had made his way to the top as White House staff secretary to Eisenhower and adviser to Kennedy, Johnson, and Nixon on defense and foreign policy. This was General Andrew Goodpaster. He had retired in 1974 after a career that just missed chairmanship of the Joint Chiefs but included Vietnam and five years as NATO's Supreme Allied Commander in Europe. From there he went to the Citadel to teach.

Goodpaster is not a typical general. He is tall, white-haired, and reserved. He's a grandfather and drives a white Mercedes. There is something pedagogic in his manner and he is exact in his speech, as befits a man who often gave advice to the powerful. When he was first asked, at Christmas in 1976, what he thought of selecting a superintendent with greater than usual academic qualifications, someone who might remain longer than the usual three years, he replied that he was in favor of it.

"Let me ask you a funny question," the chief of staff then said. "Would you consider it?"

That spring, taking off one of his four stars, he returned to active duty as the Supe. Although it was only one of the areas to which he had to give his attention, honor—and related matters—was the most important to him. It was the determining issue on which he was prepared to come back, Goodpaster says.

The honor system is as old as the school. Originally it derived from the officer's code, the aristocratic idea that an officer was a gentleman and as good as his word. Over the years the corps was so intimate and its notion of honor so close to society's that not until MacArthur's reign was there an invincible definition: a cadet does not lie, cheat, or steal. To this, unwritten at first, was added the clause: nor tolerate those who do.

The honor committee, vaguely secret, with its unobserved trials and chairman's book passed down from hand to hand, enforced the code. If a cadet was found guilty, he was expected to resign. If he refused and there were no military charges on which he could be dismissed, the tradition was to silence him—he lived and ate alone, no one speaking to him except on official matters. In the eyes of the corps he had ceased to exist. The silence lasted for life. This harsh but thrilling bit of schoolboy justice was struck down in 1973. By then, though the authorities were unwilling to recognize it, a different kind of young man had begun to enter the academy, in fact all the academies. At Air Force things were so bad that during the 1970 graduation ceremonies the new superintendent could hear groaning as certain cadets received their diplomas.

West Point failed to pick up the warning signs: earlier cheating outbreaks, changing attitudes expressed by cadets, even rumors of bribery on the honor committee. The dishonesty and cover-up in Vietnam and Washington, the years of permissiveness and protest had an effect. Like a dam breaking, the scandal of 1976 swept through company after company, in some nearly wiping out an entire class.

The most difficult part of the honor code is the toleration clause, the obligation of one cadet to report another. Although truthfulness may not be foreign to American values, informing is. MacArthur himself ironically claimed to have lived according to his parents' admonition: never lie, never tattle. The Naval Academy has no toleration clause, but at West Point a cadet who observes an honor violation and does not report it has committed a violation himself.

This is not the only problem. The code is simple, but the workings of the system are more involved and must be scrupulously taught. A cadet may not lie but neither may he quibble—tell a partial truth. Of a disheveled cadet who had reported late for duty, an officer demanded, "Where have you been?"

"Sir, I've been to the library," was the reply. It was true, but he neglected to say that was where he'd met his girl and they then spent two hours out in a field. He was tried for honor.

Nor is the question of stealing as clear-cut as it seems. Someone who sees money drop out of another's pocket and does not return it is guilty of a violation. A cadet who was at Eisenhower Hall, the social center, found that someone had taken his raincoat from the cloakroom. Raincoats are identical. He took someone else's. He was found guilty.

Self-reported violations are treated no differently from others. Nor does the seriousness of the offense matter. It is a code of iron. Fortunately it makes some exception for social situations or cadets would be monsters of candor and a foolish "I love you" could wreck a career.

Despite these almost theological intricacies, Goodpaster feels that the code is a minimum. Beyond it he sees larger questions of virtue. Of the men who were once cadets it will be asked, does he treat people with fairness, does he meet a challenge with courage, does he stand up to be counted?

Honor is the battle line along which West Point has chosen to make its stand. It is like the single square on a chessboard toward which all pieces are directed.

Joe Franklin, the brigadier general who as commandant is responsible for the military training of cadets and in charge of much of their life, says, "I feel the country looks at West Point as the honor of society. If you can't maintain it here, you're doomed."

There have been some recent changes in the honor system. Trials are now open and conducted with the participation of members of the corps at large—two from each class including plebes—as well as members of the committee. There is a legal officer who serves as a kind of magistrate, but the proceedings are essentially between cadets. If the finding is guilty, normally there is still only one punishment: dismissal. The superintendent, however, can modify the sentence.

"There are people who support the honor system strongly and there are those who don't. I'm one of the latter," a female cadet says. She is a first classman and highly regarded. "There's too much witch-hunting."

"I believe in the honor code," another says, "but I have some trouble with the system."

"Sometimes I think they carry it a little bit too far," another first classman, a male, says.

The honor captain is James Coe, six feet five, good-looking, with corn-colored hair and a slight cast in one eye, a basketball player from Minnesota who became disillusioned with the game and gave it up, never touched a ball again.

"I'd be the first to admit I'm a very naive young man," he says, "but I feel the biggest thing we try to do is teach an honor ethic—a personal ethic that goes beyond the code. On an individual level," he admits, "I think there is some discretion on the part of both reporting cadets and members of a full honor board."

Coe would like to see a return to a simpler concept. "One thing I'd like to do," he reflects, "is reduce the size of the corps. You can hide in the corps now. In the old days you could concentrate on people."

There was a time when the Army was small and a regular officer was above politics and beyond deceit, without exception or qualification. The question today is: should West Point worship an integrity that is greater than the nation's, and how much greater should this integrity be? There is an obvious danger when colonels and generals see themselves as sole guardians against corruption. On the other hand, a lack of honor among officers would be equally frightening—we saw the discolored edge of it in Vietnam.

"I don't say you don't have to compromise in the Army," a captain from the class of '69 says, "but here it should be different."

A former first captain and Rhodes scholar adds, "We haven't solved honor problems yet."

The chapel still dominates the gray granite buildings like a cathedral in a European city, but the idea that held everything firm is altered, the idea that brought a single, uniform body of young men together not only on Sunday mornings but also in daily meals, parades, and view of life. The new corps has a different identity, multiracial and bisexual, and in it are the hidden stresses found in a solid but amalgamate mass.

This May for the first time there will be women in the graduating class. As second lieutenants they will face problems nearly as great as any they have overcome. They are certain to be watched closely by everyone in the Army. Those who are marrying—about half, and with few exceptions they are marrying classmates or recent graduates—are not assured of assignments with their husbands, although the Army will make every effort to do this. And further along there are the difficulties of raising children in a house where both parents are full-time soldiers.

The women in the class of '80 entered four summers ago. Some of them may have known what they were getting into, but even these probably had an imperfect idea. Beast Barracks, the first two months of cadet life, is a period of intense physical and psychological stress and a rite of passage. There is shouting, heat, formation running, too much to be done in too little time, a nightmare of anxiety come to life. On a scale of stress from 0 to 100, where a change in residence is 20, marriage 50, and death of a spouse 100, Beast Barracks is estimated to be 300. There were women who missed their periods until November. Some, like women in concentration camps, missed them for a year.

In the spirit of absolute egalitarianism, there were, apart from some minor differences in physical training—women did not take boxing and wrestling, for example—no concessions. The women wore the same uniforms, ate the same food, and lived under the same regimen as the men.

The biggest problem was the running. Women who dropped out were looked down upon by the males. Jim Coe recalls, "I said, what are they here for? There was a woman in my squad who epitomized why women shouldn't be here. She didn't seem to try, didn't put out, didn't care about the squad."

On the last day of the summer, just before the plebes marched back from an encampment to formally join the corps, newsmen descended to interview almost all the women but only two of the men. This caused more hard feelings. And upperclassmen were saying that these newcomers had destroyed the corps by bringing in women.

Those who survived Beast Barracks found that the hostility persisted through the school year.

"Good morning, sir," a woman would say.

"It was a good morning till you got here, bitch."

The men would march behind them in ranks, muttering, "Oink, oink." Things like that.

Andrea Hollen, graduating with a Rhodes scholarship, recalls: "I stood there saying to myself, I will not cry. I will not cry."

At the same time that they were being berated by upperclassmen and told they were worthless, some of the women plebes began receiving letters from them. Something more powerful than male autarchy and rules against fraternization was at work. There were women in barracks. There were cadets with beautiful, boyish hair, like that of a shipmate on a cruise. It was an appeal that touched fantasies—on a clear autumn morning or in the winter dusk the image of a tender cheek beneath a military cap, the trace of a smile, the womanly figure in rough clothes, these brought together the affection for a comrade in arms and the aching dreams that dwelled in barracks rooms, allowing one, in a single embrace, to possess a woman, a brother, the corps.

Conservative cosmetics may be worn but not false eyelashes or excessive mascara. Dating or the establishing of any emotional relationship between upperclassmen and plebe women is forbidden. Still, "Ninety-five percent of the women were fraternizing when we were plebes," one of them estimates, "and they're doing it now."

"Before I came here," Becky Blyth says, "my father told me how blacks were treated in his time and I expected something like that, but I also expected a higher level of accepting change."

She is tense, dark-haired, beautiful, the daughter of a West Pointer. One brother graduated in '77, another is a year behind her, and a third is applying for entrance. She had always wanted to be in the Army. Her voice is low and she speaks in swift, articulate bursts.

"I'm not the same person emotionally," she admits. "I used to be very mellow. Now I tend to get upset at things. I guess I'm trying to wean myself off this bitter trip. One thing was the rumors, the talk. Someone would start a story and it would go around. When I was a plebe, they began telling about a football weekend and I was in this hotel going from room to room. An upperclassman called me in and said I was a disgrace to the corps and a lot of other stuff. I asked if I could make a statement. He said yes. "I wasn't at that football game," I said.

There are women wearing jump insignia, women who have fired mortars and driven tanks. There is a whiff of China about them, the deep socialist states. They have made astonishing achievements at West Point. Still, they will always be a minority, perhaps 15 percent in an overwhelmingly male school. "I think they perceive us as a separate class," one of them says. "There's the class of '80 and there's the female class."

"I'm not women's lib or anything, that's not my ideological foundation," Andrea Hollen says, "but this is a last battleground. I have a keen appreciation of the issues separating men and women."

"Most of you are still carrying a grudge," a man observes.

"That's true," they agree.

The bitterness passes and there seems to come a strange affection, born who knows where but slowly effacing the scars. The women's class rings are smaller than the men's. They usually wear them on the right hand. The men wear theirs on the left, the hand nearest the heart.

One last barrier remains: women are not allowed to choose combat arms, the branches that would put them in the front lines. For some this is a final ambition. They know they are tough, intelligent, and physically qualified. They not only have no hesitation about being given command in combat units, they desire it.

Lillian Pfluke, the top woman in her class physically, is slight, with pale blue eyes and brown hair. She can do seven pull-ups and run two miles in combat boots in just over thirteen minutes. She wanted infantry. "I knew I could do it, but they won't let me try."

Captain of the women's lacrosse team, Pfluke wears no makeup and is marrying a lieutenant from the class of '79. "I think I'm very confident, aggressive, and very physical," she says. "I work well with people. I think I'll be a good leader."

One thing that may be happening is that men are feeling less inhibited about their career choices. It used to be otherwise. "Guys are going noncombat arms now—you'd never see that before," a lieutenant colonel says. "The women made that possible."

There is not as much spit and polish as there used to be. There are fewer formations and parades, and breakfast, except for plebes, is optional. There has been a ruthless pruning of outmoded traditions, but what lies at the heart remains untouched.

"They still come here for the same reasons they did thirty or forty years ago," says the director of admissions, Colonel Manley Rogers. "Education is still number one."

A free education at a world-renowned school, the promise of glamour, an Army career. The profile of those admitted is markedly more conservative than at other colleges. West Point gets the achievers, the solid performers, the practical youths. Eighty percent call themselves middle-of-the-road or conservative in their outlook. Half were varsity captains in high school. Almost a third are born-again Christians.

MacArthur, who was raised in the Army, had difficulty getting an appointment. So did Grant. But the system today is more open. There are still only small numbers of blacks, nothing near the 10 percent target. The main difficulty is poor academic preparation, and the attrition rate of blacks is higher than average. Minority applicants are selected out of order of merit to try to fill quotas, but despite this they are not available.

This year the first captain, highest ranking and most visible man in the corps, is black. He is Vincent Brooks, the tall, confident son of a brigadier general and the successor to such former first captains as Pershing, MacArthur, Wainwright, and Westmoreland.

West Point is still known as the Factory. It stamps out a certain kind of man, proud, competent, not given to nice distinctions. On Trophy Point the cannon goes off at six in the morning. The sky over the eastern hills is barely streaked. Lights are on in the barracks. Shadowy figures hurry on the way to the huge dining hall. The first formation will be at 0715, bells ringing, plebes calling the minutes in the hallways. In four separate areas the corps will begin to form.

The first year is the hardest. The list of things a plebe must know is endless: the menu, Schofield's definition, the heads of academic departments, coaches and team captains, Worth's Battalion Orders. (But an officer on duty knows no one—to be partial is to dishonor both himself and the object of his ill-advised favor . . .) The pace is intense. Gone are the days when cadets studied by flashlight after taps with blankets over their heads. Now they jog in the dark with reflecting plastic collars around their necks. Late at night the lighted windows look like endless blocks of city flats.

No horse, no mustache, no woman was the ancient proscription. Essentially it still applies. Cadets live mostly in two-man rooms, the walls pastel color, two chairs, two desks, two beds neatly made, two closets, two footlockers, one stereo. Nothing on the walls and the door must be fully open during all visits between cadets of the opposite sex. No television, that's in the company dayroom. Nautilus exercise machines in the basement. Only first classmen may have cars. *The New York Times* is delivered to each room daily. On Saturday night in Eisenhower Hall there are hordes of cadets all in their identical blazers, gray trousers, white shirts. On Sunday the chaplain proclaims, "Strengthen, we pray, the instructors, the staff, the students, that we may be inspired to grow, that we may do more than follow the regulations . . ."

"Cadets are very nice people," Dr. Francine Hall, a visiting professor of psychology, says, "but a lot of them are very immature socially."

Captain Teresa Rhone, a clinical psychologist, agrees. "They're not as far advanced in getting along with other people. There aren't enough chances for it—they're in such structured situations all the time."

"I don't see them as comfortable with emotions." Dr. Hall says. "They're certainly not comfortable with women. The only roles in which most of them have seen women are as mother and dates— they come up here and it's very unreal, they have to walk on the guy's arm and so forth. I don't see the social development of the males as moving along."

Many of his classmates have marital problems, a captain and West Pointer says. "Their wives complain that they don't talk to them. The fact is, they're taught not to admit weakness or communicate doubt or insecurity, and that's what their wives want to hear."

"One should not be weak, one should not show weakness," Captain Rhone says. "We see about one cadet a year who's breaking down, maybe one suicide attempt in a year and a half. These kids are so well-adjusted that I believe those who can't handle the stress and the problems self-select out."

"They don't have time for intellectual development," Dr. Hall notes. "They don't have time to read. The norms of what you do or what you don't do are very fixed. If you're seen lying around reading a lot—it's not the thing to do."

"There's peer pressure," Robin Fennessy says. "You lose cool points. You don't wear your calculator on your belt. You don't run to class no matter how late you are. You don't wear socks with slippers. You don't date cadets."

As a college, West Point is unquestionably demanding. It requires more courses than Harvard—mathematics, physics, chemistry, history, economics, law, all are in the core curriculum. Classes are small and the once-sacred formula of a cadet reciting in every subject every day has been abandoned. The singular and narrow aspect, however, is that the faculty is almost entirely military, and of these, 56 percent are West Point graduates on a tour of duty. It is not a school where one finds famous names. This pertains to other things as well.

"You don't get so many geniuses or near-geniuses," a visiting professor of history says, "but on the other hand you don't get the very poor students."

Not the sort of place to look for a great tight end. For a long time Army did not recruit football players: they walked in. That changed with Earl Blaik in the 1940s. Even so, Blaik had to count on outconditioning and outcoaching other schools, but the level of competition has risen.

"We can't do it anymore," a member of the athletic staff says. "Once we could utilize our two hours a day better. Now, when the other team goes on six hours a week of weight work, we don't know where to look for it. And the kids we're looking for—'Do I have to cut my hair that short?' they want to know."

Further, any football player must serve five years in the Army after graduation. The present coach, a veteran named Lou Saban, is reported to have said when confronted by the high scores necessary for entrance that at Miami he had linemen who outweighed their SATs.

If Army cannot get the big, fast men that make the game, it cannot play big schools. And if it can't do this, apart from not earning the money to support other athletic programs that should be publicly funded to begin with, a great morale factor will be lost. Just as Pittsburgh, Notre Dame, and USC bask in the glory of their teams, so Army wants to have a football team to identify with, and enlisted men in tank barracks in Germany and radar operators in Alaska want to think of it as their own. It is a problem that concerns the highest levels. The chief of staff went up to West Point last winter with the question: what could be done to help the football program? Without violating the principles the school has staked its reputation on, the answer seems to be, not much.

But what about Navy, they ask? Navy seems to do well. Annapolis is a different school and operates in a different way. It is more pragmatic, more sensible, more accommodating. No one has ever said that it fails to turn out excellent officers, but it is not West Point.

West Point is a religion without a god. Its saints and martyrs are found in the statuary around the plain. It does not create, it preserves. With its beautiful stone walls, its large property, its trees, it fills the role of a great family seat and its graduates are sons. Somewhere is the inheritance that, though they will never receive it, protects them.

Duty, honor, country. On Friday night at the Thayer Hotel near the main gate the visiting teams are billeted. Young men from other schools, casually dressed, sit around downstairs. Compared to cadets they seem like inferior beings, slack, of questionable background and motives.

Across the river the lights in the house of Red Reeder, the old, one-legged colonel who wrote a series of boys' books about West Point heroes and now lives in retirement close to his beloved school, shine in the dusk.

Life
May 1980

France

Almost Pure Joy

There was Braudel which I'd never gotten around to reading. And *Middlemarch*. A senior editor at Viking long ago had told me that he reread *Middlemarch* every year. I could at least do it once. And *Parade's End. The Great War and Modern Memory*, plus three or four issues of *The New Yorker* and the *New York Review of Books*, which weighed almost nothing. All this and more was spread on the bed when Kay wandered in.

"Are you going to have room for any clothes?" she asked innocently.

"These are just some possibilities. I haven't decided on anything."

"There are bookstores in Paris, you know."

"I don't like to take chances," I said.

We were going over for ten weeks: the two of us, the dog, and Bill, a close friend. All going together. We'd been many times to France, and so had the dog, but Bill, though an art dealer and a prodigiously read man, had never been there. He loved Paris as much as anyone did—he had just never seen it. That was going to be remedied.

In the end I got everything into two bags and Kay had two of her own. In a carry-on bag I also had a bottle of 1976 Château Latour, "the most consistent great wine in Bordeaux and probably the world," to quote Hugh Johnson, for a special occasion. Château Latour 1976, then nine years old, was probably available in France, but as I said, so as not to take chances . . .

We had planned the trip for a long time and had even taken a brief earlier trip as a kind of reconnaissance. We had rented an apartment in the 16th arrondissement, the silk-stocking district of Paris, on a street called Belles Feuilles—beautiful leaves—just off Avenue Victor Hugo and not far from a brasserie called the Stella, which turned out to be the canteen of the 16th, filled on Sunday evening with chic couples back from the country, the women in mink coats and blue jeans.

Away from the avenue, in the opposite direction, was Avenue Foch, immensely wide and bordered with embassies and houses with iron-fenced gardens.

A friend in Paris had looked at the apartment for us—we had taken it sight unseen—and given it an okay. It turned out to have a terrace and, on the first floor, a German shepherd that broke out in terrific barking whenever we passed with Sumo, our dog.

Sumo was a Welsh corgi, nine years old at the time, intelligent, imperturbable, and slightly lame, although he could run like a hare when necessary. "*Oh! Le pauvre petit!*" the French women would cry upon seeing him limping along, some of their sympathy spilling over onto me. There were not many corgis in Paris, a city otherwise rich in dogs, so there were also frequent questions as to Sumo's origin. My dog vocabulary gradually grew stronger.

On the way down to the wide green borders of Avenue Foch, past the hospital, Belles Feuilles ran into Avenue Bugeaud, the street on which Louise de Vilmorin lived with her American husband and their three children before the war. Aristocratic, literary, and a famous beauty, she was one of the goddesses of her generation. The apartment building she lived in is still there, of course—that is the way Paris is constructed—and the small *tabac* near the corner is there as well. Louise de Vilmorin, restless and bored, told her husband she was going down to the *tabac* to get some cigarettes but in fact met her lover there, with whom she departed, *comme ça*, as they say, becoming divorced, later marrying a Hungarian count, and eventually winding up after the war as André Malraux's mistress and close friend. One can get an idea of her appeal from a photograph in *Vogue*, and her style from the brief but irresistible novel, *Madame De*, one of several she wrote.

Walking down to Avenue Foch, I would look up to imagine the windows of Louise de Vilmorin's apartment where her husband sat with the newspaper as she left and where, legend has it, she could look back up and see him reading.

When we arrived in Paris we went immediately to lunch, for me oysters and white wine. Then we walked or napped, I don't remember, but when we reached Bill's hotel that evening, on Rue de Longchamp, and opened the shutters, there, almost at the end of the street it seemed and blazing with light was the Eiffel Tower. It was like some unbelievable fireworks display except that it went on and on. A more dazzling welcome to the city would be hard to imagine.

We rented a car. There was an argument about that—the rental agency had confirmed a small car, but when we arrived all they had was the large touring size which they offered at no reduction in price, accompanied by helpless shrugs. We drove to Switzerland, had some adventures, then back through Germany along the Rhine. The dog went with us, of course, and most of the luggage. A few days after returning to Paris we went out to Versailles for a picnic. Bill, naturally, had never seen it.

The day was sunny and warm. We parked in the huge, cobbled courtyard, strolled at length through the famous gardens, and finished with one of the tours of the great palace itself. In the Hall of Mirrors, Kay began to feel a little funny and a few minutes later, in the gilded theater, said she thought we should be getting back to Paris.

•

I perhaps have forgotten to mention that she was pregnant, eight and three-quarters months. Despite the most heartfelt advice (*You need support, you need family around*) and pleas (*Oh, please, please don't have that baby in Paris*) and after long, lazy discussions and a final, snap decision, we had come to Paris for the delivery. Why, you may very well ask. Put it down as a romantic idea. We had taken some practical steps, visited the American Hospital in Neuilly, just outside of Paris, and made arrangements with a French obstetrician there. The American Hospital is an old and in some ways elegant institution where English is spoken, generally, and rich people, seeking comfort and dignity until the last, sometimes go to die. Among the many patrons commemorated on bronze tablets is the name Macomber, which I assume Hemingway took for use in his celebrated story.

French medicine is, in some quarters, looked upon as slightly primitive, though in my experience it has proved to be more than satisfactory. In the provinces doctors often have no receptionists, the gorgons whose purpose seems to be to make life difficult for the patient, and answer the phone and make out bills themselves. For a slight, fixed amount in France they will make house calls, and although they approach every diagnosis by way of palpating the liver, in a country of excellent food and plentiful wine, perhaps this is not misguided.

We drove into Paris in the early evening, the lovely twilight hour known as *cinq à sept*. No city is more beautiful at day's end. Bill went on to his apartment, which he rented from one of the Nabokovs, on Rue Oberkampf. He had met a Swedish girl a few days before and regained his feet, so to speak. On Belles Feuilles, we nervously timed the contractions. We had been instructed not to come to the hospital until they were three minutes apart.

At nine o'clock we went, past Porte Maillot and out the boulevard. Paris was infinite and alight. The diners everywhere were being served their entrees, the sommeliers were opening the wine.

Admission formalities at the hospital were the briefest. We went upstairs to the obstetrical section. There was only one other woman, Lebanese, I believe, there as a patient.

For an hour or so in the quiet of the labor room the contractions became stronger and more closely spaced. At about eleven, Dr. Bazin arrived. I had the distinct impression he had come from a dinner party and before that had spent a pleasant afternoon on the golf course. Perhaps it was the plaid trousers. Bazin was a slender, poised man, not given to much conversation. He was a Breton and had some of the stoicism of the breed. In his sketchy English he asked if I would mind stepping out of the room for a few minutes while he conducted an examination.

The next thing I knew, they were wheeling Kay out. I went back in to see Bazin. There were a few complications, he explained. The baby was not facing the right way and had the umbilical cord wrapped around its neck. Also there was some dark matter in the amniotic fluid which emphasized we should not delay. I was not to worry, however, he told me.

"Dr. Bazin," I said, "I am not worried. We have all the confidence in the world in you."

He nodded in modest acknowledgment and started to leave, but I went on.

"We came to France especially to have this child, in this hospital, and to have you deliver it. It's exactly as we wanted and planned. There's just one thing," I continued.

"Yes?" he said uncertainly.

"When the baby is born, we would like to wet its lips with good French wine so that it will remember the taste all its life."

This was the romantic climax. In ages past the custom was a birth ritual of French kings. Bazin looked at me for a moment or two with what seemed incomprehension. Then, glancing around, his eye fell on the bottle of Château Latour standing on the glass shelf above the sink. He went over and picked it up.

"Is this the wine?" he asked.

"Yes."

"This is not entirely a bad wine," he remarked, reading the label.

I declined his invitation to be in the delivery room and went to telephone Bill. It was surely near H-hour and the Metro closed at about this time. Then I stood in the hall, not far from the delivery room door, and listened to the groans and cries that were Kay's, the unexcited French voices belonging to Bazin, a nurse and an anesthetist, Bazin's counsel and instructions in English, the vague sound of instruments and the rest. Then I heard, and it caused a chill to go through me, the sudden, unmistakable wail of a newborn infant.

It had all been a kind of dream, the pregnancy, her tremendous happiness, deciding to go to Paris at the last minute, Belles Feuilles, everything. The baby's cry was like the sound of an alarm clock. The nurse, a good-looking girl in black net stockings beneath her white smock, came out and said, "You have a little boy." Almost at the same time, from the delivery room, I heard Bazin call, "Pull the cork!"

After wetting the little boy's lips—he was already himself, slim, cocky, serene—we drank the rest of the bottle, Kay, Bazin, the nurse, the anesthetist, and I. Real wineglasses had been produced from somewhere. Bill arrived as we were finishing.

Kay was tired, of course, drenched with triumph, the sort there is nothing to compare to. She was soon taken to her room—it turned out to be a corner suite with a white leather couch and clouds painted on the vaulted blue ceiling. They had earlier gone over her choices on the menu for the next day with her. The hospital had a genuine if unpretentious restaurant, the food was very good. French law requires the mother to stay in the hospital or clinic for a full week, in order to completely regain her strength before returning home to face whatever duties. As a foreigner, Kay was exempt from this, though she did luxuriate for days.

Bill and I went to what might be called an after-theater supper at Au Pied de Cochon, which I had first known when Les Halles, the great market of Paris, was across the street. We drank champagne. I was tired and giddy. It had all been a dream and now it was a dream again. Fog had settled in over the city. I dropped Bill off at about four in the morning and got home myself at about five after having wandered around trying to read street signs for half an hour. Dawn was just breaking, the first watery light coming through the bedroom windows. You have a little boy. I may have mentioned that to the dog.

What followed was almost pure joy. We had a list of student nurses who were willing to come in the evening and sit while we went out to dinner. Often one would come for two or three hours at midday as well. I cannot say we danced every night but we came close to it. We named our son Theo. It was the second choice, but the first was even more exotic and sounded to his grandfather like the name of a foreign radio. The franc was ten to a dollar at the time. We took taxis everywhere. We dined at Chez René and the Jules Verne, the Balzar and La Coupole. I often thought of the photograph of Scott and Zelda Fitzgerald and their daughter, Scottie, dancing all three together like a chorus line in front of the Christmas tree in Paris of the 1920s. It was like that.

It's too early to know if the application of wine to Theo's lips did its job, but having been born in Paris means a lot to him. He somehow believes he was born in the Eiffel Tower, and who are we to correct a romantic notion like that?

The Washington Post Magazine
August 13, 1995

Eat, Memory

In a sense, the connection between France and food began for me at the World's Fair in New York in 1939. The restaurant at the French Pavilion was one of the big hits of the fair. Everyone, including my parents, talked about it and the difficulty of getting a reservation. To the best of my knowledge, my father never tried.

When the fair closed in 1940, Henri Soulé, who had managed the restaurant, along with members of the staff, decided to stay in the United States and open a restaurant themselves. Le Pavillon, as it was predictably named, opened on Fifty-fifth Street, across from the St. Regis hotel, in October 1941, just before Pearl Harbor. Dedicated to perfection, it not only survived the war but also reigned as the jewel of the city for thirty-odd years. It was expensive, of course, though the prices seem laughable today. Château Margaux 1929 was, at the time, $4.50 a bottle.

I never ate at Le Pavillon either, it turned out. Too perfect, too expensive, too social. The first French restaurant, to stretch the term slightly, I ever ate at was Longchamps, part of a chain, now gone, that catered to a middle-class clientele. Creamed spinach, dinner rolls served with an adroit fork and spoon, white tablecloths, quiet conversation, an occasional laugh. I had become an officer in the Air Force, and as such, after the war, I found my way to Paris in 1950, but it was a more or less hasty visit without culinary revelations, except that the girls in the nightclubs, after a night of insisting on bad, overpriced champagne, liked to order pigeon, which was also overpriced, in the little restaurants familiar to them that, now famished, they took you to.

Four years afterward, I was stationed in Europe, and it is at this point that memories become more distinct. We went to Paris, my wife and I, a number of times and also to the South of France. There were incredible discoveries to be made. In Paris, on the Rue d'Amsterdam, there was Androuët, where everything on the menu was made from, or if necessary with, cheese. There was Les Halles and gratinée, and someplace where the waitresses were dressed as serving wenches and you ate Rabelaisian fare. There was the first steak au poivre and quenelles de brochet, and we ate at the Méditerranée on the Place de l'Odéon, unaware of distinguished patrons like Picasso and Jean Cocteau. We assumed that lobster à l'armoricaine was simply a French misspelling.

Let me just say that once you have been exposed to French cooking and French life, and they take, there is a long and happy aftermath. It's like knowing how to carve a turkey or sail a boat: it puts you a notch up. Of course, there is also Italy and all that. We cook from Marcella Hazan and *Cucina Rustica*, as well as others, but France is where Vatel, the maître d'hôtel for the Prince de Condé, fell upon his sword, his honor destroyed, when the fish did not arrive on time; where Taillevent, the most famous cook of the Middle Ages, rose from humble beginnings to actual nobility in the kitchen of Charles VI; and where Talleyrand, upon departing for Vienna in 1814 to negotiate for a defeated France at a congress of victors, told the king that he had more need of saucepans than of instructions.

Cuisine is regarded by the French as their rightful possession.

Madame de Maintenon, mistress of Louis XIV, established the Cordon Bleu as a cooking school, to become over the centuries the most famous in the world. Julia Child was among its alumni. Madame de Pompadour, also a king's mistress, was taught in her youth that food was one of the essential ways to hold a man, and she is renowned for having made good use of both. It was at Paris restaurants like Le Grand Véfour and La Coupole (well, Coupole is technically a brasserie) that the great names of France were to be found. Governments were made at Lipp, it was said, but they fell at La Coupole.

Chinon, Chaumont, a small village near Grasse called Magagnosc, Villeréal, sometimes Paris—these are some of the places we, or I, have lived in France, usually in rented houses, sometimes borrowed ones. Borrowed apartments in Paris are the best, and the best guidebook, old and familiar as it may be, for me is the red Michelin. Others have their points, but the Michelin is solid, thick, and reliable. When it was first published by the Michelin tire company in 1900 to identify gas stations, hotels, and repair shops along the road, it had only twenty pages. Over the years it has become a veritable encyclopedia covering all the towns and cities in France with a hotel or restaurant worthy of any notice—name, address, telephone and fax numbers, category, price, specialties, dates open, and on and on, even whether or not you can bring your dog. Dogs are usually allowed in restaurants in France and are almost always well behaved.

It was in the Guide Michelin that we found a restaurant, La Ripa Alta, in Plaisance, in southwestern France, one summer. It had been given a Michelin star, and the ranking was deserved. We had an excellent meal, and for dessert, figs, marvelously plump and tender, bathed in a smooth, faintly alcoholic liquid. When the owner and chef, Maurice Coscuella, came around to the tables afterward, we asked about the figs, how he had done them. The recipe was his own, he said, would we like it? I gave him a pair of drugstore eyeglasses I was reading the bill with in exchange.

Figs in Whiskey

1 package dried figs, Turkish or Greek seem best
2 cups sugar
1 1/2 cups Scotch whiskey

Boil the figs for twenty minutes in about a quart of water in which the sugar has been dissolved. Allow to cool until tepid. Drain half the remaining water or a bit more and add the Scotch. Allow to steep a good while in a covered bowl before serving.

The restaurant in Plaisance is not listed in the current Michelin. I cannot imagine Monsieur Coscuella having fallen from one star to oblivion. I prefer to think he retired after years of honest work in the kitchen, but the guide does not give forwarding addresses.

The New York Times Magazine
January 2, 2005

Paris Nights

The 1920s were the great years in Paris, the vintage of the century. The war was over, the franc was cheap, the city was at its
zenith. The painters and writers were there, amid names that have
lasted: Picasso, Stravinsky, Proust, Gertrude Stein. A. J. Liebling,
who became a celebrated New Yorker journalist, was more or less
attending the Sorbonne, and although he was too young and unac-
complished to mingle with the gods, he summons up much of the
period in *Between Meals*, his wonderful recollection of that era.

   There was a restaurant called Maillabuau on Rue Ste-Anne,
unimpressive, even shabby in appearance, known for superb food
and staggering prices. Liebling had never so much as crossed the
threshold of Maillabuau and certainly never would have had it not
been for a visit from his parents and sister. When they turned to
him for a suggestion of where to have their first dinner together,
Liebling, as if he dined there regularly, proposed Maillabuau. He had
read its description in a guidebook. The menu that night was simple:
a delicious soup—a garbure—followed by trout grenobloise, pou-
let Henri IV, and, for dessert, an omelette au kirsch. The food was

incomparable, the wines splendid, and the check, Liebling recalled, "one of the most stupendous . . . in history."

Not long ago, I was walking down Rue Ste-Anne, past Japanese restaurants, nightclubs, and travel agencies. Of Maillabuau there was not a trace. Like the legendary Le Chabanais, the most luxurious brothel in Paris, and the Hotel Louvois, where Liebling used to stay, Maillabuau had disappeared, devoured by modern times.

Of course, I knew this beforehand. I was merely strolling after lunch on Rue Vivienne, a couple of streets away, thinking of the 1920s and times past.

I came to Paris too late, not in my own life, but in the life of the city. I missed its years of glory. In the 1950s, the period of my first acquaintance, I was never in Paris long enough to have more than a vague impression of it, but eventually—I forget how—one night I walked into a restaurant that would become the restaurant in Paris for me. If I were asked to name my favorite restaurant in London, I might unconvincingly mention a place or two. The same for Rome. For Paris, however, there is no question. Not a moment of hesitation. The answer is La Coupole.

Is it because of the food? Not really. The food is good and so is the service. But it isn't just for these things that one embraces a restaurant. The crucial elements, though they don't last forever, are style and, for want of a better word, character. And in the case of La Coupole, something more: whatever the hour, but especially at night, there was the expectation of finding there le tout Paris— that is to say, everybody, from top to bottom: actors, intellectuals, journalists, musicians, along with many others whose occupation it would be difficult to judge.

Night. You cross the wide avenue, the Boulevard Montparnasse. There is the wide glass front, the garish neon letters above. People are sitting on the enclosed terrace, lingering over coffee, talking. Passing through the doors you are struck by the full sound: conversation, laughter, knives and forks clattering, bottles being opened, plates stacked. The long aisles running front to back with tables and banquettes on either side, the flood of faces. Each section has a maître, implacable as a croupier, in a dinner jacket. You know them by sight, polite but reserved. This is a profession, a life. If men like this are running the lines for the boat across the Styx, you're in luck. "You wish a table? For four?" He casts an appraising eye over his domain. "Dix minutes, monsieur." You can rely on the estimate. He'll call you in the bar.

Countless nights. I was having dinner at La Coupole once while thieves were stealing my car a few blocks away. In the police station there was a line of at least a dozen people waiting impatiently while the particulars were carefully being typed. "Ne vous inquietez pas," I was told, when I asked if this was just for the files or if patrol cars were being advised. He said 95 percent of all stolen cars were found Monday morning abandoned outside the gates of Paris—*portes* was the word he used—though it turned out that my car was in the minority and was never seen again.

La Coupole was open late. I often saw Polanski there and Gérard Brach, his screenwriter, who returned from living in England for two years, saying with pride that he had not learned a single word of the language during that time. You found Styron there, and Claude Berri. Of course, Paris is small, at least compared to New York.

These were the years when I was passing through the world of film. One unforgettable night I sat talking with an actor I had just met who was in Paris making a movie. Rip Torn. You know his face. There is a hint of the diabolic in it—this was years ago, but even then. I was fascinated as, later in the evening, he began to tell me the story of his life, but gradually a strange sensation, of being tricked somehow, being made a fool of, came over me. The details of Torn's boyhood—his years at military school, his idealism, hopes— they were all mine! How did he know all of this? No one did. How could he have known? I was watching him closely, trying to find the deceit, the slight lip quiver of falseness. He betrayed nothing. Finally, almost frightened, I said to him, "This isn't your story."

"What do you mean?"

"The one you're telling. It's not your life," I said.

But it was. Every word. I don't remember what I said, my thoughts were too confused. I was staying at a hotel not far away on the Boulevard Raspail, and I walked back to it like a ruined man. I felt weak. I could not believe what I had heard, but I could not figure out how not to believe it. There was someone almost exactly like the secret me. I felt exposed, undone.

The odd thing is that La Coupole itself is not the original La Coupole. It is a copy, refurbished after having been sold. The new La Coupole has everything the earlier one had—appearance, location—everything except one small detail, the soul. Somehow that got painted over. The timeworn quality of the restaurant, the bar that was isolated and a kind of afterthought, the feeling of being aboard an aging ship, launched in the 1920s but still holding the record—these are the things that were not passed on. Still, I cannot break the habit or resist the pull. Favorite Paris restaurant? The answer is immediate and unthinking: La Coupole. I always go back. The oysters, served on the great mounds of shaved ice, are the same, the neon sign, the front window, the crowd and the noise. For all we know, the singular lean face over there, the high forehead, is Cocteau's, and that attractive woman, face among faces further down, is definitely Djuna Barnes.

Food & Wine
October 1998

Chez Nous

A friend of mine married a Frenchwoman—something I had always had it vaguely in mind to do—and felt he had to prepare her for life in the States. There were certain things, for instance, that were never discussed at the dinner table, he told her; they were taboo—politics, religion, and sex.

"But that's impossible!" she replied. "In France those are the only things you talk about!"

You can sit in Taillevent or Lucas Carton, or maybe even on the ground floor at Lipp, something I've been able to achieve only once or twice in my life, but there's no point in eavesdropping to hear racy French conversation in these places. For one thing, they'll probably be talking English at the next table. Chez nous—at our place, as they say—is where you want to be, but the trouble is, you never get to their place. The French, and especially the Parisians, are notoriously private and probably have good reason to be: if sex is discussed at the dinner table, who knows what goes on elsewhere? In any case, an invitation to dinner is hard to come by. Despite this, there is an understandable curiosity and eagerness for any opportunity to breathe in a legendary frankness about the essential things of life.

•

The glory of France is outside of Paris, in the countryside, the centuries lying dark in the cathedrals, the timeless rivers, the impossible turns of the road through small villages in one of which is Isabel's house the likes of which you have seen many times. It's nothing, a blank facade on a street of them, four or five plain windows, traditional lace curtains hanging in the lower ones, an old door with some glass panels. Within is a small vestibule and another pair of doors, a low-ceilinged entry hall and a narrow staircase ascending to things unknown. Then, walking forward, abruptly, you enter another world. Two long rooms end to end with large windows looking out over a garden to the sea, and not just the sea but vineyards, farms and houses, the most serene landscape imaginable. A kind of vertigo comes over one, a dizziness as if seeing paradise. There is even a path that leads down to the beach, about a twenty-minute walk. It is the celebrated beach of St. Tropez, unbroken for miles. "When we bought the house, there was no one here," says Isabel. "The town was empty and poor. Next door there were stables, no, what do you call them, the place where they keep hay."

The house, in fact, had been a hotel. There is a photograph of it in the kitchen which, come to think of it, is the engine room of a small hotel, long and narrow with a great iron range and zinc counters. Colette used to stay here—her name is in the register and with it were some of her letters. The faint impression of a hotel remains but what was once dark and probably mean has been made elegant and dedicated to purity and light.

Lunch is classic, gigot and green beans, preceded by a crab and avocado salad, and with the main course, roast potatoes. The grownups are drinking wine at one end of the table and the children are at the other, talking and eating with forks too big for their hands. One of them is my son, born in Paris and now back in France on a visit—the first of many, I hope. He's three years old. The remark is made that the sweetest thing about them at this age is the way they love their mothers.

"They all love their mothers."

"Ah, non!" Isabel cries. Not her husband. His only memories of his mother are of the perfume she wore and the soft touch of her gloved hand on his cheek when she came home in the evening. "The love you receive as a child," Isabel says, "is like a bank—you give it to others later."

A tingle of anticipation goes through me as when the horses begin to line up in the starting gate. I feel we may be approaching one of the three taboo subjects and am eager to hear it talked about in the French way, perhaps in the way that the actress friend of Isabel's with the high cheekbones and great eyes that have stunned audience after audience would do it, an actress who lives nearby but who is at the moment on vacation and doesn't want to do anything, such as come to lunch and talk about love. I would give anything to hear her on the subject, and you might too, but we somehow end up instead talking about the sex life, more or less, of Isabel's father who is eighty-four and has just remarried. She's very unhappy about it. Her mother—his first wife—had died not that long ago.

"How long?"

"Four years."

"And it's the unseemly haste?"

"No, no not that," Isabel says, "but this wife is his age. What is the sense of that? He should have married someone young—that would be rigolo, at least."

The French like the word *rigolo*, which means funny or comic. Something or someone is tres rigolo. The groundskeeper of a friend of mine who has a large place in the Dordogne fell out of a boat in the middle of a pond—he was almost certainly not sober—and the owner fell in trying to rescue him. The groundskeeper liked to tell the story. He described the owner as tres rigolo.

We had some friends in another part of France, not far from Bergerac—Paul and Monique. A cosmopolitan couple, he was a former builder around Paris and she'd gone to college in California. Paul does a lot of the cooking—in my experience, all of it—and the meals are not tentative: roasts, baked fish, vegetable dishes of the region, handsome desserts, and he sits down at the table with the aplomb and apparent anticipation of a man in a new restaurant. One Sunday when we were there, the guests also included a French psychiatrist and his wife who lived in the vicinity. His wife had the sort of looks that roused my hopes. She could have stepped out of the pages of Laclos, poised, knowing, with, I understood immediately, the capacity to be entertained—there was a trace of being half amused already in her expression. They were telling a story about a merchant in town who had sold wine to the psychiatrist for years without having an inkling of his profession. It was surprising, the wine merchant said, he had no idea the man was a doctor.

"Why?" Paul had asked. "Would you have any hesitation in going to him if you were, say, very depressed?"

"I think the wife could cure me more quickly," the wine merchant replied.

Everyone laughed, including the psychiatrist. I was now following the conversation with avid interest, even accepting without wondering about it a further story of the wine merchant who'd had a smile found in a cask of his wine—I thought they said smile (sourire)—actually it was a mouse in the wine (souris). As far as I could tell, however, nothing further in the nature of sex or politics presented itself.

Later, in Gascony, we met a couple who lived in a château, and at a dinner in what could easily have been a wing of the Metropolitan, I sat next to the hostess who I immediately wished I'd met when I was twenty years younger although this would have made her about seven or eight. She was good-looking and vivacious and from the first moment we were talking animatedly and I was telling her everything I knew. Part of her charm lay in making me overlook the difference in our ages and I was trying to recall what Victor Hugo had said to a young woman to justify a physical attraction—they had in common being close to heaven, he because of his age and she because of her beauty, something like that. One thing the hostess said that I liked was that she had been trying to take up painting again. She had painted when she was younger and now she missed it. At the moment, she said, she was painting the ceiling.

Although there was someone seated on the other side of her who shared her attention, I was certain that her fascination was with me. We had begun to talk about her attempts to have children and the complete failure of them. It was probably more clinical than intimate but I felt it might fall under the heading of sex when unexpectedly, something else began to fall. Hornets from high above—the first dropped down a guest's collar at the next table, causing him to dance about in a kind of inexplicable pantomime. Then others began to fall. The hornets were apparently sleeping up in the molding and the heat of the candles or possibly of the conversations that I could not hear had stirred them, not enough to fly but to stagger forth and then lose their grip, dropping like fruit. This effectively broke up the party.

There were times they came to us, when we could say chez nous. The conversation was at our own table, though technically, it was still French.

For some reason, at one point we decided to expose Monique and Paul to authentic American cuisine, in this case, chili. There was, however, difficulty in obtaining one of the ingredients. In neither of the two small supermarchés was there any chili powder. Now, I have absolute confidence in my chili, which I've made countless times and which a friend born in Galveston and a cook himself has pronounced exceptional, but it seemed foolhardy to try and make it without the powder. We finally located a can in a specialty shop twenty-five miles away. It did not inspire confidence. It had been made in China and was being sold under an English label. Also, it was of unknown potency, as was the cayenne.

The lunch was served outside on a summer day, in a graveled courtyard, beneath the shade of a huge tree. Paul and Monique were there and a younger couple, Robert and Agnes, who it developed had only gotten to bed at five that morning after a housewarming at a friend's, a crémaillere, as they called it.

There was salad first, then the chili. It was a slight variation of the true chili, I explained, which was ordinarily made with beef and pork chunks rather than ground beef, but apart from that it was genuine. I said this with a casual air, knowing that we were sitting down to a more powerful dish than usual—the Chinese powder had proved to be of exceptional strength. "You know, there are contests in Texas every year to judge the world's champion chili," I said to divert attention. "Sort of a Super Bowl of chili."

"The bowl is super?" Agnes said.

"No. Super Bowl."

She had taken a taste. There was a pause. "How is it?" I asked.

"It clears the voice," she managed to say after a moment. Then, somewhat unconvincingly, "It's wonderful."

Her husband was tasting it. I could see him wince as he swallowed.

"Is it too hot?" I inquired offhandedly.

Fortunately Monique, who'd had it before in America, liked it. "It's supposed to be no good unless it makes you sweat," I said. "What's the word for sweat?"

"Respirer."

"Oui," Robert breathed. I thought he said something to his wife about a *ruade*, which is a kick from a horse. After lunch they were supposed to attend a first communion.

"The chili will help us sing," Agnes conceded.

To keep them from having the wrong impression, I explained that a key ingredient, the powder, had been hard to obtain and then had proven to be not what we normally employed. "There are some things that simply don't exist in France, you can't get them."

"What?" Monique demanded.

"Peanut butter, for one," I said.

"I hate it," she said. "What else?"

"Baking soda."

"You can get baking soda!"

"It's not in the supermarché."

"Of course not. You can get it at the *pharmacie*."

"What, with a prescription?"

"No, no. You ask for *bicarbonate de soude*."

"Of course," I agreed.

"What is that used for?" Agnes asked.

"Cooking vegetables," Monique said dismissively.

We never got around to sex. Their mouths must have been burning too much. The closest we came was a story of Paul and Monique's trip to Peru. They were on a train between Cuzco and Machu Picchu. There were two trains, Monique said, one for tourists and another, slower one that made many stops which was the one they took.

"A woman got aboard with a lot of baggage—really just cartons and boxes of every description—a large woman wearing four or five skirts. When she was finally installed she took up a whole row of seats. The conductor came for the tickets. She had none, she said. Why not, he wanted to know? I don't pay, she told him. You have to pay, he said. No, she said.

'When they were building this railroad, I slept with every man who worked on it. I paid already,' she said, 'I don't have to pay again.'"

I would have liked to call this letter The Woman from Cuzco, but I decided it would give the wrong idea about the candor of conversation at French tables.

European Travel and Life
Spring 1990

Aspen

Once and Future Queen

There is a restaurant in Paris on Boulevard Montparnasse that has been there since the 1920s, the decade of myth, the decade of Josephine Baker, Picasso, Hemingway, Gertrude Stein, Stravinsky, so many others. The restaurant is called La Coupole and there one saw and still sees *le tout Paris*, which translated roughly means "everyone." A certain kind of everyone, that is, the kind that writes or is written about.

La Coupole is very big and has always stayed open late. Marvelous faces, some with reputations attached, others hoping to achieve them, were there at all hours, framed by the worn red material of the banquettes, eating, drinking, and deep in conversations one could not hear or even imagine. Over it all was the haze of talk and the faint aroma of Gauloise cigarettes. You might see a dozen people you knew, you might see no one. Below was a dance hall—I don't recall ever going down to it but it lent its presence.

A few years ago the restaurant changed hands. The new owner gave it a minor facelift and much needed refurbishing. The walls were freshly painted, the banquettes recovered, the inconvenient bar relocated. The room is still huge, the service impeccable, and the prices are not much higher. There are still crowds at night and all the animation one could desire, but something is different: the place has been perfected and in the process has become a kind of replica of itself, wonderful as long as you have never seen the original.

The queen of American ski towns, Aspen, is a bit like that. At its heart, Coupole-like, is the old Hotel Jerome, the exterior looking the same as ever but, with the exception of the lobby and bar, completely done over and raised to a luxurious level. In the former Jerome the rooms were homely and the plumbing questionable and one used to be able to rent Parlor A or B, the best in the hotel, for parties. The price was about $30. The windows, then as now, looked out toward Aspen Mountain and over the glittering town which in memory was always white with snow. In those days the Jerome bar was the chief gathering place. You could ski to it right down the streets from the bottom of the mountain, and from the closing of the lifts until past midnight everyone was there or had been. One beautiful woman—the town then held only a recognized handful of them—was said to have picked up a different man there to take home every night.

No conventions or groups came to Aspen then, nothing larger than a family or two unless it was the gathering of business executives that came every other week to seminars at the Aspen Institute. Skiing was not still in its infancy but certainly in its careless youth, the days when one stuck skis in the snow at the bottom of the lift before it opened to mark a place in line and then went off to breakfast, days before double black diamonds though the runs were the same.

As a boy, a true city boy in days when one traveled by rail and the great coast-to-coast meteors had a barbershop and chefs who prepared real food, I never heard of skiing. I first encountered it in Europe about ten years after the war. It was winter and Europe was still poor but the sheets in the hotels were crisp and freshly laundered. Perhaps it was this first experience that somehow made winter and cold essential factors.

I like to ski in snowstorms and on icy days. I like snow-laden boughs and a silence that seems like that of the North. It's true one sees them skiing by on spring days in bikinis and shorts and going up in snowmobiles to steep, remote bowls in May and June—I have gone up myself after the lifts have closed for the season, climbing on mountain skis for hours and coming down, the snow wetter and wetter, in much shorter time, but to me this all seems somehow larky. For me the real days of skiing begin when summer is long gone.

There is something called the true life which I cannot describe and which perhaps varies as one sees it from different angles and at different times. At one point it is travel, at another a certain woman, at another a house somewhere with a view you will worship till you die. It is a life apart from money and to the side of ambition, a life lived in one way or another for beauty. It does not last indefinitely, but the survivors are usually not poorer for it. There was a woman in Aspen who one day confronted an old, conservative judge on the street and told him, "I've been married five times, I've run whore-houses, I've been all over the world. I'm not like you. I've lived." Perhaps that cannot be classified precisely as the true life, but something in the boast is the same.

There was a true life in the mountains around Aspen—the girl who lived year-round in a teepee up past Lenado with a white horse in the meadow and her little child, others who had cabins or old houses, new-age people never to be old. There was a true life and though diminishing it exists still, the sky dark with autumn, the wind beginning to blow, the homeless bees wandering around the shacks being insulated, alighting desperately on clothing, a dry flower, a bit of sage. Winter is coming. There will be no survivors.

Skiing all day, with someone you like, riding up together, drinking the light. Runs at the top of which you could murmur *And gen-*

*tlemen in England, now abed shall think themselves accurs'd they were not
here, and hold their manhoods cheap . . .*

Billy Kidd once listed his favorites in the West, the hardest ones.
Many were only names to me, though not Elevator Shaft or the
Ridge of Bell, which are both in Aspen, or White Out in Steam-
boat Springs, or Prima in Vail. He left out, I don't know why, the
long ones in Telluride—Spiral Staircase and the Plunge, at the top
of which, late in the day, the local desperadoes, male and female,
gather for the last descent. In the ski shop at the bottom one day I
overheard a girl talking about Spider Sabich and his being shot to
death in Aspen the day before. We listened to the evening news as
one does in wartime. It was true.

Sabich was admirable, both in character and appearance. I never
skied with him, of course—he was a professional champion, the
first real one—but I saw him occasionally on friendly terms. He was
killed in a lovers' quarrel, a crime of passion, and missed the second
half of what would have been an enviable life. It was impossible to
imagine him as ex-anything, a has-been—he was too confident and
personable for that.

So, winter with its snow, the ground all white. In the house across
the street a woman in a bathrobe opens the balcony doors, brushes
some snow from the railing, and looks toward the mountain before
stepping back into the warmth of the room. It's barely eight o'clock,
there is time for coffee, to dress. The bed will go unmade. She will
carry her skis to the gondola, the entire world of fresh snow above.
Nothing is more thrilling than a talented girl skiing—boldness, grace,
speed.

Morning. From another house, a large one, bursts a yellow Labrador followed by a black one and then a young boy who walks
them every morning, hands in pockets, long trailing ski cap on his
head. There was a time when all the license plates of town began

with ZG, and when the dogs were more or less citizens and everyone knew to whom they belonged.

I remember the day that Tim Howe, at one time in his life a marine biologist but for far longer a veteran figure of the ski patrol, went up the steps of the courthouse in the uncharacteristic outfit of blazer and tie to defend his dog against the charge of running loose. The dog, a handsome old black Labrador wearing a bandanna around his neck, was arthritic and nearly blind. He had to be carried into the courtroom.

He had lived all his life accustomed to freedom, his owner pleaded, it had been his birthright, and it was inhumane to expect him now to be attached to a leash.

The charge sheet read that the police had to chase him for six blocks. Was this correct, the judge asked? Yes, sir. "It doesn't speak well for the fleetness of the force," the judge observed. "Mr. Howe," he then said, "you have to understand that Aspen has changed—it's no longer a place where dogs can sit in the middle of the street or run free."

I forget the outcome; perhaps there was a fine. One might claim it was the sale of the Aspen Ski Corporation to non-skiing billionaires, or the advent of Hollywood stars at Christmas, or the construction of the huge Ritz-Carlton Hotel, but in my memory it was the trial of Spade, Tim Howe's distinguished old dog, that marked the vanishing of the old queen and the coronation of the new.

Rocky Mountain Magazine
1994

They Call It Paradise

From the air, the first view comes after forty minutes of flying over the rugged mountain country west of Denver: forests, snowy peaks, lost blue lakes, and only the rarest glimpse of habitation. Suddenly, there is the town. It lies in an irregular valley and seems quite small, as if it would fit in the palm of one's hand. In the winter, ski runs plunge down the slopes above the town like broad mountain roads. In the summer, the large ranches seem to speak of plentiful land. As you get closer, you can make out houses clustered on the lower slopes.

The drive from the airport into Aspen leads past grazing horses and lodges set at the edges of meadows. There are buses, pickups, bicycles, people running. A certain giddiness begins to take hold, and it is not attributable to the simple fact of having arrived at your destination after a heroic journey. Aspen is 8,000 feet above sea level, an altitude at which dogs do not have fleas. It is considerably higher than similar resorts in the Alps, and being short of breath, especially for the first few days, is not unusual. The climate is also extremely dry, which contributes to the fine quality of the snow but has an alarming effect on the skin. The effect is the reverse of that in Shangri-La—here one dries out on arrival and suddenly feels like the Grand Lama, 600 years old.

Main Street is long and very wide, with many Victorian houses and a few surviving majestic trees. Toward one end is the downtown area, four or five blocks square. Here, new buildings are mixed with the old; by law, none of them stands more than four stories high. There are restaurants, shops, bars, and bookstores. Some of these businesses are temporary, some well established. Anything ten years old in Aspen is old. Anything twenty years old is a tradition. There's a pleasant, easygoing feeling everywhere. The crowds on the streets are made up of some people who are obviously tourists, some who seem to know their way around, and others who clearly belong; the dividing line between these last two groups is vague. Galena, Durant, Mill—the names of the streets come from the mining days. Above the town, surrounding it, are mythic forests, mountains, and streams, readily accessible and open to anyone with a pair of hiking boots.

"How long have you been in Aspen?" Saul Bellow, who visited occasionally during the '70s, once asked a beautiful resident.

"Oh, a long time," she said. "I couldn't think of living anywhere else."

"After five years, you can't leave," someone explained.

"It's like the Magic Mountain without TB," Bellow said bemusedly. He was never completely taken in by the town; he more or less saw through it. "These young people," he observed, "you can see it in their faces—the meaning of existence is themselves."

Aspen is the chief bauble of American resorts, combining luxury and simplicity, the ephemeral and the enduring, in a spectacular way. Like Paris, Aspen is a city of light, gaiety, generally civilized behavior, and agreeable streets. It is thought of as a sexual paradise, and in fact there is a vast array of available partners of both sexes, for the most part with enviable tans. There are beautiful shops and extraordinary apartments and houses tucked away in places one would never expect. There are cinemas, museums, and art galleries.

There is no "society" in Aspen, no old and distinguished families. The rich who arrived early and the large landowners occupy a certain special position, but the rest is pure democracy. Everyone is on a first-name basis. The girl helping at a dinner party is as likely as not to be dating one of the guests.

Good looks and a hint of background can take one far. Aspen isn't unconquerable; even the clever locals can be fooled. A store owner I know once saw a particularly good-looking couple come in. They were dressed in western clothes—not the kind you buy in Bloomingdale's but the authentic clothing of people who own a ranch. The man, who was tall, was wearing a magnificent weathered Stetson.

"Where did you get your hat?" the storeowner asked.

"My hat? In New York," the man replied.

"You're not from New York, though?"

"Yes."

"But your hat," the storeowner protested. "Your hat looks so real. I was sure you were from Montana. That stain . . ."

The man took off his hat and looked at it.

"Oh, that," he said. "That's béarnaise."

Aspen was virtually a ghost town when a Chicago businessman named Walter Paepcke drove by to have a look in 1945. What he saw were the beautiful bones of what had once been a thriving silver-mining town. Everything perishable had wasted away, and only the skeleton remained. All around were mountains and forests of incredible splendor. A river, the Roaring Fork, flowed past scenes of haunting desolation, empty meadows, broken streets. And yet it was, as an Aspen carpenter I knew once said of his old saw, "better wore-out than another was new."

Paepcke brought Aspen back to life. European in his taste, his ideas leaned toward quality rather than size. He had a vision for the weary town—one in which the unrecognized beauty would be made whole again and preserved. For almost fifteen years, until Paepcke died in 1960, Aspen developed largely according to these ideals. It remained small in scale and aristocratically unstylish. The agreement now is that these were the golden years.

Paepcke encouraged his friends and acquaintances to buy houses and fix them up, and he bought a good deal of property himself—though not for speculative reasons. He then came up with an ingenious idea to put the town back on the map. The two-hundredth anniversary of Goethe's birth was in 1949, and the authorities in Frankfurt were somehow persuaded by Paepcke (who was of German descent) that the bicentennial celebration should be held in Colorado, in a remote spot that had been Indian wilderness when Goethe was born. Celebrities such as John Marquand, Gary Cooper, and Norman Cousins were already frequent visitors, and now Thornton Wilder, Arthur Rubinstein, Ortega y Gasset, Gregor Piatigorsky, and the Minneapolis Symphony Orchestra came to Aspen. Albert Schweitzer—it was his only visit to America—gave the dedication address. A tone was established that somehow endures. Today, for all the town's swinging dentists and gilded youth, there are still Nobel Prize–winning physicists and great musicians playing tennis, having lunch on the mall and hiking the trails.

In addition to the people Paepcke first brought in, there were others who somehow heard about Aspen, came, and stayed. Some had been members of the 10th Mountain Division, which had trained in Colorado at Camp Hale during the war. Others were the black sheep of prominent families, forever on the prowl for new haunts. There were young people, eccentrics, and talented unknowns. For a long time, Aspen was a kind of "in" secret, a refuge too perfect to be spoiled, and those who moved there were aware of their good fortune.

"It had everything I was really looking for," says Andre Ulrych, who came to Aspen in 1968. He had been designing and building houses in the East. "It had a small-town quality without a small-town mentality. An interesting mix of people. Then there was the natural beauty of the place and the climate."

Ulrych taught skiing for several years, opened a successful restaurant with his wife, and afterward launched the most elegant disco in town. He doesn't seem like the owner of a gin mill. Born in Warsaw, where his father was a government minister, Ulrych has a degree in architecture from the University of London, good manners, and clear blue Polish eyes.

Andre's, as Ulrych's establishment is called, occupies an old restored building in the middle of town and has become the summit of Aspen nightlife. On the first two floors are the restaurant and bar, on the third is the discotheque. In a long room pulsing with strobe lights and roaring with sound, a gala goes on every night. Along the wall are deep sofas and chairs piled with fur coats and parkas; in the morning, packets of white powder are occasionally found between the cushions. There are beards above white turtlenecks, long hair, warm smiles exchanged beneath cowboy hats. In the beginning Ulrych sold memberships, and there was the impression that the club was exclusive, an answer to the desire of some residents for the kind of establishment one finds in St. Moritz—luxurious, private, and a natural resting place for Viva clones and young women who like to travel in private jets. In fact, Andre's is open to everyone for a small fee. The liveliness increases as the evening wears on, and toward midnight the town's waiters and sommeliers, finished with work, begin to show up at the bar to see who's new. At 2:00 AM. everything closes, and almost anyone can go home with somebody. This is called the two o'clock shuffle, and last-minute consultations can be seen on every corner when the dance halls and bars empty out.

Strangely, all this success strikes a melancholy note in Ulrych. "I see this town going completely crazy now," he says. "The people we all knew years ago who were into a certain kind of lifestyle can't afford to live here anymore. There are so many people coming in, especially in the winter.

"I see an incredible degeneration in the human race in this country," Ulrych says sadly.

The owner of the Jerome Bar, a popular establishment three blocks away, has a more positive view of things. Michael Solheim, like everyone in town, comes from somewhere else—in this case Chicago. Good-natured, sleek, he was running an espresso house in Sun Valley when he met the then mayor of Aspen, who took a liking to him. "I'm the mayor," he informed Solheim. "The city has a lease on the Jerome Hotel, and you can run the bar."

It wasn't to be quite that easy. Solheim did in fact come to Aspen, but he had to run a paint and wallpaper company for five years before he could convince the new owner of the Jerome, who had bought the hotel in the meantime, that he could turn "a badly lit room full of African spears and winos" into a successful bar. Solheim finally took over in 1972, redecorated the interior in the style of fashionable San Francisco bars he admired, and met with immediate success.

The Jerome Hotel is one of the landmarks of the town. A massive brick structure, it was built in 1889 at the height of the silver boom. Never seriously modernized, it remains one of the most interesting places to stay in Aspen. The food in the bar is nothing exceptional, and the most popular drink is white wine ("We'll go weeks without making a martini," Solheim says), but there is the spirit of the place: it is pure Aspen. People have been known to ride through the door on horses. "Of course, there's no sign saying that's specifically prohibited," Solheim allows.

The clientele tends to be young and dazzling, with a few nostalgic men of forty thrown in. It seems as if the casts of several hit movies as well as characters from the pages of *Vogue* and *Interview* have been spilled over the tables and chairs of the two rooms. As with all such places, one section is more desirable; at the Jerome it's the front, where the bar is located. Normally, you can't get a seat there after five in the afternoon.

The bar's success is due in part to its reputation as a hangout for Aspen's most notorious figure, gonzo journalist Hunter Thompson. Thompson lives in a secluded valley about ten miles from town and usually shows up late in the day or in the evening, sometimes during the last quarter of a football game. He was once a sports columnist, and his interest in such matters has not diminished. He usually stations himself near the coffee maker and television at the end of the bar; when irritated by the game or by life in general, he will throw food or drink at the screen. Thompson does leave his mark, but as Solheim comments philosophically, "A high-pressure hose gets rid of most of it."

There are only two seasons in Aspen—winter and summer. The winter is bigger; more money is spent then. Skiing begins in early December, depending on the amount of snow and the number of tourists expected. It is great skiing, as good as any in the world. Aspen doesn't get huge amounts of snow, but it always seems to get enough—and the snow is wonderful, often so squeaky and cold that skiing on it is like gliding on velvet. There are at least 300 miles of trails on four principal mountains: Ajax (as the locals call Aspen Mountain), Highlands, Buttermilk, and Snowmass. There are some difficult runs, but most of the skiing is exciting, not frightening. The views alone, the vast panoramas of blue peaks in brilliant sunlight, are worth the price of a too-expensive room or condominium and the long waits in restaurants and supermarkets.

The winter ends in Aspen on the day the lifts close. There is often still plenty of snow and—because spring storms are frequent—sometimes some of the coldest, purest skiing of the season. But around Easter Sunday, on a date that the lift owners have decided on long in advance, everything stops. The curtain descends. It is as if the town breathes a sigh and collapses. For weeks afterward, it is like a beautiful house the morning after an unforgettable party.

There is a vast exodus of all those who have worked feverishly since November—ski instructors, restaurant help, maids. They trade

one paradise for another, heading for Hawaii or the beaches of
Mexico.

One of the last of the ski bums, his thirties drawing to a close,
sits in the sauna after the final day. On his face is the imprint of
nothing but pleasurable years. His knees are gone, he says. They can
only take so much, so many bumps, no matter how strong they are.
When they're gone, the veterans agree, that's it. He's heading for
California, the fading champion says. He's going to Esalen. He wants
to find his true center before it's too late.

For a few months in spring, Aspen is virtually closed. In the old
days, in the '60s, it was a time of never-ending mud, as the spring
thaw turned the unpaved streets into quagmires. Now, it is merely
a mournful time of watching the snow vanish week by week from
runs whose very names recently had the icy feel of terror: Cork-
screw, Lower Stein, Franklin Dump. They are slowly becoming
naked and harmless, covered in the end, like battlefields, with green.

The other season, summer, begins in June with the International
Design Conference. The restaurants reopen; there is a feeling of
awakening. Although nights can still be very cold at this time of
year, the real crowds have not yet arrived, and there is a certain
sense of privilege—something of the feeling that existed in the '50s
and '60s, the feeling that made people fall in love with the town.
The huge cottonwoods are smudged with green. Independence Pass,
over which the original settlers came, is white with snow in the
distance. The pass is 12,000 feet high; there are snowfields almost
year-round, and the air is so thin it seems metallic. A narrow,
breathtaking road crosses the pass and is usually open from June
through October, depending on the weather.

The real activity of the summer, beginning in late June, is music.
Since 1949, the Aspen Music Festival has featured some of the world's
greatest artists—Penderecki, Britten, Perlman, Zuckerman, Milhaud.
The concerts take place in a large tent in a meadow surrounded by

beautiful views and million-dollar houses. There is a music school with 900 students, master classes, operas, and string quartets. Students perform at outside restaurants and on the mall, and for two months Aspen comes close to the dream that was Paepcke's.

In addition to the music there is ballet—Ballet West comes from its Salt Lake City home every year—the Physics Center (a serious convocation of physicists that goes on throughout the summer), and various activities of the Aspen Institute. The Institute was created by Paepcke as the intellectual arm of his spa, aimed at exposing successful men to great ideas. Executives who have read little of importance since college days undertake two weeks of Aristotle, Adam Smith, John Stuart Mill, and the like, discussing what they read in seminars. After Paepcke's death the Institute drifted, if not exactly to the right at least into the arms of the establishment, where it is now virtually indistinguishable from other foundations closely connected with government and business. Its present offices are in New York, and Aspen is only its bohemian grove—one of the places where the many problems facing us in these chaotic times are discussed and predictable reports are written up afterward.

I once sat on a terrace overlooking Hallam Lake, a small nature preserve near the Institute, with one of the visitors who had risen high in the world. It was late in the afternoon. The lake was silvery. Swallows darted in the air. Over the leafy town fell a perfect, clear light.

"Let's go in," he said.

"What's wrong?"

"Nature upsets me," he said.

The last concerts are at the end of August. Unlike the winter, summer drifts slowly to an end. There are still white-clad figures on the tennis courts, and on the bulletin board outside a restaurant called The Shaft flutter slips of paper placed by people urgently seeking housing or selling climbing boots and skis, as well as by those making proposals of a more striking nature:

Two girls heading to Minneapolis end of August. Need ride. Will
trade ass for gas.

The leaves begin to turn. The sky is a deeper blue. The tree for
which the town is named (Aspen was originally called Ute City) has
small, shimmering leaves and a whitish trunk like a birch. In some
places it is called the trembling poplar. Chaucer and Pliny wrote of
it, and there is a legend that the original Cross was made of it. The
bark was once used as medicine. About the first week in October,
the vast groves on the mountainsides become gold overnight. In a
last sweep of color, the summer is gone.

America's oldest cities date back only to the seventeenth century, and some of the largest merely to the nineteenth. An entire
growth—and in some instances decline—has taken place in the
wink of an eye. In less than a century, Aspen already has a buried past: an old town covered by a new one, and beneath that still
another layer—there are mining tunnels everywhere under the
present city, abandoned vessels of bewildering scale. A little way up
Ajax is the entrance to the old Durant mine. You can still enter and
walk into the chilly depths of another realm, into absolute darkness where shafts soar toward an unknown surface and tunnel walls
have collapsed to reveal galleries large enough for the Jerome Hotel
to disappear in. All this, all the lives devoted to it and the wealth it
brought forth, is forgotten. Beneath the modern town is a Homeric
ruin, and though it is invisible, it has an influence and provides a
quality that other places do not have: the sense of having been built
on something other than the pursuit of pleasure—on something of
consequence. Without this submerged order, Aspen would be like
Snowbird or Vail, both of which are pleasant but made-up. They
lack the authenticity that Aspen, for all its foolishness, still possesses.
Yet the town seems to have rapidly traveled the path that leads,

in the case of resorts, from discovery by an adventurous few to full-fledged ownership by the rich and prosperous. Some of the early people were well-off, but they were part of the jaunty days of an unconventional era. A number of them, not much older-looking, are still around thirty years later, burnished by the sun and preserved by years of fresh air. But just as there are two theaters, the one the audience sees and the one backstage, so there are two Aspens—the one in plain sight and the invisible one withheld from the visitor. What happened over the years was that certain members of the original cast, far from being content with the beauty of an ideal life, started buying up the theater. When the great land boom began in the early '70s, the ambitious had stockpiled real estate, and the dreamers, tinkerers, and exiles drifted away to Santa Barbara or New Mexico.

From glorious, primitive winters and shared communal joy, Aspen turned into real-estate offices and boutiques. Dogs once sat serenely in the middle of the street. Now they are on leashes, and the hip young cops drive blue Saabs. Not that there is crime here. One can sleep sweetly and in peace. A certain amount of thievery and housebreaking goes on, of course, unlike the days when doors were never locked. But there are virtually no crimes against the person; the last murder occurred five years ago and was attributed to a maniac, Theodore Bundy. Bundy is alleged to have killed a young woman in Snowmass, a satellite resort about ten miles from Aspen, and to have dumped her naked body in the snow along a road. The case was never tried, Bundy having first thrilled the town by jumping from the second-story window of the courthouse—he had been left unguarded to look something up in the legal library—and disappearing on the streets in broad daylight. The radio warned people to lock their doors and windows, but as it turned out, the fugitive had no interest in disturbing anyone and wandered about miserably in the woods for several days before he was recaptured trying to leave the valley in a stolen car. On his second escape attempt, he fled to Florida, where he was tried and convicted for a series of murders he committed there.

The county sheriff, Dick Kienast, was embarrassed by the escapes but regained his dignity among the locals by taking a strong stand against the ways in which drug laws are enforced. His position, reported with zeal by the national press, was that most drug use, at least in Aspen, takes place in homes. He came down on the side of privacy, refusing to cooperate with federal agencies and even facing a grand jury as a result.

There are reasons to believe that a significant amount of cocaine—or Bolivian marching powder, as it is affectionately called in Aspen—is passed around. There is a general understanding within sophisticated circles in cities like New York, Los Angeles, and Dallas that Aspen is a place where good times can be had, in the modern sense of the term.

Jane Smith and Susan Olsen own a shop called Heaven next to the ancient brick building that houses the Isis, Aspen's oldest movie house. They are right out of an updated *Gentlemen Prefer Blondes*—sassy, warm-blooded, and wise. In Heaven one can find chic clothes, unusual and expensive: jackets woven from silk and Samoyed hair, suede chaps as erotic as spike-heeled shoes, leather belts for $250, skimpy tops and fur coats of coyote or Japanese raccoon.

They opened their shop two years ago, although Jane has been in Aspen for ten years and has already owned or managed three similar places. Jane is the brunette—beautiful facial bones, dark eyes, and dazzling smile. She was born in Alabama and studied interior design in college. Every year she goes on a six-day juice fast (two hour-long massages a day, an enema, and plenty of juice) under the supervision of "an old lady who comes up from Florida." "I had a friend who kept saying, 'You'll love Aspen,'" she says, "and I did." She was in her early twenties at the time. She started a clothes shop, ran it for a while, and then started another one, called 20th Century Fox.

The name Heaven was inspired by a girl friend who always said, talking about Aspen, "Here in heaven . . ." The clientele includes

Cher, Anjelica Huston, and Tatum O'Neal—as well as a lot of wealthy Mexicans and South Americans. The shop has been doing well. "But I think it's a tough town for a girl," Susan Olsen says. She is a stunning Californian with a contemptuous mouth, the sort of woman men would give anything to possess. You see her on the street, long-legged and golden, and think she cannot have a care in the world. "It's tough to make ends meet," she says. "It's hard to find a niche in this town and make some money. It's very unstable. A lot of people go through a lot of problems. They get caught up in the fast life. It's too casual. Guys take advantage of women here."

The myth dies hard. There are those haunting visions of a unique happiness. Meanwhile they drive, they fly, they come over the mountains in blizzards and storms. The drive from Denver is four to five hours long—but it can take days. Getting to Aspen is part of the legend.

Still, it is there: the steep blue mountains, the wood fires, the trees bearing fresh snow—like a mistress, in Browning's words, with great, smooth, marbly limbs. Morning comes. The river is covered with ice. There are occasional breaks in it, fissures that run in the direction of the current like wounds. The water is black, but the trout are surviving the cold. Not half a mile from town are animal tracks in the snow leading down to the bank. A few miles farther and you are in the wilderness, in a world without men. Here you can breathe, see the country as it was, as it will be forever. Here in heaven.

Geo
November 1981

Snowy Nights in Aspen

In those days we got dining room chairs, as well as other items, from the dump. This was in Aspen. The grocery store was in the basement of the opera house and ran charge accounts. Houses, most of them from the mining days, were selling for five figures.

It was the 1960s. The town still had a vague air of destitution and most streets were unpaved. It was a ski town, a kind of legend even then. I had a house near the Meadows with two bedrooms and a small brick basement, the bricks unmortared. In the winter the snow came down, almost horizontal as it swept past the windows, heavy and white, unending, like silent applause. In the fireplace, logs, which in early autumn we had virtuously cut and split, were burning with a furious sound. It's hard to think of a feeling of greater well-being: storm without, fire within. What was going on in the rest of the world? It little mattered. The porch was buried in snow, the skis leaning against the wall. People were coming to dinner.

It seems, looking back, to have been the dinners. They were countless. Friends, and sometimes their friends, people from out of town, people met skiing. There were dinners when the candlesticks fell over on the sideboard and the frame of the mirror caught fire.

Nobody noticed until flames were running up the wall. There were triumphant dinners and dinners that were simply disasters, when the meat was like cardboard and Gordon Forbes's passionate daughter threw it on the floor—by unfortunate coincidence the potatoes were underdone that night.

There were dinners when marvelous things were said, confessions and opinions that would never have come forth but for the company and the wine, and dinners when guests, in need of a little fresh air, went out and were discovered, after an hour, sleeping on the woodpile.

Somewhere along the way we began to jot down a few lines as a reminder of who had been there and what was served, mainly to avoid repeating the menu, and over time there crept in brief comments, a record, like notes one might make in the margin of a book.

Thus were created The Annals, Robin Fox dramatically reciting Swinburne, Lorenzo unexpectedly appearing, as if at the opera, in a fur-collared coat—that was the night when the exotic-looking wife of a painter was the sexual star of the evening. She had high cheekbones and arched eyebrows. She had been to France, she said—it seemed to have a special meaning.

Leafing through the notebook in which all this was written, one comes across loose pages and others that are water- or wine-stained, difficult to make out. But there is also a strange feeling, almost of accomplishment, in thinking of bygone evenings—no matter what else, life has been lived. Names I have forgotten are there, and others I simply don't recognize. "Four bottles of Bordeaux," is one succinct entry and beneath it, "Spaghetti carbonara like glue." There were five at the table that night, and the couple later got divorced. It happened in an odd way. The husband had had a long affair which he knew his wife was aware of and was causing her unhappiness. He was very fond of his mistress but decided the marriage came first and one day announced to his wife that it was over.

"What's over?" she said.

"Me and Maya."

"You and who?" his wife said.

Many nights, apparently, there was poker, not the grown-up kind but congenial games, the value of hands sometimes written out for women who had never played or who had forgotten. "The Judge was losing and left early," is an entry. He eventually left town as well, but the memory of him is vivid. He was squire-like and cordial, but could be abrupt and unyielding. In younger days he'd once jumped from a window to end it all, in love and rejected, but the window was only on the second floor.

On another evening advances of more chips from the bank were being written for convenience on the label of a bottle of wine. Tom Hubbard had been losing and several times he, as well as other players, had replenished their chips. Weary and having lost yet another pot, he inquired plaintively, "Is there any room left on the wine bottle?"

There is someone's unattributed description of the sensuous life in Cuba before Fidel. Perhaps we were smoking cigars. "In Havana," it reads, "the woman takes the cigar in her palms and warms it over a lamp. Then she dips it in a decanter of dark rum and rolls it again. Then she puts the end in the flame of the lamp. The man takes two puffs . . ." I try to imagine who was delivering this alluring account. Was it Abigail, Portia, Krista-all—names I cannot attach a person to—or the orchestra conductor or former lieutenant governor? Nor can I identify the minister on the evening when there was written only, "Man of God got drunk." Irene was there that night. She was young and from the South, attractive to both sexes and with the most knowing smile imaginable. She'd been married once briefly, to a man named Thorndike. The reception, she liked to say, lasted longer than the marriage.

Did we ski the next day? There is no telling. In my memory it is more often after a day of skiing, filled with that matchless, almost lightheaded exhaustion, that we sat down to dinner. The talk was of runs and gear, of the snow on Powderhorn that was more perfect than it had ever been. The temperature was just right, cold, about twenty degrees, and no one had been down it; the tracks we made were a declaration of happiness.

I wonder why, unrelated to anything else, I find Joe Fox's six rules for being the ideal weekend guest. Fox was a senior editor at Random House. He had been the editor for a book of mine but more notably had edited Truman Capote, Philip Roth, and Peter Matthiessen as well as others. A Philadelphian through many generations, he had certainly been to great houses. From that February evening, there are these unexplained but most likely unimpeachable rules: 1) Never arrive too early 2) Bring a gift the hostess will love 3) Stay to yourself for at least three hours a day 4) Play all their games 5) Don't sleep in the wrong bed 6) Leave on time.

The days of winter and skiing are perfect days. If asked to explain why, I can only say, somewhat helplessly, because one loves them. The fire in the evening, the fatigue and ease, the lack of guilt at having spent the day in no more than pursuit of pleasure, and finally the warm, convivial dinner. Abbodanza. If leaders of enemy peoples could ski together, much hardship could be avoided.

One night just after Christmas someone brought a houseguest, a young Japanese. He was probably perplexed by the customs but being, as it turned out, the son of a former prime minister of Japan, he was both socially adept and polite. He sent a thank-you letter which still hangs, framed, on the wall in the kitchen. Somewhat faded, it reads, "It was very nice to know you. Thank you very much for inviting me for a great dinner. I enjoyed your cocking very much." The slight misspelling which makes the letter a classic is the writer's. Courtie Barnes, who read it a few weeks later, remarked admiringly, "Incredible we could have gone to war against such a charming people."

In the beautiful winter, on snowy nights, the people are all like that.

Colorado Ski Country USA
1997–98

Notes from Another Aspen

Well, it all depends what you mean by the old days. For people like Tom Sardy and Judge Shaw, who were prominent figures in town when I came for the first time in 1959, the old days were when you could buy a house and lot in the West End for $25, including all the furnishings. Judge Shaw used to buy them for even less, for unpaid back taxes which were pennies. When I arrived houses were selling for $10,000 to $20,000. Now they're probably even more.

Judge Shaw was a chain-smoker and breathed with a wheeze. He persisted in calling Tam Scott, who is now a judge, "Cam," despite respectful correction, and lived with his wife in a large house at the east end of Triangle Park, which has since passed into more-renowned hands. Land Rovers, in fact, were not even invented when the judge was around. Sushi was unknown. My lasting image of the Shaw house was after his widow's death. The mattresses were pushed out of the window and slit open in a search for gold coins thought to be in abundance, I suppose.

One of the early magnates of the present, or skiing, era was Ed Brennan, who paved the way for Gerald Hines and Mohamed What's-his-name who built the Ritz. The Ritz back then, of course, was the Jerome. Except for the post office and a café or two it was the center of everything. The fire siren was mounted on the roof and I believe the hotel had the only switchboard in town. When the siren went off the firemen had to drive by the hotel and ask where the fire was. The Jerome bar was the bar. Everyone skied all the way down to it at the end of the day and not infrequently made arrangements for the evening. Later at night there might be an invitation to go upstairs, which was like going to a badly maintained fraternity house room, but drunk with love, who cared?

The great days of the Jerome bar, most of them under the reign of Mike Solheim, seem now to have been the heart of a long democratic period, the 1960s and '70s, when the rich and poor of town, so to speak, rubbed shoulders and were on cordial terms. The bar even served as campaign headquarters when Aspen politics were, unfathomably, of national interest, and Steve Wishart, at one time a Jerome bartender though barely tall enough to see the customers, once ran for the city council more or less from the bar. The night of the election it was packed, and when the returns came over the radio, Wishart had won! He was standing on the bar with a bottle in each hand, and with a shout of triumph dove off into the crowd. Fortunately, they caught him, and as he was set upon his feet he said, "I just wanted to see who my real supporters were."

To return to Ed Brennan, however, when I first came to Aspen he blanketed the town. Whichever way things went, he was prepared. There was Ed's Beds, his low-end lodge; Ed's Express, which inspired FedEx; and Trader Ed's, which exists in a haze of memory as being where the Hyman Avenue Mall is now, with papier-mâché palm trees and local wahines in grass skirts, very authentic. There were no moral guardians in those days, and the annual wet T-shirt contest, perhaps one should say pageant, at the Red Onion was more popular than the Super Bowl.

My first memory of skiing in Aspen is lying on my back at the bottom of Spar Gulch, due to some faulty snow, and averting my face as a glamorous couple I knew slightly came past with an instructor. I didn't want to be recognized and they probably would have taken pains not to recognize me, and one of us had to do something. I had a broken arm, though not as a result of the fall—I'd broken it on Main Street the night before and it had been set and put in a cast by one of the town's two doctors. The bill must have been $25 or so.

A few years later I was given a pair of Graves skis. I skied on them for four or five seasons. They were made of some indestructible material or put together in a unique way and were guaranteed for life. The company, naturally, went out of business. The skis were a dark maroon with the name in bold white letters. In the lift line people always noticed them. "Graves," they would say, "who makes them?" I didn't know. To one persistent questioner I said, "The same company that makes Bayer aspirin." But I liked the skis. They carved well and I was counting on the guarantee, but they eventually delaminated.

Aspen is now a resort. It wasn't always; it was a ski town, hard to get to and the best in the country. The streets weren't even paved. In the fall there was mud, in the spring mud and dust. Eisenhower was president, practicing putting in the Oval Office. I wasn't impressed by him but I didn't know what would come later. I don't remember how we first got here; I think it was by train and someone picked us up in Glenwood.

Aspen Airways was in its infancy, to say the least. There was only one plane, later a few. Early models carried five passengers, one of them in the copilot's seat. Later models had metal patches that seemed suspiciously like bullet holes, and the "No Smoking" signs were in Spanish.

Back then, traffic was a problem only twice a year when 10,000 sheep walked through town on their way to or from high ground, as it was called, though I never found out where this actually was. The sheep filled Main Street almost from one end to the other, and are probably still talking about how the town was in the old days, if they're like everyone else.

Aspen Magazine
Winter 1996–97

Writing and What's Ahead

Once Upon a Time, Literature. Now What?

The first great task in life, by far the most important one, the one on which everything else depends, can be described in three words. Very simply, it is learning to speak. Language—whatever language, English, Swahili, Japanese—is the requisite for the human condition. Without it there is nothing. There is the beauty of the world and the beauty of existence, or the sorrow if you like, but without language they are inexpressible.

Animals are our companions, but they cannot, in any comparable sense, speak. They do not have, even the most majestic or intelligent of them—whales, elephants, lions—a God. In whatever form, our apprehension and worship of God is entirely dependent on language: prayers, sermons, hymns, the Bible or other text. Without language God might exist but could not be described.

In the richness of language, its grace, breadth, dexterity, lies its power. To speak with clarity, brevity, and wit is like holding a lightning rod. We are drawn to people who know things and are able to express them: Dr. Johnson, Shakespeare. Language like theirs sets the tone, the language of poets, of heroes. A certain level of life, an impregnable level, belongs to them.

There is not just one language, however. There are two, the spoken and the written. The spoken is like breath, effortless and at hand. The written is another matter. Learning to read and write is a difficult business, the second portal. Once through it, you are into the open, as it were, the endless vistas. The biblios is there for you. I made up the word. It means library, archive, vast collection. A made-up word here or there is not much. Shakespeare made up nearly one in twelve of the more than 20,000 he used overall; at least no previous use of them is known. The King James Bible by comparison contains only some 8,000 different words.

In the biblios are books, manuscripts, newspapers, printouts of Web sites, letters, all manner of things. The books are the most important. It is from reading them that one gets the urge to be a writer, or so it used to be. The first book that I believe I read in its entirety and on my own was *All Quiet on the Western Front*. I can't say that reading it made me want to be a writer, or that I became an avid reader, but the confidence and simplicity of the prose made a deep impression.

I remember lines from it even today. Sixty years have passed. I later heard that Erich Maria Remarque had been the editor of a German fashion magazine and decided to quit his job and write a novel. You're crazy, they told him. But the issues of *Die Dame*, or whatever it was, the lunches and dinners and perhaps the models have all disappeared, but not the novel.

I understood, of course—it was dogma—that a true education was based on being well read, and for ten years or more I read all I could. These were wonderful years of voyage, discovery, and self-esteem. I would never catch up with those for whom reading was a passion, but I had climbed high.

I read less now. Perhaps it's loss of appetite. I read fewer books—reading is a pleasure, and I'm supposed to be working—but I am not less interested in them. They have not moved from their central position in my life.

At one time I thought frequently about death. It was when I was barely thirty and said to myself, "More than a third of your life is gone!" Now, for a different reason, I have started to think about it again. I like the image of the ancients, the crossing of a river. Sometimes I think of what, when the time comes, I might want to have with me. I can go without an expensive watch, without money or clothes, without a toothbrush, without having shaved, but can I go without certain books and, more than books, things I have written, not necessarily published?

The other day I was reading an essay by Deborah Eisenberg, a writer I have never met, called "Resistance." Very well written, it brought to mind the lucidity and aplomb of Virginia Woolf. The subject of the essay was writing, and I came, midway, to a sentence that ended, "part of the same disaster that has placed virtually every demanding or complex literary experience beyond our culture's confines."

I stopped there. I was unable to go on until I had sorted out a number of thoughts that had been aroused. "The same disaster . . ." It brought to mind Kazantzakis's observation that the Apollonian crust of the world had, in modern times, been broken. From somewhere beneath, the Dionysian had poured forth.

Then the last words of the sentence, "our culture's confines." There came the persistent question: What is culture and what has become of ours? The dictionary definition is vague, "the sum total of the attainments and learned behavior patterns of any specific period or people." Let me list instead what I consider the components. I would say culture is language, art, history, and customs.

We know that what is called popular culture has overwhelmed high culture with consequences not yet fully realized. Pop culture's patrons, youth and a large number of those who were formerly young, have rewarded it with immense riches, advancing it further. Junk like George Lucas's *Star Wars* trilogy or quintet becomes the most consuming and widely discussed, sometimes in terms appropriate to masterworks, artistic endeavor. Are we witnessing a mere collapse of taste or the actual genesis of a new myth worthy of replacing the outdated Trojan War or of standing beside it? As with the glorious stock boom, age-old standards of value are henceforth cast aside.

We seem to have seen it already, those of us old enough to remember. It was then called *Flash Gordon*, with similar location and cast, a cruel and omnipotent villain, a beautiful girlfriend of the hero, a wise old counselor, futuristic weapons, spacecraft, distant planets, air armadas. It was only a comic strip then. Schoolboys followed it. In its new form it has become a mine for academics and for those undergraduate courses called film studies.

When I wrote movies, which I did for about fifteen years, thinking of Graham Greene and John Steinbeck, who were writers as well as film writers, I was for a long time unaware of what it all looks like viewed from above, a writer as someone who must be employed preliminary to the real work.

And the balance between what I wrote and what was made was low, about four scripts written for each one shot, with the best work often ending up in the trash. The waste was depressing and also the venal stench that is the perfume of the business. Still, the ascendance of movies is irreversible.

The life-giving novel, like the theater, despite occasional flare-ups, belongs to the past. There is a limited audience. Céline, in an interview in *The Paris Review*, said, "Novels are something like lace . . . an art that went out with the convent." Literature is not dead—students still read Dostoyevsky and Whitman—but it has lost its eminence. The tide is turning against it.

I have heard figures of authority say that the Beatles' songs will be played three hundred years from now, and that Richard Wagner, were he alive today, would be a movie director. Can these things be true? We are not in a position to know, nor can we even be sure which way the great ship is turning.

Only a few things seem certain. The future, as DeLillo put it, belongs to crowds. The megacities, like cancer, have appeared with their great extremes of poverty and wealth, their isolation from what was called the natural world with its rivers, forests, silent dawns, and nights. The new populations will live in hives of concrete on a diet of film, television, and the Internet. We are what we eat. We are also what we see and hear. And we are in the midst of our one and only life.

More and more I am aware of people who are successful in every visible way and who have no sensitivity to art, no interest in history, and are essentially indifferent to language. It's hard to imagine that anything in their experience other than the birth of a child might elicit from them the word *transcendent*; ecstasy for them has a purely physical meaning, and yet they are happy. Culture is not necessary for them although they like to keep up with movies and music and perhaps the occasional best seller. Is culture essential, then? Not pop culture but something higher, something that may endure?

Perhaps not. Whether humankind or nations advance or decline is a matter of unimportance to the planets and what lies beyond. If civilizations reach a new zenith or if they founder is a concern only to us and not really much of a concern since individually we can do so little about it.

At the same time it is frightening to think of a glib, soulless, pop culture world. There is the urge toward things that are not meaningless, that will not vanish completely without leaving the slightest ripple. The corollary to this is the desire to be connected to the life that has gone before, to stand in the ancient places, to hear the undying stories. Art is the real history of nations, it has been said. What we call literature, which is really only writing that never stops being read, is part of this. When it relinquishes its place, what is there to substitute for it?

It was Edwin Arlington Robinson, I think, who when he lay dying asked that his bed be taken out beneath the stars. That's the idea, anyway, not to breathe your last looking at some TV sitcom, but to die in the presence of great things, those riches—the greatest of all riches, in fact—that can be in the reach of anyone.

Writers on Writing, Collected Essays from **The New York Times**
2002

Words' Worth

When a wrecker's ball divides the facade of an old building, or a switch is thrown to ignite efficient charges at its core, you see how the physical work of years can be undone instantly. There's less show to the death of a tradition. It's hard to fix the moment, or sequence of moments, at which breath goes out of it and decay takes hold of the remains. Yet every so often you do get to watch a tradition disappear almost as expeditiously as a blown building. A report in *The Washington Post* in October 1995 describes what has happened to literature in post Soviet Russia. "For more than a century," writes *Post* reporter David Hoffman, "Russian writers occupied a special place in society. Literature was at the forefront of opposition to power, and in the Soviet era totalitarian rulers went to great lengths to bend writers to their will." But writers resisted, risked prison and death, and fought back with words. For their words, their alternative prose visions of the society, there was a vast audience.

Now writers in Russia are free, and the good ones seem not to matter at all. The literary journals essential to cultural life a decade ago barely survive, their sales not a tenth of what they were. Capitalism's triumph has made them beside the point. Television owns the platform now—"Look! Look!" has replaced "Hear! Hear!"—and visual sensation is still so novel to the Russians that they don't mind if it flickers to the rhythms of an elevator prose as nondescript as elevator music. "There is great literary prose, and there is junk," says one despondent Russian writer. "It's only junk that you can earn money from."

Sound familiar? The displacement of literature, the devaluation of the word, and mass indifference to nuance have been a longer time coming in the United States, and their insurgency can't be attributed to arriviste capitalism (commerce and literature worked out an arrangement like partners in a cold marriage who stay together for the sake of the furniture). Who can recall the last time the publication of a book that might reasonably be called literature—that aspired to more than an extended author's tour and a celluloid afterlife—raised the nation's hackles or lifted its spirits or shook its premises? In a country where Maya Angelou passes for a poet, Tom Clancy for a novelist, and Tony Kushner for a playwright what hope do words have? How do we stay alert to the spark of unwilled pleasure struck by words placed against each other just so, in a line, through a paragraph, over pages? The truth is we are less interested in words' beauty these days than in their ugliness. The perceived insult to physical condition or sex or race rouses us easily, mechanically. We're not so conditioned to respond to what is uncommon and miraculous.

It's not that we lack words, Lord knows, or books for that matter, which can be bought in spaces the size of hangars. Those aisles of books are mostly for burning, though a whole stack of them alight would not give off the heat of *Othello*. We don't expect enough of words anymore, that they be crafted, beautiful, purposeful, careful, true. The edge has gone off discrimination (it's on its way to becoming the "d" word), and fine judgment has flattened almost to the horizontal. We're losing the disposition to read closely, listen critically. Why so? An odd lot of suspects seems to have worked at the reduction, but there's no evidence of a conspiracy, and space to indict only a few.

Start with the media (irresistible: each now wears a neon "kick me" sign), with television, for example, the same television whose glow has enchanted the Russians and whose deeper infection they are yet to feel. On TV news shows, the standard patter is strictly anodyne, and the standard patterers as individual as Pringles. Their words, the means through which tens of millions of citizens get a fix on the world, work like a narcotic on the memory of eloquence and complication. On midafternoon dramas, charmless actors prattle, strip, couple, and scatter farcically, but the truest confusion is often grammatical: "A selfish person who always expects to get their own way better not look to Dawne and I for favors." On talk shows—circuses that are all freaks and clowns and no acrobats—participants use a common language of sentiments borrowed from psychos and psychotherapists. They have learned this language, these emotions, from the media, and they live for the opportunity to demonstrate what good students they are, to show-and-tell their constricted hopes and blasted dreams in home room. These shows insistently exploit race and class in America, yet there is in them none of the sometimes-fierce poetry of the lived vernacular, flung straight as a weapon or a curse. Borrowed words only, and secondhand passion.

Consider the language of computer communication, the use of words as blunt instruments—you type the fewest needed to trigger the electronic impulse and provoke a response. Blithe souls on the Internet can communicate in a language that seems to be in its infancy, and in the very process of learning itself: "Say, Cherry Red, does mountain air cool?" "Yes, Blue Fox, and anger messes." I beg your pardon? This is not Milton, and not even Beckett, but so what to the souls who've bumped electronically? Will there someday be collections of e-mail sendings to rival the great correspondence collections of the past? What a lax and indifferent archivist the SAVE key may prove.

Our civic discourse is bland and evasive. "Senior citizens," the verbal equivalent of a pat on the head for the family dog, gets the tone just right. Every wrenching issue invites a pulled punch, like this from a pro-choice advocate explaining a particularly grim abortion practice: "The foetus is demised" before its skull is cracked. We've recently seen a million-man march that wasn't quite, and we read daily of presidential hopefuls who seem neither. Even the most celebrated of our political figures doesn't help. We have a president who's wound up to talk without taking a breath into the new millennium, but for whom words and their intent have the substantiality and the staying power of soap bubbles; to be told by this man "You have my word" is to know true fear.

The most high-minded culprits in the drive to sideline literature work at institutions that once knew better, our universities. We read (accurately?) of faculty members in literature classes who are there not to celebrate texts, let alone be in awe of them, but to unmask them, like so many yapping Totos pulling the curtain. Language is construct, snare, and subterfuge. Every text is just a text, to be eyed with suspicion, every sentence much as good as any other. You are taught not to love literature but to be wary of it. Words subvert the intention of their author, and they will trick readers too. The value of a work is not aesthetic but mechanical—artifice maybe, art surely not. This seems akin to ignoring a great building's breathtaking shape, elegant skin, and material audacity to study its elevator shaft. One does not wish to impinge on the freedom of these folk to give students the shaft, so long as they situate it in its proper place. We live in an "age of theory," and we'll just have to muddle through, as past ages endured massive outbreaks of plague. The great mystery is that theory should have had such ascendancy in the academy when so many of its exponents cannot speak or write plainly about what they do: language takes revenge on them by simply crossing its legs to their blandishments.

If true, it is depressing that teachers should be reluctant to make aesthetic judgments about the worth of words, to say that these, arranged in a line, a chapter, a book, have a beauty that is worth your attention, as those do not, and to explain why that should be so. *Beauty, truth, preference, order, value* are words to make the new-knowing wince and wink. Uncomfortable with style, these individuals leap instead on lifestyle and fey anthropology, which may explain some of the strange scholarship that's bred in literature departments these days: stuff on cross-dressing, the iconography of Jackie Kennedy or Madonna, the imperialistic reach of Walt Disney. Will anyone read these books in five years? They should be carried by skeletal models on fashion runways, for they will stay current no longer than the season's prized synthetic.

Have the universities engaged in a great leveling process in the presentation of literature, as in much else, and, by so doing, have they forsaken traditional notions of what a liberal education should be? Such an education has to be about discrimination, dismissive and embracing judgments, differences calculated with an unclouded eye. Let technical vocational skills be uniformly imposed: the bridge should remain suspended, the tunnel unflooded, the spacecraft aloft, the ship afloat, the accounts in balance, the patient alive. Let liberal education champion value, disagreement, rank, all the elements celebrated by guileful Ulysses in Shakespeare's *Troilus and Cressida*: degree (not the same thing as a university's production-line piece of paper), priority, place, course, proportion, form, office, custom, in all line of order. He could be offered no campus presidency, this eloquent, slippery man ("Wouldn't he be a good fund-raiser?"), but universities have done worse: "Take but degree away, untune that string, / And hark what discord follows. Each thing meets / In mere oppugnancy." Which is where a lot of America meets now.

The "canon," about whose hegemonic hold on curricula we have heard too much in recent years from those uneasy with degree, is really no more than an A-list of things to consider reading. Life is choice, you have x amount of time to spend reading, apportion it wisely. If you're a serious reader, look here. It's a list both porous and expansive. What's canonical is so, by and large, because it has for some time satisfied minds and hearts, not because it has met some Noah's ark notion of inclusiveness. Those who scorn the very idea of a canon had better come up with a powerful alternative. It won't do to mandate that work be read because it represents the cat-egory of, say, hermaphrodite fiction—and right-handed hermaphro-dite fiction at that, sinister hermaphrodite prose being a separately privileged genre. All literary texts are not created equal, and their worth is not in their provenance or their good intentions, just as their achievement is not to be gauged by their conformity to the moment's panethnic pansexual Panglossian social or political enthu-siasms.

Imagine that in time the society will divide into readers, who want information and don't much attend to the form in which it comes, and Readers, who want music, implication, wit, transfor-mation, resistance. You can guess who'll be in charge. The Readers will shrink to a circle as sealed as the Druids', and as irrelevant and doomed. At least the tree folk lost out to Rome and Christianity. Where's the glory in Reading your fate on a pulsing blue screen, or in a friend's shrug and blank stare?

Talk given at Woodrow Wilson Center
October 25, 1995

Acknowledgments

Grateful acknowledgment is made to the books and journals in which the pieces in this volume were originally published.

"Some for Glory, Some for Praise." In *Why I Write: Thoughts on the Craft of Fiction*, edited by Will Blythe. Back Bay Books, 1999.

"The Writing Teacher." *The New York Times Sunday Book Review*, March 8, 2005.

"Odessa, Mon Amour." *Narrative Magazine*, Spring 2009.

"Like a Retired Confidential Agent, Graham Greene Hides Quietly in Paris." *People*, January 19, 1976.

"An Old Magician Named Nabokov Lives and Writes in Splendid Exile." *People*, March 17, 1975.

"From Lady Antonia's Golden Brow Springs Another Figure of History." *People*, February 24, 1975.

"Ben Sonnenberg Jr." *Men's Journal*, May 2001.

"Life for Author Han Suyin Has Been a Sometimes Hard But Always Many Splendored Thing." *People*, November 8, 1976.

"D'Annunzio, the Immortal Who Died." *The Paris Review*, Fall/ Winter 1978.

"Cool Heads." *Joe*, 1999.

"An Army Mule Named Sid Berry Takes Command at the Point." *People*, September 2, 1974.

"Ike the Unlikely." *Esquire*, December 1983.

"Younger Women, Older Men." *Esquire*, March 1992.

"Karyl and Me." *Modern Maturity*, April–May–June 1997.

"When Evening Falls." *GQ*, February 1992.

"Talk of the Town on Bill Clinton." *The New Yorker*, October 5, 1998.

"The Definitive Downhill: Toni Sailer." *The New York Times*, November 7, 1982.

"At the Foot of Olympus: Jarvik, Kolff, and DeVries." Typescript, May 26, 1981.

"Man Is His Own Star: Royal Robbins." *Quest*, March–April 1978.

"Racing for the Cup." *Geo*, December 1982.

"Getting High." *Life*, August 1979.

"The Alps." *National Geographic Traveler*, October 1999.

"Offering Oneself to the Fat Boys." *Outside*, December 1995.

"Passionate Falsehoods." *The New Yorker*, August 4, 1997.

"The First Women Graduate." *Life*, May 1980.

"Almost Pure Joy." *The Washington Post Magazine*, August 13, 1995.

"Eat, Memory." *The New York Times Magazine*, January 2, 2005.

"Paris Nights." *Food & Wine*, October 1998.

"Chez Nous." *European Travel and Life*, Spring 1990.

"Once and Future Queen." *Rocky Mountain Magazine*, 1994.

"They Call It Paradise." *Geo*, November 1981.

"Snowy Nights in Aspen." *Colorado Ski Country USA*, 1997–98.

"Notes from Another Aspen." *Aspen Magazine*, Winter 1996–97.

"Once Upon a Time, Literature. Now What?" In *Writers on Writing, Collected Essays from* The New York Times, introduction by John Darnton. Times Books, 2002.

"Words' Worth." Talk given at Woodrow Wilson Center, October 25, 1995.

Index

ABOUT THE AUTHOR

James Salter was a novelist, short-story writer, screen-writer, and essayist. Born in 1925, he grew up in New York City and was a career officer and Air Force pilot until his mid-thirties, when the success of his first novel, *The Hunters*, led to a full-time writing career. Salter's potent, lyrical prose has earned him acclaim from critics, readers, and fellow novelists. He was the recipient of a PEN/Faulkner Award and the PEN/Malamud Award, among other honors. His novel *A Sport and a Pastime* was hailed by *The New York Times* as "nearly perfect as any American fiction." His other books include *Cassada* and *Light Years*. He died on June 19, 2015, at ninety years old.